America's Theologian

America's Theologian

A Recommendation of
Jonathan Edwards

ROBERT W. JENSON

New York   Oxford
OXFORD UNIVERSITY PRESS

Oxford University Press

Oxford   New York   Toronto
Delhi   Bombay   Calcutta   Madras   Karachi
Petaling Jaya   Singapore   Hong Kong   Tokyo
Nairobi   Dar es Salaam   Cape Town
Melbourne   Auckland

and associated companies in
Berlin   Ibadan

Library of Congress Cataloging-in-Publication Data
Jenson, Robert W.
America's Theologian
Bibliography: p.
Includes index
I. Edwards, Jonathan.—1703–1758.   I. Title.
BX7260.E3J45   1988   230'.58'0924   87-14037
ISBN 0-19-504941-1
ISBN 0-19-507786-5 (PBK.)

2 4 6 8 10 9 7 5 3 1
Printed in the United States of America

For Kari and Robert

The increasing knowledge of God, in all elect creatures, to all eternity, is . . . a reality infinitely worthy to be in itself.
—*Miscellanies, 1225*

Preface

Americans have heard about Jonathan Edwards. Until recently, what we heard was often wrong. This has not only been an injustice to Edwards, for his thought and fate so touch the truth of our nation that ignorance of him is an alienation from ourselves. In part, misrepresentation of Edwards has resulted from ideological animus. But mere lack of information has had a big role. So long as it was not fully appreciated that key parts of his thinking are not mediated by the published editions, but are recorded only in unpublished notebooks, a true representation of his work was not possible.[1]

It was Perry Miller's virtuosic *Jonathan Edwards*[2] which in 1949 inspired the contemporary rediscovery of Edwards.[3] We may expect that Edwards scholarship will continue for some time at a lively rate; there is still room for many studies of particular aspects and connections of Edwards' thought. But a more general book, such as that here offered, may need justification over against Miller himself, whose book should long continue to be read.

Two justifications are possible. The first is the ever-given possibility of standing on a giant's shoulders. The second has more specifically to do with the scope of this book.

For one rereading of Miller, I happened to use a copy which previous and remorseless readers had much annotated. Early on, Miller makes a recurrent claim of his study: that in all Edwards' writing there is a method of concealment, "an exasperating intimation of something . . . held back, some esoteric divination that the listener must make for himself." "Edwards' writing," wrote Miller, "is an immense cryptogram, the passionate oratory of the revival no less than the hard reasoning of the treatise on the will."[4] By this there is the annotation: "Is this secret, faith in God? To Perry Miller that must seem cryptic."

That is indeed the characteristic of Miller's study that makes another work a plausible undertaking: Miller did not share Edwards' secret.[5] That faith in God *is* a mystery, only to be approximated by discourse, was of course a dominant tenet of Puritanism, which we will have recurrent occasion to consider. But that the Puritans indeed cultivated this mystery is itself no secret. Moreover, the mystery is one that can be shared, and that Edwards labored with every utterance to share.

One who—Puritan or other Christian—believes with Edwards in Edwards' God, must take Edwards seriously in a certain way: as a Christian theologian, whose propositions are claims on the present apprehension of truth. It is the proper question of theology that, in my hope and intention, guides this study. Given the history of the Christian gospel in American life, what may we learn from Edwards about the *truth* of the gospel in our community? And about the truth of our community, still so much determined by the erstwhile dominance in it of the Puritan version of the gospel?

I in ho way suggest that Miller's interpretation, always concerned to abstract from Edwards' faith and therefore always slightly across the grain of Edwards' own goals and connections, is not legitimate or even of the very most fruitful sort. But room is left for another kind of interpretation, that evaluates Edwards' views not only by their originality or power or historical fruitfulness, but by their intention of truth. One may ask not only, "Why was Edwards great?" but "Was Edwards right?" One may ask not only, "Was Edwards right?" but "Is he?"

The same hermeneutical shift also distinguishes the present study from those with more particular focus. I hesitate to claim that readers will find in this book many special discoveries not made before. But Edwards himself did not think he was doing aesthetics, metaphysics, speculative science, moral philosophy or psychology, as these disciplines are now known. He intended all his thinking as one unified project of specifically believing reflection; and studies that abstract from that project are again crossways to their matter, though surely justified and fruitful in their own ways.

Finally, prospective readers should know that the nationalism signaled in the title does indeed characterize the entire study. Perhaps a bit of autobiography may be permitted. As with many American theologians of my generation, the great post-Enlightenment Europeans were those on whom I initially exercised my reflection. For many years Blanche Jenson, one of whose interests is American intellectual history, rebuked the anomalies of this situation: that, for example, I knew in some detail what happened in early nineteenth-century Berlin and almost nothing about what happened in early nineteenth-century Princeton. Eventually, I was persuaded to lead a seminar of excellent students through a menu of "American theologians," and found several to admire and one to love. I have exercised my reflection on him for many years now and have found that America has indeed an American theologian and that I am, for better and worse, an American Christian. I trust that Europeans who read this study will find much to learn from its hero. I hope that Americans may profit more particularly.

I owe various debts. Blanche Jenson is, as noted, to blame for the book, and has taken her usual part in its creation. Milton Kotler and Leopold Bernhard, the latter now deeply mourned, accomplished much of my initiation into that political way of thinking about America which so characterizes the work. Paul Ramsey knows the variety of ways in which he must be thanked. Thomas Schafer permitted me to use his transcripts of the *Miscellanies,* deposited with the manuscript in Yale University's Beinecke Library; and that library's staff facilitated my reading with every courtesy. Gettysburg Seminary provided sabbatical leave and additional support for a main period of research. And finally—and, I think, exceptionally on such lists—I must thank the reader to whom Oxford Press sent the typescript and whose name remains unknown to me; her or his suggestions for improvement were of a generosity and precision that cannot go unacknowledged.

Gettysburg   R. W. J.
July 18, 1986

Contents

IV
COMMUNITY

America's Theologian

1

America and Enlightenment

I

It has become a truism, that Jonathan Edwards is America's greatest theologian, in the sense that his achievement in the discipline of theology is the most weighty to have appeared on this continent. The thesis of this book is rather different: that Edwards' theology meets precisely the problems and opportunities of specifically American Christianity and of the nation molded thereby,[1] and that it does so with the profundity and inventive élan that belong to only the very greatest thinkers.

The insufficiently quelled smallpox vaccination that killed Edwards just as he was prepared to write his long-planned major works, and so buried much of his system in the heap of his notes and drafts, worked a great historical accident. It is as if America had been given its Hegel and had not noticed. Between Edwards' death in 1758 and the Civil War there was, to be sure, a strong identifiable presence of Edwardsean ideas in American theology. But the availability to Edwards' admirers of his fully developed thought on the particular topics of bondage of the will, original sin, virtue, and America's apocalyptic destiny, and the unavailability of the comprehensive vision within which these topics had for him their force, gave his influence an unfortunate twist. His address to the great spiritual movement of his time was obscured, and his thought thereby robbed of its potentially recreative power.[2] By now Edwards has become for educated Americans the horrid old fanatic who frightened "Sinners in the Hands of an Angry God."

The fit between Edwards and America, to be described throughout this book, may be stated here in utmost schematization: Edwards knew what to make of the great eighteenth-century Enlightenment, and America and its church are the nation and the church the Enlightenment made. The European and American theological task of the eighteenth century was to be at once believing and Enlightening; this book will argue that Edwards brought it off, as perhaps no other theologian quite did. As to

3

America, all Western nations and all parts of the Western church were shaken and reformed by the Enlightenment, but only America and the American church were created by it. It is the latter point to which this preliminary chapter bows.

The politics of all Western nations were profoundly transformed by the revolutionary impact of Enlightenment political theory and the new bourgeois reality the theory explicated. But the polity of the United States was deliberately invented in accord with the prescriptions of those "improvements" which the "science of politics" had "lately received."[3] Other Western nations' economies were bent and invigorated by the new capitalist energies. But America had little antecedent economy to be changed, so that while elsewhere capitalist slogans have been hypotheses to be considered, in America they have had the sanctity and power of myths of the Beginning. The European universities of theology and humane letters were shaken by and accommodated the new disciplines of empirical science, historical critique and practical technology. But most American institutions were founded only after these disciplines had come to dominance. The history of all Western Christianity since the end of the eighteenth century has been very largely the history of efforts to deal with the Enlightenment's rejection of authority and historical contingency. But the Enlightenment has been American Christianity's fate in special degree, for our dominant modes of Christianity were given us by the same groups, the English and Scots Calvinists, who were the pioneers of Enlightenment.

This book is not about the Enlightenment, but about one of the enlightened and enlightening, and I am therefore doomed in this chapter to the distortions and superficialities of all attempts quickly to characterize a great historical movement. That disclaimer entered, it may be suggested that the following mandates make the substance of Enlightenment, for the limited purposes of our story.

II

Karl Barth once said that the defining phenomenon of the eighteenth century was its "Mensch," its specific sort of human person, and described this person as "absolutist." This is the human person "who discovers his own power, his own ability, the potential that slumbers in his . . . humanity simply as such, and who understands this as something final. . . . , i.e., as something . . . in itself justified and authorized and mighty, and who therefore sets this potential in uninhibited motion in every direction.'' [4] The definition doubtless hits the target, and also displays how very much ''American'' is still synonymous with ''Enlightened.''

It was the intellectual leaders of the century who themselves presented their work as ''enlightenment,'' as a campaign of the human mind to carry its light into all the dark places of superstition and prejudice. No authority should rule the mind except such as could justify itself *to* the mind, and do so otherwise than by appeal to other authority. Thus another favorite self-designation of the enlighteners, and the word with which Immanuel Kant summed up all their work, was ''critique,'' the stance of those from Missouri over against all initial appearances of truth. We need not leave our own nation to hear the archetypical utterance of the century: ''I have sworn upon the altar of God eternal hostility against every form of tyranny over the mind of man.'' [5]

In the eighteenth century's distrust of authority and passion for the critique of appearances, it but drew lessons from the experience of the previous century. The seventeenth century's great triumph was its natural science, personified for all subsequent memory in the mighty Isaac Newton. The century's great hope was for the extension of that science to embrace our more specifically human concerns; the legacy of this hope was transmitted above all by the writings of John Locke. The century's great disaster was the wars of religion, which seemed irrefutably to discredit every final reliance on authority, as this was represented above all by the warring post-Reformation Christian confessions.

Most elements of the ''method'' of modern science were platitudes of antiquity and the Middle Ages. Three things were new: the actual mathematics to do what Western thought had always said mathematics should do, the eschewing of teleological explanations, and the rigorous critique of appearances. It was the latter two that were culturally decisive; I will take the second of them for the thread of my exposition.

Thus it certainly appears that the sun goes around the earth; the founding deed of the new science was the audacity to say, with persistence and investigative energy, ''But does it really? Might we not discover truth by supposing the opposite?'' It is not mere ''observation'' that is characteristic of the new science, but rather precisely distrust of initial observation, of nature's immediate self-presentation, the determination to ''put nature to the question'' and *then* observe what happens.

No sooner was the critique of natural appearances undertaken than it proved a magic key, loosing in the seventeenth century an unprecedented flow of new and useful knowledge. With a record of success, it was inevitable that the dream should arise of extending the method to the heretofore intractable problems of humanity's own life. The dream may

well have been delusion, but that is beside the present point. And—again
two Englishmen!—Thomas Hobbes and John Locke promptly began the
effort to write the sciences of humanity. By the time the United States'
Constitution was to be created, American Enlighteners were confident
that the science of human societies had received such "improvement"
that that they could know how the devising of polities was best done.

General Enlightenment thus seemed actually feasible—indeed, well
in hand. And the Enlighteners were sure where the darkness was: in the
shadow of the great systems of religiously based authority. One did not
need to be unbelieving or even unchurchly to interpret history so; English
and American Puritans saw papacy, Laudian Anglicanism, Stuart absolutism and sheer ignorance as one vast system of oppression. So John
Adams, Puritan and Enlightener: "Thus as long as this confederacy [of
papacy and monarchy] lasted, and the people were held in ignorance
. . . , one age of darkness succeeded another, till God in his benign
providence raised up the champions who began . . . the Reformation.
From the time of the Reformation to the first settlement of America
knowledge gradually spread; and in proportion . . . ecclesiastical and
civil tyranny . . . seem to have lost their strength."[6]

But the attack on religious authority could not consistently be restricted to those systems of which particular Enlighteners otherwise disapproved. Since classical Christian theology based all its most controversial assertions on authority, Enlightenment critique was at its center critique
of inherited theology simply as such. In England and America those critics who came to consistent results were called "deists"; in their teaching
there was indeed, as more radical Christians insisted, little left of the
specific Christian gospel. It is vital to remember that the American revolution was a joint enterprise of Puritan Whigs and deistic Whigs, and
the United States' polity a product of the deistic wing.

That Christian theology and the Christian confessions were caught
in the eighteenth century's critique of authority was theology's own fault.
It had been the historic task of the medieval church to work out the
dialectic between the West's two sources of truth: the gospel and Socrates. All Western thought and practice has been carried by two religious
messages: the gospel-proclamation of the God who raised Jesus from the
dead, and the call to Greece's metaphysical quest for true deity. There
was and is no way for Western civilization to be deaf to either message;
medieval theology's millennial effort to obey both was obligatory. What
was perhaps not so salutary was the way this was regularly done.

In Western theology's affirmation of Socrates and his successors, it
possessed a body of theology which it knew it shared with the unbeliev-

ing: that God is omnipotent, omniscient, invisible, etc., that the human soul is a free moral agent, and that the soul's reward is somehow to participate in God's eternity. The usual explanation of this circumstance was that the shared theological truths are those attainable by the power of that created reason which, if the doctrine of creation is true, believers do indeed share with all humans; so much religion and theology are "natural" to us. But then the gospel's teaching about God, manifestly so very different from that of Socrates and not shared with him or his successors, must bring knowledge that is *not* "natural" to us, nor yet of course "unnatural," and so "supernatural"; and it must therefore not be mediated by reason but by revelation, by an "authoritative" communication from God. When the eighteenth century—in large part taught so by the gospel—rebelled against doctrines laid down by mere authority, it was precisely the specific Christian teaching that appeared under the rubric.

It is a paradox at least arguably true that America has been able to remain nominally Christian longer than other Western nations just because the specificities of the gospel, the promises and offenses not plausible to the natural, i.e., Socratic, religionist, were blunted almost from our religious beginning. Where the Enlightenment has won its most essential goals within the church, its critique does not need to be external and obliterating. In America there have been few Tom Paines and many like Jonathan Edwards' contemporary Charles Chauncy, whom we will repeatedly encounter as an urbane and verbally orthodox critic of religious extravagance in general and Edwards' Christian radicalism in particular. In this connection, there is a further circumstance worth noting. Through the late eighteenth century, the Enlightenment was cultivated in this country's centers of religious and scholarly influence especially in the specific form it had taken in Scotland. In Scotland, church and Enlightenment had found ways of mutual accommodation, under the shared banners of "common sense" and civil utility. The bitter conflicts of the French and even English Enlightenments never tore Scotland; there the Enlighteners in the church were known as the "moderates" and dominated the establishment. Even David Hume was a friend of the clergy.

III

Equal to the Enlightenment's passion for critique was its passion for order. It is easy to see why this was so. If the human mind is to illumine all reality, all reality must be amenable to mind; this amenability is what we mean by "order." The demand for order was hardly novel, but the Enlightenment pursued it with new energy and self-consciousness.

All creation, the Enlightenment insisted, must be a strictly harmonious whole. But of what sort? Our civilization harbors two proposals of universally encompassing order: the biblical word of a dramatically coherent total history, and Greece's vision of a cosmos, of a stable interrelation of moving parts. The normal Enlightenment could entertain only the Greek proposal, for history is constituted by precisely the tradition and authority the normal Enlightenment feared. Moreover, the new technology offered a powerful image for such order, the image of the machine. And perhaps most decisive, the two greatest triumphs of the new science, Copernican astronomy and Newton's laws of motion, seemed at the time to cast exactly the vision of the universe as a perfect cosmos-machine.

The vision of nature as the harmony of a well designed mechanism was a problem for Christianity generally, flatly incompatible as it is with the reality of the Bible's living, deciding, acting God. As village freethinkers of all strata asked, and received no good answer: If God made the machine right to begin with, what is he doing interrupting its function with resurrection, new creation and other miracles? But peculiarly decisive for America was the extension of mechanics to the understanding of human phenomena.

The American polity was constructed according to a self-aware political technology which conceived human persons and groups as inertial masses, their needs, hopes and histories as inertial vectors, and their interactions as governed by analogously Newtonian laws of motion.[7] As the deists' God is a universal Engineer who followed Newton's laws in the construction of the cosmos as the marvelous mill of all his blessings for us, so Madison and his fellows set out to construct a polity that by an exact arrangement of "checks and balances" would grind out liberty and justice mechanically, that is, independently of the personal dedication to liberty and justice of those who at any moment are the polity's cogs and levers. Interest is opposed to interest, faction to faction, power to power, to the greatest good of the greatest number. Through all remodelings of the mechanism, the vision has remained unchanged: nowhere but in America could the public question after each crisis be, "Did the system work?"

Only a powerful ideology could make one think of polities as machines, or attempt to design a polity by mechanical analogies, for the analogy is intrinsically most implausible. A polity is the forum of a community's moral decidings, of its argument and decision of what sort of community it *should* in future be. To appear authentically in this forum I must not appear there as an inertial mass of inalterable interest. The polity is the arena in which we trust to the transformative power of deliberation, to bring us from what we severally *want* to what we together declare to be *best*.

Therefore it is not surprising that the United States' machine-government has very nearly eliminated politics, properly so called, from our national life. The polity, with us as with the socialist states, has been absorbed by the economy. The economy is indeed a sort of machine, in which persons and groups appear only as bearers of interests; to compel politics into a mechanistic system is to assimilate political decision to economic decision and civic worth to managerial or entrepreneurial power.

The seventeenth-century dream and its eighteenth-century ideology extended the new science not only to the human community but also to the human individual. The archetype was the psychology of John Locke; nowhere was Locke received with such ready assent as in America. And as the grip of the traditional humanistic curriculum upon our schools has failed, psychology in all its sects and specialities has become our main path of self-understanding, displacing the historical studies we fear. We have been above all the psychological nation, with our tests and therapies a wonder to the Western world.

There is a twist to the notion of scientific psychology as a means of self-understanding; the twist has been fateful for American culture and religion. The new science is done, as a principle of method, from the closest possible approximation to the position of an uninvolved observer or technique-wielding agent. But all human self-understanding occurs within the mystery of personal self-transcendence: in that I seek to know and will *myself,* I am somehow beyond myself to be a subject with myself as my object, I am somehow beyond myself to be an object of a subject that is myself. What then if this subject is trying to be an observer and technician? Then personhood and its transcendence become the kind of inner alienation that was and is America's special kind: then I become not the doer of my life but its observer and manipulator. Then I see myself doing what I think I ought not, and it does not occur to me simply to stop; instead, I seek the psychic and social explanations of my behavior, as if some other will than mine were therein displayed, and summon the appropriate technicians to undertake the repair.

IV

Finally in this chapter I must trace certain national boundary conditions of theology in the stricter sense.[8] There is such a national natural theology, for, as we have already noted, our polity and its relation to the economy institutionalize an historically particular apprehension of God. Puritanism was the Calvinist Reformation in the Church of England. When Stuart absolutism made Reformation in England seem hopeless, thousands went to *New* England, to carry on from there. It should also be remembered that Puritans were not only in New England; 75 percent of the population of the revolutionary colonies had a Puritan religious background.

It was characteristic of Calvinism that, unlike the radical sects or Lutheranism, it maintained unaltered the general conceptual structure of classic Western-catholic theology. That theology, in response to its double religious source, had a double vision of God: on the one hand, of the timeless and so distant Ground of the world's correspondingly timeless structure; on the other hand, of the One who raised Jesus from the dead, the temporally active Power who effectually contradicts the established world. It cannot be claimed for classic theology that it had done much more than set these two identifications of God alongside each other, and *assert* that they were of the same God. Each identification even had its own chapter of theology. The Socratic identification was expounded by the doctrine of the one God's "eternal being"; the gospel's identification was expounded by the doctrine of the Trinity, which makes God's temporal history with Christ constitutive for God's own reality.

In the system of medieval catholicism, the dual vision of God was internally reconciled by the mere existence of the church that lived by it. The medieval church was a rationalized institution, but what was institutionalized was miraculous grace. It was a main structure of the standing order, but it administered eschatological transformation. Remove this church, leaving all else where it was, and you have the truly astonishing inner conflicts of the religion English Puritanism brought to America: between cool rationalism and christocentric religious passion, between a world-encompassing static metaphysics and the daily expectation of miracle.

English-American deism and "evangelical" Christianity may plausibly if schematically be described as the products of the inevitable decay of this weak synthesis. Each of the two apprehensions of God left something behind when it emerged into new independence. The God of deism left behind even such historical potency as Greek deity had possessed, to become a pure Origin and Guarantor of the status quo; and the God of evangelical Christianity, invested with all the gospel's transformative passion, left behind his claim on the public universe and the public society.

The American religious settlement institutionalized the division of the Puritan God. On one side, the national founders created a mechanistic polity that is plausible only on the assumption of deism's God, and put that polity explicitly under his aegis. On the other side, since no religious movement descended from Puritanism could fully abandon the public realm, evangelical religion created a second public arena on a privately voluntary basis. It is in this privately public arena that the actual moral history of the American people has occurred: the evangelization and civilization of the West, abolition, prohibition, female enfranchisement, the social gospel, and in its black section the civil rights movement.

Neither God is able to be God by himself. Each of our public spheres has had to depend on symbiosis with the other: the deist state has drawn on national Christianity's sources of purpose and dedication, and the evangelical crusades have drafted the state when it came to action. It is the decay of also this symbiosis that now undoes us. When Madison's polity severs all ties to Christianity, it becomes indeed a machine, blindly grinding down all human transcendence and community. When the God of evangelical religion is no longer even vaguely identified with the God of the state, he loses power over outward reality, and "religion" becomes indeed a "private matter," destructive in its turn of transcendence and community.

V

My sketch of American Enlightenment has become a Puritan "jeremiad." I turn from its generalities to the particular Puritan and Enlightener who is our subject. Jonathan Edwards was born to the manse of East (now South) Windsor, Connecticut, October 5, 1703. In the fall of 1716 he matriculated at Yale, where he remained as a collegiate and ministerial student until 1722. At Yale he read—among many others—Newton and Locke.[9] And in the meeting between his special piety and the new science, a vision and policy of Enlightenment opened to him that was very different from that of others: a vision of *triune* harmony and a policy of critique in the service of the *gospel*.

In 1727, after a period of false starts, Edwards settled into what would be his life. He married Sarah Pierrepoint, a member of several illustrious New England families and a notable personality. And he entered the pastorate at Northampton, Massachusetts, for the first two years as assistant to his maternal grandfather, the formidable and influential Solomon Stoddard.

In Northampton, Edwards encountered the dubiously Christian side of American religiosity, called it "Arminianism," and in pastoral combat with it triggered in 1734 the first great American revival. Turning his critical passion to the analysis of this surprising phenomenon, he produced a body of published work that created and still crowns a new intellectual genre, the critique of religious appearances.

In Northampton he also encountered what was to become the standard American solution to the problem of the relation between the civil community and the community of the church, pioneered by his grandfather: Solomon Stoddard had taken into full communicant membership all who accepted the outward discipline and doctrine of Christianity, that is, all who wished to be within the New England community. In effect Stoddard proposed first to christianize sinners and only thereafter to convert them. Attempting to reverse this collapse of Puritan ideals, Edwards irrevocably offended his congregation.

Thus in 1751 Edwards found himself Indian missionary, school-teacher and pastor at the frontier post of Stockbridge, Massachusetts. Amid the distractions of this unsuitable labor, he matured plans for a synthesis of Christian wisdom: a *Principia* of saving harmony, and a rational-critical assertion of Christianity against "Arminian" and "deistical" religion. He had been storing ideas and drafts throughout his ministry, most particularly in the numbered journal called *Miscellanies;* a few parts were now in fact published: the books on *Freedom of the Will, Original Sin,* and *True Virtue.*

Then long overdue academic employment was offered. After anxious hesitation, he became president of Princeton, but died one month after assuming office, March 22, 1758. His tomb is in a row of Princeton presidents in the town cemetery. His last words, as reported, were: "Give my kindest love to my dear Wife, and tell her that the uncommon union which has so long subsisted between us has been of such a nature as I trust is spiritual and therefore will continue forever." [10]

I

THE FOUNDING INTUITION

> The eternal heaven surrounds Christ not merely as an house surrounds an inhabitant . . . , but rather as plants and flowers are before the sun, that have their life and beauty and being from that luminary
> —*Miscellanies*, 1122

2

Beauty and Reason

I

Jonathan Edwards'[1] intellectual life and achievement instance a phenomenon that is perhaps commoner than we think: that a lifetime of investigation and reflection, despite all twists and starts, explores and elaborates an interpretation of reality that is whole from the moment of its conception. With Edwards, the moment was the meeting between an intense piety of a very particular sort and the new world-interpretation of modern science, as mediated by Newton and Locke in the first flush of its power. In this chapter, it is the piety I will describe, under two chief rubrics.

It is not certain how far back into Edwards' youth we may trace a sharply profiled religious life; the problem is that usual with great thinkers' retrospective accounts. It is anyway clear that the decisive period for our purposes was the last years of his study at Yale, and we need not further solve the biographical problem, since all accounts present the same picture. So far as the available evidence tells us, there never was a religiously aware Jonathan Edwards whose piety was of a different *sort* than that which carried his life's work. Edwards' religion was from its root—with or without what he could have called conversion and with or without Newton and Locke—a sheer adoration of God's majesty, and that is for Edwards to say, a sheer beholding of God's beauty. As the famous *Personal Narrative* describes the paradigmatic experience, "And as I was walking there and looking up into the sky and clouds, there came into my mind so sweet a sense of the glorious *majesty* and *grace* of God, that I know not how to express. I seemed to see them both in a sweet conjunction . . . it was a sweet and gentle, and holy majesty; and also a majestic meekness."[2] Again, of a bit later, "I remember the thought I used then to have of holiness. . . . It appeared to me that there was nothing in it but what was ravishingly lovely."[3]

The spring of Edwards' whole system is in these descriptions, whether they are those he would contemporaneously have given or are interpreted by further experience. Central is the equation of holiness with *beauty*,[4] which in turn is interpreted as the harmonious reconciliation of opposites;

15

in amazing variation and fecundity, these equations will provide the animating dialectic of all Edwards' thought. In the first entry of the *Miscellanies,* the huge collection of notes and drafts he began immediately after
leaving Yale, it is already fully at work, encompassing now God, the
human soul, and their relation: "Holiness is . . . the highest beauty and
amiableness. . . . It makes the soul a little sweet and delightful image
of the blessed Jehovah. . . . What a sweet calmness, what calm ecsta-
sies, doth it bring to the soul. How doth it make the soul love itself . . .
how doth God love it and delight in it; how do even . . . the sun, the
fields and trees love a humble holiness. . . . It makes the soul like . . .
a garden planted by God . . . where the sun is Jesus Christ, the blessed
beams and calm breeze, the Holy Spirit."[5]

There is a set of motifs I must point to in these evocations. First is
the constant presence of the natural world. Beauty is not an abstract concept for Edwards, it is his word for what he immediately loves in reality
as it presents itself to him. So it is while walking the river watching the
clouds that he is given "a sense" of the beauty of God; and conversely
as his apprehension of God deepened, "The appearance of everything
was altered; there seemed to be . . . a calm, sweet cast . . . of divine
glory, in almost everything."[6] As to wherein natural beauty consists, he
is provided with an explicit doctrine from the start, by the nature of his
experience of it: "The beauty of the world consists wholly of sweet mutual consents, either within itself, or with the Supreme Being."[7]

A second motif is the concept by which Edwards grasps the relation
between God's beauty, the soul's beauty, and the beauty of nature: the
concept of *image.* This is an ancient notion of late-antique Platonism and
all its Christian continuations. In this tradition, the notion is theologically
and metaphysically loaded; it carries its full burden as it appears in Edwards' language, shaping not merely his theory of the beautiful, but the
experience itself.[8] To be an image is, in this tradition, to belong to a
particular class of being. An image is not its archetype, yet neither is it
anything other; it is precisely *of* the archetype. Thus in the cognitive
order, an image reveals the archetype where the archetype is itself un-
seen; in the causal order, an image is the means of the archetype's action;
and ontologically these two relations are not finally distinct.

It is exactly images in this sense that Edwards saw when he gave
himself over in attention to the natural world. To choose a jolting example on which Edwards spent much thought: the fires that are the bodies
of the sun and fixed stars are an image of God's wrath,[9] as their regular
movement is of his moral harmony;[10] in the stars' final collapse, follow-

ing the inherent law of their movement, they will make the actual conflagration of divinely ordered punishment.[11]

II

Indeed, an entire metaphysical vision springs so directly from this vision of the world as beauty imaging God's beauty, that if Newton and Locke had not provided the occasion of its statement, Edwards would certainly have found other occasion. It is therefore proper to sketch it in this chapter. "As to the corporeal world . . . , the sweetest and most charming beauty of it is its resemblance of spiritual beauties."[12] "Spiritual" does not here have primarily the sense of *invisible,* but rather of *personal,* indeed *communal.* There is a world of spirits, comprising human souls, other created spirits, and God; and its personal and communal harmony is the beauty imaged in the corporeal world: "When we think of the great harmony of the parts of the corporeal world, it fills us with such astonishment that the soul is ready to break. Yet [it all is] but shadows of excellency, in comparison of those beauties and harmonies that may be in one finite spirit. That harmony of the world is indeed a very true picture and shadow of the real glories of religion. . . . The glories of astronomy and natural philosophy consist in the harmony of . . . the corporeal shadow of a world; the glories of religion consist in the harmony of the . . . more real worlds with themselves, with one another, and with the infinite fountain and original of them."[13] So heaven will be the sheer perfection of harmony "between all . . . minds and Christ Jesus and the supreme Mind,"[14] and hell will be simply the perfection of mutual hatred.[15]

There is only one possible word for Edwards' intuition, though it must be kept free from some nineteenth and twentieth-century associations: the deepest and encompassing event, according to Edwards, is sheerly *aesthetic* ecstasy. The moral order and the order of laws and covenants, to which Puritans were supposedly so bound, emerges only within and derived from the aesthetic order. The derivation runs so: the heart of the harmonious creation is the harmony of minds, the harmony of created minds is established by the "moral government" of their Creator,[16] and *so* there are commands and works and covenants. Or, coming at it slightly differently, the harmony of minds, whether among humans or between humans and God, depends on their communication, and the act by which communication is maintained is the act of moral government.[17] Indeed,

even the necessity of final moral Judgment is in the last instance aesthetic. An unrevealed beauty is no beauty at all, and short of a final
judgment the harmony of the world's moral government is hidden: "since
God has made the beauty . . . of the natural world so publicly visible
. . . , 'tis much more requisite the moral beauty and regularity of his
disposals of the intelligent world should be make publically visible." [18]

III

As so far described, Edwards' piety may well seem to be of a familiar
and not very remarkable sort. He apprehends God in beauty, connecting
God and natural beauty by various traditional Platonic borrowings. If
someone wishes to call such piety "mystical," there is much justification, and the mysticism would be of a fairly standard sort. But two further motifs, one that appears in my initial citations and one that does not
but must properly be introduced here, disturb our ready classifications.
The first: the God into whose beauty Edwards is led by the beauty of
nature is no nature-God or God of natural theology, but from the very
first and essentially the *triune* God of christological faith. The beautiful
soul-garden, we may remember, is planted by the Father, animated by
the Son, and watered by the Spirit. This is no mere metaphor. "God has
appeared glorious to me, on account of the Trinity"; the "direct view"
of God that sees his beauty is a view "of the glorious things of the
gospel" as these belong to God's own being in "that he subsists in three
persons: Father, Son and Holy Ghost." [19]

Nor may we dismiss this triunity of Edwards' supreme aesthetic object as conventional or merely traditional, since neither convention nor
tradition suggested it. The Western tradition has well enough understood
the triune story of Jesus the Son and his Father and their Spirit as the
story of our way *to* adoration, but has been much less able to let that
triunity characterize God as *object* of adoration. Moreover, that the Christian
God's triunity has any direct function at all for piety, or must be a war-
rant of theological argument, was by no means obvious to seventeenth-
and eighteenth-century Puritans. They did not dispute the doctrine, but
they did not much use it. So William Ames, the "chief theological men-
tor of the New England puritans," [20] in his main work, the *Medulla Theologica,* divides the doctrine of God into the doctrine of his "essence"
and his Trinity. The doctrine of God's essence is prior to, independent of
and almost entirely uninfluenced by the impoverished and sketchy discussion of Trinity, and comprises a deduction from allegedly self-evident

truths of God's unity, aseity and immutability, of his attributes, of his identity and of the fact and character of his power, his predestining choice, his creating and his governing. Even the fundamental Puritan doctrine of covenant is derived under the last-mentioned head, quite without reference to Christ or any part of the biblical narrative.[21] After Edwards, the "New England theology" was to become explicitly heterodox in the doctrine of the Trinity, out of sheer incomprehension.[22]

In distinction from such theology, all the great Augustinian image-relations are reborn to vital function not first in Edwards' systematic construction but already in Edwards' "view" of God. The harmony of each soul, of which astronomical and physical harmony is but a shadow, is the harmony of "the spirit itself, and its understanding, and its will," and this "is in resemblance to the threefold distinction in God."[23] Heaven is and will be the "exquisite spiritual proportion" between all created minds and between them and God, in reflection of and dependence on that "among the persons of the Trinity, the supreme Harmony of all."[24] And where Augustine himself stops short of enveloping more than spiritual reality in the christological-trinitarian imaging, Edwards pushes on. Adapting the patristic doctrine of creation as an act of Christ, the "Second Person" of the Trinity, he writes: "the Son of God created the world . . . to communicate himself in an image of his own excellency. He communicates himself properly only to spirits. . . . Yet he communicates a sort of shadow . . . of his excellencies to bodies. . . . So that when we are delighted with flowery meadows and gentle breezes . . . , we may consider, that we only see the emanation of the sweet benevolence of Jesus Christ."[25] Thus also the "views" of Edwards' walks by the river are specifically christological-trinitarian apprehensions of God.

The second unconventional motif of Edwards' vision is that it is indeed merely by convention that he and we keep calling it "vision," for Edwards' paradigmatic art is music. All discourse about the "beauty" of nature conceals a metaphor, for the first home of our experience of beauty is not in passive reception of the world but in the activity of art. If we ask what art was most immediate to Edwards, and provided the metaphor of his aesthetic descriptions, the answer is unambiguous: singing.

Our attention is first drawn by Edwards' accounts of the initial wave of revival. Of all the manifestations of new religious vigor that occurred in the services themselves, only one receives his unqualified approval, and of the aesthetic manifestations—good or bad—that must have occurred, only one receives his notice. "Our public assemblies were then very beautiful. . . . It has been observed that there has been scarce any part of divine worship, wherein good men amongst us have had grace so

drawn forth . . . , as in singing. . . . Our congregation excelled all that
ever I knew in the external part of this duty before. . . . But now they
were . . . wont to sing with unusual elevation of heart and voice." [26]
Edwards' personal experience was the same: when "engaged" in "sweet
comtemplations" of God, "it always seemed natural to me to sing, or
chant forth my meditations." [27]

Contemporaneously, Edwards can state the matter in principle: "The
best, most beautiful, and most perfect way that we have of expressing a
sweet concord of mind to each other, is music. When I would form . . .
an idea of a society in the highest degree happy, I think of them . . .
sweetly singing to each other." [28] So the final version of Edwards' evocation of heaven is a stunning change on the usual notion of mystical
vision: the eschatological "exquisite spiritual proportion" will be that of
a "very complex tune, where respect is to be had to the proportion of a
great many notes together." [29] With only slight pressure on the texts we
may say: if, for Edwards, the whole of reality is a great harmony, it is
not the harmony of a cosmos of architecture or painting but that of a
fugued melody. The universal beauty that is Edwards' immediate object
of experience is thus spread out in time rather than in space, in precise
and necessary pairing to his apprehension of the specifically triune God,
of the God whose beauty is told by a story.

IV

Were I to rely only on Edwards' retrospective accounts of his founding
religious life, and close this chapter with the preceding paragraph, I would
have described a straightforward pietist, though of a very interesting sort.
But in the writings which themselves come from the period Edwards'
pious accounts describe, we find a different Edwards: a born rationalist.
His "view" of God is there revealed as a thoroughly intellectual vision.

Thus the eighteen-year-old Edwards' first longer writing was an entirely a priori and speculative proof of the reality of God. The manuscript
draft-essay "Of Being," must be briefly described, for it is a remarkable
manifestation of Edwards' native habit of mind, in the first freedom of
its deliberate exercise.

Edwards begins with the utmost speculative abstraction: "That there
should absolutely be nothing at all is utterly impossible. The mind can
never, let it stretch its conceptions ever so much, bring itself to conceive
of a state of perfect nothing. . . . And if any man think that he can think
well enough how there should be nothing, I'll engage that what he means

by 'nothing' is as much something as anything that ever [he] thought of in his life. . . . So we see it is necessary some being should eternally be."[30] We note two features of this argument: the equation of inconceivability with impossibility, and the jump from what is actually proven, that there must always be something or other, to what is asserted, that some one thing must always be. The first marks Edwards' uncomplicated location in the central tradition of western metaphysics, his full confidence in the mind's necessities as a guide to fact. The second is a formal fallacy which he quickly repairs, by an argument to the identity of what cannot not be: "Space is this necessary something. . . . We find that we can with care conceive how all other things should not be. We can remove them out of our minds, and place some other in the room of them; but space is the very thing that we can never remove."[31] That is, if we think away all that we can think away, we are left precisely with "empty space," which is not nothing.

Now, since sheer absence is as inconceivable at particular places as at all, Edwards argues that eternal being must be omnipresent as well. But if space is necessary, eternal and omnipresent, "I had as good speak plain: I have already said as much as that space is God."[32] With this brazenly speculative proposition, Edwards reaches a position that will remain through his entire development: that God *contains,* envelops, all other reality. And within a year after writing the just-cited passage, Edwards returned to his draft and added a statement of *how* God contains other reality: as a consciousness contains that of which it is conscious. It is, he now argues, as inconceivable and therefore impossible, "that something should be from all eternity, and nothing all the while be conscious of it," as that there should absolutely be nothing. The space that is eternal and omnipresent is the space of a consciousness.[33]

As with Edwards' adoration of beauty, so with his confidence in reason the picture is chronologically uniform. At no period of which we have any knowledge did there exist for Edwards any threat of a clash between reason and the gospel—in the Enlightenment's terms, between reason and authority. Few major thinkers have kept and left so complete a record of daily reflections as did Edwards in the *Miscellanies* and other manuscript collections; in these there is, early and late, no trace of the supposition that provided equally the energy of eighteenth-century "infidelity" and the bad conscience of believers: that revelation and reason are alternative cognitive passions.

What one finds throughout Edwards' published and unpublished works is instead a manifold assertion of the reasonableness of faith, in every sense of the phrase. According to Edwards, it is reasonable to think that

God reveals himself; the alleged truth proposed by the actual revelation to Israel is satisfying to reason; and the processes by which we become convinced of this revelation's actuality are rational processes. Edwards can and regularly does sound like the most unchastened rationalists of his period. One may dip in the *Miscellanies* at random; thus in an entry from his mature years, Edwards explicitly agrees with Matthew Tindal that reason must judge "whether there be any revelation, or whether any pretended revelation be really such." [34]

Accordingly, in the entries from his years at Stockbridge, argument after argument begins with the posit of "a Creator," made in common with the deists, and argues that "without a revelation, mankind must be forever in the most woeful doubt" about all the most important "things that concern their welfare"—the future state, the content of God's will, the possibility of forgiveness, etc. This would accord ill with God's general care of his creatures,[35] as it would leave us without "necessary means, for the exercise of that religion, which becomes us, towards God." [36] Bluntly: If God never speaks to us, why should we speak to him? Why any religion, including the deistical?[37] And if "a Creator" is not granted, he will argue that too: that "the first . . . principle . . . from which results the being . . . and sweet order of the world, is properly an intelligent willing agent such as our souls only without our imperfection, and not some . . . unintelligent necessary agent, seems most rational" because of all agents we know of, only our souls originate as does the agent of the world.[38]

V

It might be thought that the character of young Edwards' contemporary writings casts doubt on the accuracy of his later recollections of piety.[39] But there are no grounds for this suspicion other than our own inability to unite our cognitive and aesthetic lives. What we must finally for this chapter understand about Edwards is the native unity of speculation and adoration in his life. Edwards' free metaphysical speculation is precisely his way of "viewing" God's beauty. As the thesis of this chapter, I offer: with or without Newton and Locke, Edwards was and would have developed as a rationalist contemplator, whose ecstatic object was the specific beauty of the specifically triune God.

3

God Against the Machine

Edwards was with and not without Newton and Locke; the two great saints of Enlightenment were in fact the interlocutors of his full systematic reflection. Edwards' religion was from the root adoration of God's beauty, that is, of his inner harmony; in the world as Newton and Locke described it, Edwards recognized the answering harmony of created being. From his first reading of the *Principia,* the *Optics* and the *Essay,* he seems never to have doubted but that modern science's distinctive policy toward reality, primally exemplified in these works, was simply right. Evidently, he also never shared the eighteenth century's typical construal of that policy, which then and since has created so much antagonism between science-inspired ideologies and faith. For Edwards, Newton and more problematically Locke were sheer theological inspirations.

I begin with Newton. The direct document of Edwards' meeting with physics is the manuscript collection *Natural Philosophy,* comprising draft essays and notes entered at intervals from Edwards' first year of post-collegiate study, 1720–1721, through his early years at Northampton.[1] Included are the draft-essay "On Being," another "Of Atoms," two numbered series of notes, and sundry other items.

In the earliest entries, we find above all sheer enthusiasm for vast cosmological investigations, for example, "To know the shape of the spheroid of the world by observation of the Milky Way," or "To write concerning the use of comets to repair the wastes of heavenly bodies." One begins: "To find out a thousand things"[2] And in the very next entries we find the meaning of this enthusiasm: "To show how all nature consists in things being precisely according to strict rules of justice and harmony,"[3] and "how infinite wisdom must be exercized in order that gravity and motion be perfectly harmonious."[4] The bulk of *Natural Philosophy* continues the amateur passion of the earliest entries, with proposed empirical projects, hopeful demonstrations of various theorems, and hypotheses garnered at some random. Many were not far off; for example, Edwards supposes that the sun's energy results from the compression produced by its enormous gravitation.[5] And in all, *what* is to be discovered is one or another cosmic harmony.

Beginning, perhaps, in 1723, Edwards undertook also a direct philosophical analysis of this valued harmony. In another series of notes, *The Mind,* the first entries define "excellency"—or, as Kant has taught us more dolefully to say, value.[6] Since "excellency" is in these notes explicitly equivalent to "that which is beautiful and lovely,"[7] it is interpretation of Edwards' central vision that is offered. He accepts a contemporary definition of excellency as proportion, but finds it unanalyzed.[8] He summarizes his own, lengthily derived, proposal: excellency is the "consent of being to being."[9] Substitution of "consent" for "proportion" achieves two purposes. It directs attention to the mutuality of relations, as against the way in which "proportion" construes them for an external observer. And it places the discussion within the field of a root metaphor of *community.* "One alone . . . cannot be excellent."[10]

One further question is answered in this same passage: Why should proportion be value? It is because "being, if we examine narrowly, is nothing else but proportion."[11] This doctrine, appearing so suddenly, is mysterious until we remember that God is above all *harmonious,* so that to be disproportionate in the whole, ill-placed in reality, is to be against the source of being. According to Edwards, to be is to be harmoniously related. And thus a disproportionate patch of entity is a denial of each other being, quite literally a refusal of "consent" to it.[12] But excellency is what "pleases," and "pleasedness in perceiving being always arises, either from a perception of consent to being in general, or of consent to that being that perceives."[13] Therefore proportion is excellency.

Plainly, this dialectic, which remained a permanent key in Edwards' thinking,[14] works only within the root metaphor of community, just noted. Neither this root intuition, nor the doctrine that to be is to be in proportion, are compatible with Newton as many others understood him, to describe a world-*mechanism* made of self-subsistent material bits. It is time to consider a decisive character of Edwards' appropriation of Newtonian physics: from the beginning it depends upon philosophical *critique* of the metaphysics then associated with Newton's physics. Apparently from his first reading, Edwards was unerringly drawn to the systematically unresolved places in mechanics. An instance is perhaps already before us: the duality of "gravity" and "motion." That these are "harmonious" is indeed not explained by Newton; gravity, as an "action at a distance," is the very sort of thing for which laws of mechanical motion can make no provision at all.

That Newton's physics cast a vision of universal harmony was much of its appeal to all and not just to Edwards. But specifically Christian theology, and even many kinds of mere theism, were put off from creative appropriation of the vision by the apparent necessity of conceiving that harmony as the established internal reciprocity of a great mechanism. Whatever may have been Newton's own dream, the God of the eighteenth century's reception of Newton was an omniscient and omnipotent Engineer, who had fashioned a universal machine for his own pleasure and to be the maintenance-free mill of his blessings for others. The Christian God is manifestly incompetent in this role, for his actuality is invested precisely in the *transformation* of established reciprocities: he is real in Jesus' resurrection and ours, in the Spirit's unpredictable dynamism, the forgiveness of sin, and other "miracles." When religionists tried to combine Jefferson's God with the God of the gospel, they only set themselves up for devastating critique of internal incoherence.

II

Edwards grasped the problem clearly and unabashedly. It was the goal of his philosophical reception of physics to show "that there is no such thing as mechanism, if that . . . is taken to be that whereby bodies act each upon other, purely and properly by themselves"[15] And he grasped equally boldly wherein lay the conceptual heart of the mechanistic ideology. The heart is the unanalyzed assumption that "bodies" are the sort of thing that either can or cannot act "properly by themselves," that is, the unthinking application of the ancient Western notion of *substance* to physics' conception of masses in motion. The "substance" of any real thing is the supposed hidden, intrinsically potent subject of its overt attributes and actions. That there is no "mechanism" is established in Edwards' argument by proof that "the certain unknown substance which philosophers used to think subsisted by itself, and stood underneath and kept up solidity and all other properties . . . is nothing but solidity itself."[16]

Moreover, he saw *why* the application of the substance-category to physics' masses in motion was bound to cause confusion both for Christian theology and for thought in general: the category of substance is part of a notion of deity, so that its application elsewhere is either polytheism or mere confusion. If philosophers "must needs apply that word . . . , they must apply it to the divine Being. . . . And here I believe all those philosophers would apply it, if they knew what they meant themselves."[17] Edwards' critique of mechanism is an encompassing piece of demythologizing: there are no little self-sufficient agencies beside God, natural entities are not godlets, and therefore the world harmony is not self-contained.

Edwards' insight is profound and accurate. We inherit the notion of substance from Greece's attempt to describe its own appropriate God. A substance is the possessor and asserter of its attributes, maintaining itself in being by the security of its grip on them: "this chair" is the thing *that is* stable, can uprightly accommodate, etc., and it remains this self just so long as it retains stability, upright accommodation, and so on. Thus to say that something is a substance is to say that it possesses and asserts itself against time; the constitutive hopes are of self-retention and persistence. Thus also, only immortal entities are fully substances, only the gods or their philosophical sublimations. And if Greece's development and use of the category of substance for all real things thus claims potential divinity for all things, that is exactly what Greece meant to claim.

Christian theology's adoption of the category of substance was therefore a chief misstep in its delicate and necessary negotiation with Greek religion. The category fits even God ill, as the gospel interprets him, for the gospel's God is not God by his self-preservation and immunity to history—quite the contrary! Edwards was right in calling even God substance only because others "must needs apply" the term. Nevertheless, the baneful influence of traditional theology's application of the category of substance to God was mitigated by the doctrine of triunity. In that patristic and medieval thought then went on to speak also of creatures as substances, still less tractable problems were created, but within pre-modernity's person-centered worldview, also they could be contained. Are soul and body one substance or two? Just how are created souls immortal? No fully Christian answers to such questions were ever devised, but workable approximations were. The contradiction finally became disastrous only when the reality also of Newton's masses in motion was unquestioningly guaranteed by regarding even these as substances. Christianity can do nothing with a world of rule-obeying, acting and reacting *things,* when these are taken to be timelessly self-contained.

"Substance" is a God-concept. In older Christian thought, its use of others than God was tolerable, since all remained within the economy of history and its personal agents, open and correlated to the gospel's active and purposeful God. It is the elevation of an ahistorical and therefore purposeless world-system and its constituents to the title of substance that is the nihilist strain in vulgar modernity. That atoms or other masses should be, even if created once upon a time, self-possessing in their being and action denies God, whatever else may be asserted. Edwards was one of the first to see this with full clarity.

Edwards had no quarrel with physics' operational concept of matter; it was an inspiration to him. At the end of the metaphysical reconstruction whose goal we have just described he insisted: "We would not, therefore, be understood to deny that things are where they seem to be, for the principles we lay down . . . do not infer that. Nor will it be found that they at all make void natural philosophy, or the science of the causes or reasons of corporeal changes." As to the laws of physical process, he wrote, "the case is the same . . . whether we suppose the world only mental"—devoid of material substance—"or no."[18] Whatever "mass" or "matter," or "space" or "motion," mean *within* Newton's laws, they mean for Edwards. It is Aristotle Edwards wants to be rid of. In the philosophy of science, narrowly conceived, Edwards was a phenomenalist and an operationalist, rescued by faith in God, as we will see, from these positions' usual deficiencies.

The draft essay "On Atoms" begins with one of the century's standard theses, that all bodies must be "atoms" or "composed" of atoms, and defines an atom as a body "whose parts cannot by any finite power whatsoever be separated one from another."[19] "Parts" is the right word, since so far as geometry is concerned, matter must be indefinitely divisible.[20] Thus if the parts into which a unit of matter are geometrically divisible are actually inseparable, this is strictly a fact, requiring explanation. Next step in the argument: since what makes an atom an atom is indivisibility, and since it is essential to matter to have atomic structure, to divide an atom would be simply to dematerialize it.[21] Therefore solidity, which is resistance to being divided, is in the case of atoms "the resistance to be annihilated, or the persevering to be." That is, solidity is the being of atoms and so of body: "The very essence and being of bodies" is resistance to division; "body and solidity are the same."[22]

Thus the question is inescapably posed: *What* resists the division of some geometrically divisible portions of body? What holds the potential parts of atoms in fact together? That is, what exerts the being of atoms and so of all body?[23] The usual answer was that the substance that "is" whatever the atom is—the x that "is," for example, rectangular, solid, etc.—is the doer of this resistance. But Edwards has eliminated this answer by his argument that solidity itself—not an x "that is" solid—is the whole being of atoms. He has debunked the godlet hidden in each fundamental mass, posited by the standard language of the time. An obvious alternative is that the real God assumes the function.

Edwards takes that alternative. His argument is provided by his entirely unoriginal definition of the atom. The power that resists an atom's division must be superior to "any finite power whatsoever," that is, must be infinite. Which is "as much" as to say "that it is God himself, or the immediate exercize of his power, that keeps the parts of atoms . . . together." And then Edwards continues with a move entirely typical of his mind, unhindered by pieties of language: "And if any say that [merely] the nature of atoms is an infinite power, [they] say the same that I do."[24]

The demythologizing speeds on: "solidity results from the immediate exercise of God's power, causing there to be indefinite resistance in that place where it is." And since "body and solidity are the same . . . , it follows that all body is nothing but what immediately results from the exercize of divine power in such a particular manner."[25] And therefore, if we "must needs" use the word substance, we must say "that the substance of bodies becomes . . . nothing but the Deity acting in that particular manner in those parts of space where he sees fit."[26]

Masses thus accounted for, their motion is quickly incorporated into the scheme. Motion is "the communication of this resistance, from one part of space to another successively," and is therefore equally God's immediate act. The Newtonian laws of motion become "the stated methods of God's acting" of this sort, "and the stated conditions of the alterations of the manner of his acting." The laws of motion are but the regularities of God's spatial resistance-setting. And so "there is no such thing as mechanism."[27] There is instead the harmony of God's "immediate," that is, personally present, agency. If God's triunity is the harmony of what God is, the laws of motion are a harmony of what he does.

Gravity also fits easily into this system. Edwards' severely empirical eye viewed the alterations of motion at a boundary by the solidity of the body setting the boundary, and viewed the alteration of motion which we call acceleration and attribute to gravity, and saw the same phenomenon in both.[28] Newton himself regarded gravitation as the action of some as yet unanalyzed agency, and various thinkers, to whom Edwards refers, had proposed God for the role.[29] Since Edwards in any case regarded God's immediate agency as the substance of solidity, it is an obvious step to say that "Solidity is gravity," indeed, that the "essence of bodies is gravity."[30] The agency that *holds* atomic bodies together, and the agency that *draws* them to each other must be the same, only in different degrees. The agency is God in person.

One step remains in this construction. Space is the field of God's immediate activity. We have already learned, from "Of Being," *how,* according to Edwards, space is God's field: space is the field of the universal consciousness that God is. Thus the immediate power that impells and resists at points in space and so creates masses in motion is the power of thought; God thinks resistances at places and times and literally "communicates" them. God conceives a harmony other than himself and so it is. And the laws of motion and gravity are the logic of this part of God's thinking. That the world is "only mental" characterizes it not only by what it is not, made of impersonal substances and chained to mechanism, but also by what it must then be. God thinks a world and so, without intervening steps, there is one.

With this turn to the phenomenon of consciousness, we have turned also to the other side of Edwards' appropriation of the Enlightenment, his discussion with Locke. Locke's place in history is as a founder of that tribe who have tried to make consciousness, communally and individually, the matter of sciences conceived in analogy to Newton's. But before continuing on this second line, I should pause to say that the truth of Edwards' philosophical use of physics does not depend on the particular state of physics in his time.

Modern physics has no idea of atoms in the original sense, of geometrically but not factually divisible units of matter. Edwards' argument that divine immediate agency is needed to account for atoms is therefore now empty. But this is only because the mystery to which he penetrated has been incorporated by scientific theory itself. Physics now posits *no* entities that satisfy the concept of substance, just as Edwards insisted it should not. That does not eliminate the question: What, finally, are physical equations *about?* It only throws the question wide open. One can, of course, sheerly declare the question out of bounds. But whether that procedure or Edwards' is more rational, is yet another question.

III

I return to Edwards' use of Locke. He documented it in the manuscript notebook *The Mind,* which once begun he seems to have worked over much of his life.[31] He accepted chiefly two things from Locke. The first is an interpretation of mind or personhood.

"Well might Mr. Locke say that identity of person consisted in identity of consciousness." That there is a person, a continuing self-identical someone, is the same as that there is a more than momentary consciousness; about so much Edwards gratefully agreed with Locke. But then he used Occam's razor in the way he had learned to use it in the case of bodies: he rejected Locke's posit of a spiritual substance, "a spirit,"

behind and maintaining the temporal extension of consciousness. According to Edwards, Locke "might have said that identity of spirit, too, consisted in the same consciousness. A mind or spirit is nothing else but
consciousness and what is included in it. The same consciousness is to
all intents and purposes the very same spirit."[32] There is no x, other than
awareness, to "have" awareness: "certainly there is something that immediately produces and upholds [each new] thought. . . . It is not antecedent thoughts, for they are . . . gone. . . . But if we say 'tis the
substance of the soul, if we mean that there is some substance besides
that thought, that brings that thought forth . . . , that has no properties,
it seems to be absurd."[33]

With the Lockean interpretation of mind, stripped of substantialist
hesitations, Edwards is in position, second, for a new attack on the notion
of material substance, this time from the side of created mind. Locke
conceived consciousness as a field, for what "is included in it," to use
Edwards' rendering. These contents are "ideas," and by conceiving these
on the analogy of atoms, and the activity of mind as their mechanics,
Locke thought to lay the basis for a Newtonian science of experience. A
double causal structure was posited. The motion, resistance and attraction
of ideas among themselves make one causal network, analogous to Newton's. Since what is thus afoot is to be cognition, the ideas and some of
their motions are themselves supposed to be caused by solidities outside
the mind, in a straightforwardly Newtonian way. In this last connection,
Lockeanism offered abundant opportunity for philosophical critique.

When "ideas" are thought of as *caused* by external actuality, it
instantly becomes obscure how they can be ideas *of* external actuality.
The redness I experience must be caused in me by characteristics of the
"red" object, but why should we then call the object itself red? What
can it even mean to speak of a redness "in the object"? My pain is
doubtless caused by characteristics of the needle, but the needle has no
pain. Locke's own recourse was the notorious distinction of primary from
secondary qualities. Secondary qualities such as color or smell are indeed
not in the object but only in the mind, but are caused there by primary
qualities that are in both the object and the mind. The primary qualities,
that are really out there, are those that appear in Newton's laws. Edwards
was not the first and would not be the last to understand that this distinction would not do.

So far as unprejudiced registration of what appears in consciousness
takes us, Edwards says, we could better suppose that color is primary
and the Newtonian qualities secondary. "The idea we have of space [that
is, here, extension] . . . is only [of] *colored* space, and is entirely taken

out of the mind if color be taken away; and so all that we call extension, motion and figure is gone if color is gone."[34] If we nevertheless insist that some of the qualities that make our experience of bodies, mass and motion, are outside the mind, to cause all of them in the mind, this is founded on no analysis of experience but only on a metaphysical insistence that bodies must somehow be substances. For Edwards, it is, vice versa, a decisive argument against the metaphysics of material substance that it supports so arbitrary a distinction.[35] And so the conclusion: if we grant, as "is now agreed upon by every knowing philosopher," that "colors are not really in the things . . . , but are strictly nowhere else but in the mind,"[36] then the reasonable conclusion is that all that makes up what we experience as body is "only in the mind."[37] Note that it is precisely empirical reality that is thus saved; it is because we suppose that the ideas in mind are *caused* by things beyond the mind, that those things threaten to become themselves sensibly unreachable. Edwards' doctrine is not that the world is my dream but that consciousness *envelopes* what it apprehends, and that the enveloping is the "being of beings."

It is created minds we are now talking about. This sets a problem: When God thinks the universe of bodies, when he thinks resistances and accelerations in coherent series, what "exists in the divine mind," since all these things are now shown to exist in *our* minds? Edwards answers with his customary willingness to face every consequence. What exists in the divine mind is God's "determination, his care and design that [our] ideas shall be united," within each mind and perspectivally among all, *as* the ideas of such-and-such resistances and accelerations.[38] God directly "communicates" to each of us the ideas that are the content of our consciousnesses,[39] and it is this communication that is his thinking and so his creating of the universe of bodies. Thus Edwards' final metaphysical proposition is: "And indeed, the secret lies here: that which truly is the substance of all bodies is the infinitely exact and precise and perfectly stable ideas in God's mind, together with his stable will that the same shall gradually be communicated to . . . other minds, according to . . . established . . . laws."[40]

Truth in this system is the success of this communication; all empirical truth is an agreement of our "ideas" with the "series in God" that is the being of objects.[41] The external world remains external and the object of empirical knowledge. One must understand: Edwards is concerned precisely to save and affirm the externality of the material world, both to God and to us. But what has "existence out of" created minds, "the very substance of the body itself," is "nothing but the divine power, or rather the constant exertion of it."[42] As for God's mind, the universe is external also to it, since his thought of it is a self-*communicating* thought. In the very first entry of the *Miscellanies,* Edwards had a full vision of the latter point: "Man . . . is the consciousness of the creation whereby the universe is conscious of its own being . . . of the actions of the Creator . . . with respect to it. Now except the world had such a consciousness of itself, it would be altogether vain that it was. . . . For the creation was known as much . . . from all eternity as it is now, to the Creator."[43]

Expounded as Edwards had to, and as I have followed Edwards in doing, this metaphysics must seem awkward and round about. But in fact its animating intuition is breathtakingly simple and quite possibly true. Reality is a community of minds; and it is an actual community, that is, one engaged in communication. Minds in community are "the only proper . . . beings."[44] The world of bodies is the *between* of their communication, the perspectival field in which persons can come together while each remaining an *other* from all the others. The world of bodies is what God thinks in order to think a *communal plurality* of consciousnesses, who are to think and feel each other's thoughts and feelings while yet remaining plural. Edwards appropriated Newton's physics by replacing the hidden substance-category's posits of self-possession and stability with the posit of intersubjectivity. And so he abolished control of our world-image by the metaphor of mechanism.

Finally in this chapter, therefore, we must give an initial account of this community of divine and created consciousnesses, as Edwards interprets it. The spiritual community is, as we have already noted, the fundamental harmony of being: "As nothing else has a proper being but spirits . . . , therefore, the consent of bodies to one another, and the harmony that is among them, is but the shadow of excellency. The highest excellency . . . must be the consent of spirits one to another. . . . [T]he sweet harmony between the various parts of the universe is only an image of universal love."[45] But what is a spirit?

Edwards locates the difference between true mind and the intelligence he attributes to animals in the reflexivity of self-consciousness: "the main difference between men and beasts is that men are capable of reflecting upon what passes in their own minds: beasts have nothing but direct consciousness. Men are capable of viewing what is in themselves contemplatively."[46] The reflexivity is, moreover, not merely contemplative; thought is distinguished from mere perception in that men have "voluntary actions about their own thoughts."[47] Thus when Edwards comes to define consciousness as such, he defines it as "the mind's perceiving what is in itself" as "a sort of feeling within itself." "The mind feels when it thinks, so it feels when it desires, feels when it loves, feels itself hate, etc."[48]

As may be seen from these last expressions, it is what would later be called *"immediate"* self-consciousness that Edwards proposes for the key anthropological role, despite some freedom of expression elsewhere in this connection. Indeed, so immediate is self-consciousness, according to Edwards, that to *know* acts of the mind can only be to *perform* them again. "[I]deas of what is internal or spiritual . . . are the same thing over again";[49] for example, "to think of love, either of our past love . . . or of the love of others . . . we either so frame things in our imagination that we have for a moment that love . . . , or we excite for a moment that love which we have, and suppose it another place."[50]

Clearly, Edwards was on the way to creating a doctrine that consciousnesses are substances by virtue of their self-relatedness, by their metaphysical independence as *self*-consciousnesses. Just such doctrine was to be created by the German idealism of the next century. And indeed, Edwards taught that the "nearer in nature beings are to God, so much the more properly are they beings, and more substantial; and that spirits are . . . more substantial, then bodies."[51] He even wrote in his *Miscellanies:* "Many have wrong conceptions of the difference between . . . deity and created spirits. The difference is no contrareity, but what naturally results from His greatness and nothing else, such as created spirits . . . more imitate, the greater they are in their powers. . . . So that, if we should suppose the faculties of a created spirit to be enlarged infinitely, there would be the deity to all intents and purposes, the same simplicity, immutability, etc."[52] Nor did he ever reject these propositions. But this was not a way he could pursue to the end, with his clear insight into the polytheism of taking any creatures for "substances." Thus after a period in which he accepted Locke's teaching that continuity of consciousness is by itself self-identity of person, he broke the metaphysical independence also of self-consciousness, by making continuity of consciousness a necessary but insufficient condition of personal self-identity.[53] Also minds, as continuing entities, have their substantiality only in God's mind, they exist only in that God forms and communicates a coherent "series" of ideas.[54] They are indeed God's images, they are consciousnesses as he is, but they are dependent and therefore always behind his clarity. He communicates to them, and so they have being.

But if we as minds are not substances, and if God and we are alike minds and just alike *as* minds, is not also God robbed of his "substantiality"? For Edwards there is only one possible reply: God is independent mind, as we are not, in that he is in himself communal, as we are only with him. God is triune. "That God is as it were the only sub-stance" would better be stated as "the perfection . . . of his knowledge, wisdom, power and will"[55]—note the Augustinian Trinity. Of God, it can be true that he "infinitely loves himself"; just so, "his being is infinite."[56] And this can be, with *him*, "excellence" because "he exerts himself toward himself no other way than in infinitely loving and delight-ing in himself, in the mutual love of the Father and the Son. This makes the third, the personal Holy Spirit . . . which is his . . . infinite consent to being in general."[57]

In Edward's interpretation of being, the triune God, as harmony in himself, thinks other true partners of this community, and so there is also the world posited by physics, as the intersubjectivity of the expanded community. It is surely worth considering whether some such interpreta-tion of Newton's world is not that demanded by faith—or even to pre-serve a natural moral self-interpretation by the human community. Be-hind all the nihilisms of modernity is the vision of our world as a deaf and dumb apparatus, within which we live but to which our converse is irrelevant. Perhaps the issue may be put most simply: Does it make any sense to *pray* for and with one another? Even if, as in most current inter-pretations, the world-system is supposed to involve real contingency, the question is still: Does the world take place in the *kind* of contingency in which our addresses and pleas can participate? Is the world within a *free-dom?*

America has been more than other nations undone by alternate fear of science itself and capitulation to usually jejune science-inspired ideol-ogies. Insofar as we have tried to reunite ourselves with our world by psychological ideologies and techniques, by taking up Locke's enterprise and assimilating also ourselves to the mechanical environment, we have turned also our society and our individual psyches into alien and silent prisons. In its participation in this self-alienation, one-half of the Ameri-can church has become simply unbelieving, disguising its abandonment of prayer by doing other things—meditation, self- or group-therapy, etc.— and calling them prayer; the other half thinks it can maintain belief only by relativizing the Newtonian harmony and making God an extra entity who sometimes "intervenes." The American civil community is flattened and perverted by the same religious triviality and ideological demonism. Our "liberalism" and our "conservatism" are but the atheist and super-stitious branches of the same capitulation before a dead universe. And it is all a delusion. There is; in reality, no mechanism—or so at least the most Enlightened of all our teachers asserted.

4

The Melody of History

Even deeper than the standard Enlightenment's divorce of *personality* from the world described by science was its divorce of *history* from that world, for personality itself is founded in the sequences and connections of time. Also this divorce has been particularly fateful for America, that in any case so uneasily possesses its history. Regularly, to be sure, we exhort ourselves to recover "a sense of history" or some such virtue, but self-help resolutions only confirm the timelessness of the world we suppose ourselves actually to inhabit. We can be freed only by discovering the truth: that our ahistorical environment is mere illusion. And perhaps there is one recovery that might help us see this, for the final outcome of Jonathan Edwards' metaphysical revisions was an understanding of reality as temporal in root and twig.

In traditional Western metaphysics, created reality is temporal, but as a deficit. It is composed of substances that give hostages to time only by weak spots in their being, by insecurities in their grip on their essential attributes. In Edward's metaphysics, exactly per contra, it is the rule by which a *sequence* of changes is generated in the divine mind—it is, to press Edwards' thought hardly at all, their tune in God's ear—that is the very being of a creature. There are continuing entities other than God because God associates momentary other consciousnesses with predecessors and successors, and resistance-events with predecessors and successors, in a—one can only say it so—musically coherent way.[1] To specify a created thing's identity is thus to run over at least some stretch of its sequence. The word "history" has acquired for us a sense not quite available to Edwards; with that sense it exactly states his thought: the being of creatures is their history.

Moreover, creatures are histories because God is. In traditional Western theology, God is God because he suffers no deficit of substantiality, that is, is altogether immune to time. In Edwards' theology, God is God because his life is triune and so is musically harmonious in itself, as against

creatures who are coherent sequences only with and by him. Also of God
it holds: being is history.

Thus Edwards must include also the apparently ahistorical realms of
reality in an historical whole. He knew three such: the cyclically moving
cosmosmachine, heaven, and the angelic creation.

Unlike many Enlightenment theorists, Edwards' cosmology is not
"steady-state"; the seemingly cyclical revolutions of the heavens have,
he asserts, a goal. "These revolutions are not for nothing. . . . The sun
don't go round day after day and year after year for no other end, but
only to come to the same place again from whence it . . . set out."[2]
The cosmic harmony from which Edwards with his century infers an
intelligent and voluntary first cause, must, in order to evidence that particular intelligence in which Edwards actually believes, be a harmony
primarily in time and only so in space. The harmony is "that the state of
one thing may be conformed . . . with the state of another and also to
something to come, to some end to be attained";[3] this end can only be
"in another state that is to succeed" "these revolutions,"[4] attained as
the conclusion of "various successive states of the world . . . as connected in a scheme."[5] For God, the cosmos is itself a particular, which
exists as a continuing entity in that he composes and hums its tune.

Therewith we arrive again at the community of spirits. Its priority
to the harmony of physics is now seen as the priority of a goal to that of
which it is the goal. Man is "that creature for whom all the rest is made."[6]
This is not, as in some theology, a claim of superior present endowment.
Human creatures are the goal of creation in that they will "enter" the
state after "these revolutions," and in that thereby the entire creation has
purpose. For man is the *consciousness* and so will be the memory of the
cosmos. To cite again a key passage already instanced: "Man is the consciousness of the creation whereby the universe is conscious of its own
being and of what is done in it. . . . Except the world had such a consciousness of itself, it would be altogether vain that it was. . . . For the
creation was known as much . . . from all eternity as it is now, to the
Creator. Now it is evident the world is as much in vain, if this consciousness lasts but a little while and then ceases, as it would be if there were
no consciousness of it."[7] If "the intelligent beings of the world" do not
"remain after the world comes to an end," nothing will have been *attained* by the world's existence.[8]

The material creation is correspondingly conceived. It was from the
broad Platonism of western tradition that Edwards came to grasp material
things as images of spiritual reality. But the tradition normally located
the superiority of spirit in stability and the dependent character of matter

in its flightiness. In exact reversal of the tradition just at this fundamental point, Edwards teaches instead: "The fixedness of . . . animate parts of this lower world is really an imperfection," is that wherein they are "below the things that are spiritual." In the last state, material entities will be "most flexible, moveable and agile," "susceptible of mutations from the presence of Christ"; and in this age it is the "animated parts" of this lower world "that are most beautiful, because they most accurately resemble the beauty of spirit."[9]

That the universe has an end, after which comes its fulfillment, is not to be inflicted merely by supernatural intervention. The laws of physics and the initial boundary conditions are such, according to Edwards, that the world-system is inherently perishable; only so can it have a purpose beyond itself.[10] Edwards, in the style of some modern cosmologists though not with their time-frame envisions a collapse of the universe back upon itself, into a concluding infinitely energetic singularity. Even if Scripture did not tell us of the fall of the heavens and a final conflagration, "philosophy," he writes in his notes, would "tell us that the motion of the several parts of the visible world must, in a great length of time, gradually cease; and that if it ceases, it will come together into a common heap; but if it does so, it must necessarily be involved in a great conflagration."[11] The fixed stars are "worlds of fire" like our sun; at the end they will traverse their "infinite" spaces with "prodigious velocity . . . into . . . one huge conflagration."[12] Just such expectations, we may note, have been taken by scientistic ideologists right through Lord Russell as disproofs of the gospel; Edwards finds in them precious confirmations.

It is already apparent that Edwards must describe also the goal, the perfected community of spirits, as above all lively, as the very opposite of eternal relaxation. I must devote a later chapter to that matter, and can leave it here with this mention. But also short of the Kingdom, there is not only earth with its changes, but heaven where the souls of departed saints dwell already with God. Surely their state is, at least in the interim, beyond history?

"Heaven," for Edwards as for the antecedent medieval and Calvinist though not Lutheran or sectarian, traditions, is that part of creation God made to be his own place in his creation and into which to receive the finally perfected creatures. It is distinguished, by Edwards, from the rest of creation precisely by its lack of resistance to spiritual dynamism, by its fluidity.[13] Thus created spirits now already there are *not* cut off from the history of God's work in his creation. "Tis manifest that the saints in heaven . . . do behold and rejoice in the prosperity of Christ's Church on earth and do rejoice in those . . . glorious events by which

Christ's kingdom is set up in the world."[14] The saints "happiness" is "in a like progression with the church on earth."[15] Edwards can recount the entire history of salvation from their viewpoint, as their history.[16]

As for the angels, a reader of the *Miscellanies* may well wonder why the themes of their test, by which some fell, and of the others' eventual "confirmation" in eternal righteousness, so occupied Edwards. After a bit, one sees why. In order for the spiritual community to be truly communal, it must be neither naturally undifferentiated nor practically hierarchical. The angels are created spirits naturally superior to humans, yet set by the Creator to serve these inferiors. The proclamation of this plan was the test against which Satan revolted and in which the good angels stood; thus they too acquire the history of human salvation as their own history. Indeed, the position and history of the angels establishes metaphysically the chief principle of saving history, that creatures' exaltation is not by natural endowment but by God's grace.[17]

The final result of Edwards' work with Newton and Locke is a metaphysics and worldview that necessitate, drive, and perfectly accommodate three great preoccupations: Edwards' passion to interpret the "end for which God created the world"; the importance for him of knowing the principles of historical change; and his lifelong exegetical labor on the apocalyptic parts of Scripture. The first two of these are the remaining matter of this chapter.

II

Edwards' interpretation of God's final purpose for creation runs through the whole sequence of his notes. There is also a finished though only posthumously published work from the years of his mature thought, the *Dissertation Concerning the End for Which God Created the World.* In the *Dissertation,* the problem set is one that was always acute for the Calvinist tradition: does God create for our sake or for his own sake? It is apparent that either answer is likely to support destructive religiosities. If we say God creates for the creatures' sake, it will be hard to combat the cult that has, as Edwards feared, come to be the practiced religion of most Americans: of the "loving," "unconditionally accepting" God, who has no intentions of his own and is ever more transparently a mere device of our self-help. If we say God creates simply for his own sake, it is hard to know why we should care. Edwards foresaw the dangers of both answers and labored to show how their disjunction does not fit the biblical God.

One supposes Edwards must be writing in the 1980s, attacking one or another program or manual of religious self-help, when he writes in the *Dissertation,* of the biblical saints: "It would be absurd to say, that in their ardent exclamations [of praise to God], they are only giving vent to their vehement benevolence to their fellow creatures, and expressing their earnest desire that God might be glorified, so that his subjects may be made happy by this means."[18] Absurd it may be in saints, but Edwards saw it as a pressing danger in New England Christianity, and spent his life attacking the correlated interpretations of God's end in creation. As to what a relation to God might be like, that is *not* self-serving, and how it is possible, these are large questions to which Edwards devoted a major part of his literary production.

Edwards thus begins with the other possibility. God must have himself as his end in creating, since as Creator he is source of all good, must therefore be the ultimate object of every just "regard," and therefore must be the ultimate object of his own infallibly just regard.[19] But he establishes this standard Calvinist position only in order immediately to conduct a trinitarian-christological analysis of it, aimed at deriving our good within God's. In the bare bones of his metaphysics, Edwards can achieve this purpose with great despatch: "For God to glorify himself is to discover himself in his works, or to communicate himself in his works, which is all one, for we are to remember that the world exists only mentally, so that the very being of the world implies its being perceived or discovered."[20] It is, however, precisely in the present connection that we can learn just how trinitarian and christological this metaphysics is.

Necessarily, Edwards' analysis of God's self-regard begins with something about the object that God thus regards, that is, God. Edwards' teaches that "the glorious attributes of God . . . consist in a sufficiency to certain acts and effects."[21] With that, his whole argument is determined. The first step: in that God, necessarily and rightly, supremely values himself, he supremely values also his "acts and effects," since his own attributes are nothing but sufficiency to these. Second step: given the nature of divine being, God's acts are communicatings, and their effects therefore knowledge, so that in supremely valuing his acts, God supremely values other minds' knowledge of them, and that is, of himself. Finally: since God is good, to know him is to be blessed; therefore in supremely valuing himself, God supremely values our blessedness.[22] Which, it would seem, is what was to be proved.

But there are further questions. For one, it may be asked how this doctrine accounts for created *history,* why it does not altogether empty the notion of God's purpose. Why did not God simply bring forth at once

a perfected knower of himself? "For what reason . . . was it requisite
that God's intelligent creature should first be in a state of probation before
he is in a state of confirmed happiness?" [23] Much evil would have been
avoided. Edwards' answer is again beautifully Calvinist: the history between the first creation and the end is needed in order that *all* God's
glorious attributes may be displayed, and the creature, whose happiness
is the beholding of God, not left in an incomplete blessedness. "Without
[a period of testing] there would not properly have been . . . a divine
moral government over intelligent creatures. . . . But it is chiefly by the
exercize of moral government that God displays his moral perfections,
which are in a peculiar manner the glory of the divine nature." [24] The
glory of God simply is such as to be only historically communicable.

A second question takes us deeper. Can it also, conversely, be said
that in valuing us God values himself? Must not that identify God's love
of himself and his love of us? And must not such an identification, at
least within Edwards' system, finally identify God and us? Yet if this
converse cannot be said, we are back with the disjunction between God
and creatures as ends of creation.

Edwards does not shrink from the reflection. Our knowledge and
love of God are, he says, a "conformity" to God's holiness, to his
knowledge and love of himself—as of course follows directly from the
foregoing. And since God's "sufficiency" thus to communicate his spiritual attainments is infinite, our spiritual conformity to God must eternally
increase. [25] But God *is* spirit—this Edwards hardly bothers to note at this
point. Therefore, he continues: "the more those divine communications
increase in the creature, the more it becomes one with God; for so much
the more is it united to God in love . . . , and . . . more and more
conformed to God. . . . [A]nd so the good that is in the creature comes
forever nearer and nearer to an identity with that which is in God." [26]
God's act of communication is infinite, and therefore we eternally ap-
proach but never arrive at identity with God. But that is from our viewpoint; "[i]n the view . . . of God, who has a comprehensive prospect of
the increasing union and conformity through eternity, it must be an infinitely strict and perfect . . . oneness. . . . In this view, those elect
creatures which must be looked upon as the end of all the rest of creation,
considered with respect to the whole of their eternal duration, and as such
made God's end, must be viewed as being . . . one with him. They were
respected as brought home to him . . . and as it were swallowed up in
him, so that his respect to them finally coincides . . . with respect to
himself." [27]

Edwards has here repristinated some of the most problematic positions of the mystical tradition. It will already be seen that he does so only within a trinitarian habit of thought;[28] yet initially this only increases the threat of a pantheistic blurring of the line between Creator and creature, and of an abolition of history. Edwards seems to anticipate Hegel and make the perfected creature as a whole, and not Christ, the second divine hypostasis, God's perfect object of love who just so is God again. All the emanationist language of pagan antiquity and the most precariously Christian mystics—soon to be revivified by German Idealism, and when imported into America called "transcendentalism"—comes flooding into the *Dissertation:* "all that is ever spoken of in Scripture as an ultimate end of God's works, is included in that one phrase, *the glory of God.* . . . [This] is the emanation and true external expression of God's internal glory and fulness."[29] In the *Miscellanies,* God's glory is "the infinite good as it were flowing forth or the infinite fountain of light as it were shining forth."[30] There is in God himself a "propensity of nature to diffuse of his own fulness," and therefore it can even be said that without the perfected creature God would be "less happy."[31] From our side: "in the creature's knowing . . . , loving . . . , and praising God, the glory of God is both . . . received and returned. Here is both emanation and remanation."[32]

And yet all this language is in fact christology, though only tentatively unveiled as such in the *Dissertation.* For the perfected society of spirits is *Jesus'* society: "the holy Scriptures teach us that Jesus Christ is the head of the moral world . . . ; the chief of God's servants, appointed to be the head of his saints and angels, and set forth as the chief and most perfect pattern . . . of goodness." Therefore it is "what *he* sought as his last end," that is God's last end in the creation of the world.[33] And that is to say, precisely the *redemption* he worked is the end of creation.[34] This is another subject to which I must return; here one remarkably blunt passage may suffice: "The creation of heaven was in order to the work of redemption . . . to be a habitation for the redeemed. . . . As to this lower world, it was doubtless created to be a stage upon which this . . . work of redemption should be transacted."[35] Therefore the more precise trinitarian statement is: "And as the happiness [of blessed creatures] will be increasing to eternity, the union will become more and more . . . perfect; *nearer* and more *like to that* [my emphases] between God the Father, and the Son."[36]

The "procession" of the eternal Son, his reality as the object of perfect Love, is in Edwards' thought given before there are creatures—for Edwards is not, after all, Hegel. Thus the identity of self-love and communicating love is accomplished already in God by himself: "God is glorified within himself . . . (1) by appearing to himself in his perfect idea . . . , (2) by . . . delighting in himself by flowing forth in infinite love towards himself . . . in his Holy Spirit."[37] But that seems to undo the previous paragraph and pose the question anew: "Why then, did God incline farther to communicate himself, seeing he had done [it] completely" in his own triune life?

Edwards' answer takes us finally to the center of his systematic reflection, to—"as it were"—his notation of the universal melody's fugal structure: "To this I say, that the Son is the adequate communication of the Father's goodness. . . . But yet the Son has also an inclination to communicate *himself,* in an image of his person that may partake of his happiness: and this was the end of the creation, even the communication of the happiness of the Son of God. . . . Therefore the church is said to be the completeness of Christ."[38] It is as and only as a factor in the plot of the triune God's inner life, that God has a need to overflow. In the *Miscellanies,* Edwards is beautifully simple: "The end of the creation of God was to provide a spouse for his Son Jesus Christ, that might enjoy him and on whom he might pour forth his love. . . ."[39] "[H]eaven and earth were created that the Son of God might be complete in a spouse."[40] The church is *with* Christ the object in the triune love and so the purpose of creation.

Western Christianity, since the Enlightenment, comes always too late with its gospel. We preach to souls presumed imprisoned in a natural world indifferent to the message of Christ's history. If history is allowed any reality, we then preach to souls presumed antecedently determined also by a history detached from Christ's history. In Europe, it was Karl Barth who finally broke through to a post-Enlightenment recovery of authentic Christian vision: of Christ's story as the encompassing story of all reality. But the best efforts of Barth's admirers have never been able to make the American church see the point of his thought, perhaps because natural science remains uninterpreted in it. Americans may therefore rejoice that our own teacher arrived at a similarly encompassing christological vision two centuries sooner, and not in spite of the Enlightenment's elevation of physics and psychology, but by virtue thereof.

The very Enlightenment that blinds us to the universality of Christ's action and suffering illumined Edwards' eye, to see through every apparent confinement of Christ within a special history. Christ is the agent and beneficiary of all events from creation to fulfillment; "as Mediator [Christ] rules all events . . . so as to conduce to the good of his church, and to bring to pass the ends of his mediation,"[41] for since "God created the world to provide a spouse . . . for his Son," so "the spiritual marriage of the spouse to him, is what the whole creation labors . . . to bring to pass."[42] And Edwards does mean "whole creation," for the material universe is, we must remember, but the intersubjective field of the community of spirits that makes history. Thus he can, with supreme sophistication and naïveté, say, "the whole course of nature . . . [is] subservient to the affair of redemption,"[43] or again, "Every atom in the universe is managed by Christ so as to be most to the advantage of the Christian."[44] It may be hard to believe so much. But it may be doubted that anything less can, in the Enlightened world, be *believed* at all. Ahistorical religion is, of course, always possible.

Contemporary American religiosity mines all mystical traditions, Christian, antique and Eastern, in the desperate search for relief from the mechanical cosmos and random history we have posited for ourselves. And indeed, this has been a continuous American occupation from the very next generation after Edwards. Edwards, as is clear not only from the passages I have cited but throughout his works and from the evidence of his life, was a far more natural and intellectually devoted mystic than any after him. It is thus salutary to see that his mysticism moves oppositely to our normal variety. It emerges in the discovery not of God's good in ours but of our good in God's. And that is to say, the God the soul enters is the triune God, so that the soul can be one with God while yet God works his own will that is not necessarily ours; and the universality the soul appropriates is the encompassing fact of Christ's history rather than of the soul's own religious aspiration. I must quote one more piece of Edwards' beloved spouse-mysticism, of a drastic Christianity I am not sure is elsewhere found: "There was, [as] it were, an eternal society or family in the Godhead, in the Trinity of persons. It seems to be God's design to admit the church into the divine family as his son's wife."[45]

III

It was the consistent intention of Edwards' life to write a *summa*, a complete "body of divinity" on the scale of the great medieval and Protestant-scholastic masterworks. By the time of his call to Princeton, he felt ready to begin, and described the project in a letter to the Princeton trustees. The work, he said, would be "in an entire new method," and as we read his description, we see that the claim was justified. Merely the proposed title, as a title for a dogmatic theology, shows how Edwards anticipated some of the most vaunted insight of nineteenth- and twentieth-century theology: the "great work" was to be called *A History of the Work of Redemption*. He described the method: analysis of "the affair of Christian theology, as the whole of it, in each part, stands in reference of the great work of redemption." Edwards' claim for the virtue of this method reveals much about his thought: by displaying the topics of theology in their various references to saving—and just so universal—history, "the admirable . . . harmony of the whole" will appear as it had not before, and just this makes the method itself "the most beautiful and entertaining."[46]

The *summa* was never written. How exactly the various dogmatic loci would have been turned into comment on universal history can only in part be discovered from what Edwards left behind. The *Dissertation*, however, is in itself a complete Christian vision, at once of history and of doctrine, and may perhaps be taken as a paradigm of the great project. On that supposition, the organizing doctrine would have been the eschatology, the stipulation of the "end" of God's ways and of his creatures.[47] As in later parts of this book we consider what Edwards did say about many of the classical *loci* of dogmatic theology, we will find that his treatments are in fact eschatologically molded.

Moreover, in 1739 Edwards had preached a set of sermons, in an attempt to rekindle the Northampton revival, with the very title that he proposed for his summa, and from them and other sources we can recover the principles of at least one side of his vision of saving history: his theological interpretation of universal history itself.

It was Edwards' first principle that all the changes and revolutions of history are to "make way for the coming of Christ,"[48] whether at the Incarnation or at the End. All events are "so wonderfully ordered by the infinitely wise governor of the world," that they conduce, finally, only "to this general design."[49] The "all" is unrestricted; it is indeed the "nations" that are the subjects of revelation, apostasy, etc., as Edwards tells the history.[50] And he does not shrink from specificities; we learn, for example, that Canaan was chosen for the place of Christ's coming because it "was the most conveniently situated of any place in the world for . . . the spreading of the gospel" and that just for that reason the devil directed emigrations to such distant parts as America;[51] or that pagan philosophy flourished just before the decisive revelation in order to make clear what human wisdom could and could not achieve.[52]

It is what the theological tradition has called "providence" that is here to be discussed. With Newtonian harmony arrayed before it, Enlightenment theology accepted the divine ordering of nature as a matter of course, but was reluctant to regard history in a similar way. Over against this hesitation, Edwards insists that it "may be worthy to be considered whether it is not of as great or greater importance, that the law . . . of righteousness between the supreme *moral* [my emphasis] Governor and his subjects, should be maintained."[53] Besides God's governing of all things by his mere decree, there is a governing by commands and sanctions, that is appropriate to the place of created spirits within creation. "God . . . governs . . . all events concerning [brute creatures]. And rational creatures, are subject to the same sort of government. . . . But rational creatures . . . are the subject of another kind of government . . . with respect to their voluntary actions. [This is] moral government, and consists in . . . giving laws and in judging."[54] Were there no such government, God's provision for those creatures that are the goal of creation would be less than for others; the world of moral agents would lack its specific beauty; and communication between God and humans, both of whom are moral agents, could not occur.[55]

The end of God's moral government, as we have seen, is redemption. This doctrine determines Edwards' understanding both of the nature of God's historical agency and of the general pattern of God's historical plotting. I will describe the latter first.

A division runs through the history of Christian theology between those for whom the concrete actuality of the Incarnation, in Jesus' cross and resurrection, occurs within a providence of God that in its basic intention might not have included it, and those who read the whole plotting of God's providence from the cross and resurrection. The division runs between those for whom Christ's atoning work is contingent to the sheer fact of sin, and those for whom the fact of sin is contingent to God's intent to redeem. Some cannot and some can join the medieval hymn in praise of the "blessed sin, that occasioned such great redemption," or the carol that rejoices in Adam's sin, since otherwise "our Lady" would not have been "heaven's queen." Edwards is decidedly in the second group, with the Franciscans, Luther, the supralapsarian Calvinists, and Karl Barth.

"God hath made man's emptiness and misery," Edwards preached to his congregation, "into which he sank by the fall, an occasion of the greater advancement of his own glory . . . , in this, that there is now a more universal and apparent dependence of man on God."[56] Precisely in redeeming from sin, God "acquires a greater right to the creature" than he had even as Creator, "as he hath redeemed [it] from a state infinitely worse than nothing and brought it to a state vastly better than its former being before the fall."[57] Since knowledge of God and of our dependence on him *are* our good, it must be said that by Christ's redemption "is our happiness advanced highly above" what it would have been without sin,[58] in that we have become what we would not have been without redemption, God's "members, his spouse."[59] Nor can God's heightening of good by overcoming sin be understood as merely his taking advantage of contingency: even if "there were any such thing as . . . mere contingence," "it would have been very unfair that God should have left it to mere chance, whether man should fall or no. . . . [It is] certainly . . . more fit that an event of so great importance . . . should be disposed . . . by infinite wisdom."[60]

Edwards can say that the tempting promise of the devil to our first parents, of becoming like gods in the true knowledge of good and evil, was allowed by God and turned into a prophecy that is in blessed fact fulfilled.[61] The fallen angels' attempt to ruin humankind became the means of bringing to pass the plan to unite lowly creatures to God, against which they had rebelled. For Edwards just this connection is the supreme instance of God's wisdom.[62]

Indeed and explicitly: "the fall of the devils was wisely permitted and ordered to give occasion for a redemption from that evil they should introduce."[63] Temptation, fall and sin are not the less terrible because God's wisdom encompasses them; by "procuring the fall of men and . . . the death of Christ," Satan "snapped the pillars of the universe to bring all upon his head in flaming fire." "The great Creator that made all those stars . . . has been murdered . . . in this system and on this earth—and no wonder that this breaks down the whole frame and fetches all down in vengeance."[64] Nor does sin's necessity for redemption solve the problem posed about God's justice by his allowing it; Edwards seems to regard the problem as insoluble.[65] As to the compatibility of encompassing redemptive Providence with creaturely free responsibility, Edwards was to write one of the two or three greatest books on that millennially plumbed subject.

Since the inner connections of history's determining events can be so described, the pragmatism of all history is cruciform: "God's manner is in almost everything to suffer 'em first to be undone and then to build 'em up again in a more glorious state . . . than before. . . . When he has anything very glorious to accomplish, he . . . builds it up out of ruins . . . , hereby manifesting the glory of his sufficient power."[66] Specificity is Edwards' very point: the low estate of the Jews over against other nations just at the time of Christ's coming was a necessary preparation;[67] the persecutions were most intense just before Constantine;[68] high-church persecutions in England and sufferings in the American wilderness created the holy commonwealths.[69]

IV

The final matters of this chapter must be the nature of God's historical agency and of historical ordering, as Edwards conceives them.[70] It is already clear that Edwards has overcome all notion of a causal relation between God and temporal events, and indeed all notion that God's agency is in any way external to them.

The being of creatures is simply God's thinking, in that God thinks some of his thoughts as thoughts to be communicated. And since what God thinks is precisely tunes, coherent sequences of events, the fact that the created world has history requires no further explanation. Now we must only recall: within the triune life, it is specifically the *Son's* self-communication in which God's communicative thought overleaps the bounds of God's self. The Son thinks the fellowship in and by which he responds to the Father's self-communication, and *so* there is a world. Thus God's providential and moral agencies are simply modes of the communal reflection of Father, Son and Spirit.

On this basis, Edwards can appropriate a motif of traditional Christian speculation far more radically than was otherwise possible: from the fall to the end, *Christ* is the agent of created history. "[W]hen we read in sacred history what God [did] towards his church and people, and what he said . . . , we are to understand it especially of the second person of the Trinity."[71] Edwards tells the whole of universal history as the cummulative steps in Christs' "investiture" as "head over all."[72] And then Edwards adds his own special doctrine, that the periodic impetus of history, at the points where history breaks out of stagnation and gathers itself for the Kingdom, are "carried on by remarkable pourings out of the Spirit of God . . . at special seasons of mercy."[73] Putting it all together: creatures are providentially and morally governed in that they are included in God's triune life.

Within this interpretation of divine agency, vexed traditional problems simply vanish. What is the difference between God's agency in nature and his agency in history? Between his agency in history generally and his agency in the events narrated by Scripture? Between "naturally" explicable events in the scriptural narrative and "miracles"? Between his agency in the broad world and his agency in the soul? To all these questions Edwards has the same answer: there is no difference in principle. The only difference is that whereas "all natural operations are done immediately by God, only in harmony and proportion," miracles, great saving events, and "gracious operations on the mind" are in their several ways "done in the most general proportion, not tied to any particular proportion, to this or that created being; but the proportion is with the whole series of acts and designs from eternity to eternity."[74] The sprouting of a seed is right and rationally comprehensible within the tune of one organic life; the resurrection of Jesus or the making of a believer is right and rationally comprehensible within the tune of the universe.

One of Edwards' two principles of historical order is thus already before us. The great reversals of history, whether the resurrection or an individual's conversion, are thought by God "in the most general proportions" only, and so are unconnected to their immediate temporal environment by stipulable laws; they are "most arbitrary."[75] But this does not mean that they are *irrationally* arbitrary, or even that their rationality is wholly unknowable to us. We have to hear the great melody; then every note sounds in its necessity. Or, as Edwards was likely to say in his later writings, the mode of harmony appropriate to God's "arbitrary" agency is that appropriate to agency within free *community;* this mode of harmony he called "propriety."[76] Apart from regard to "fitness and propriety," he says, the whole "mediatorial scheme" of history "might have been set aside" for the whole of the scheme is the "means and methods" of propriety.[77]

The word "means" had a very exact sense for Puritans: "means" were the natural events ordained by God as the necessary but insufficient conditions of supernatural grace;[78] such as are, on Calvinist interpretation, baptism, preaching, and the Lord's Supper. Thus Edwards' doctrine is that the whole course of history, ordered to the final miracle of the gathering of Christ's spouse into God, proceeds as an ordering of occasions each necessary but insufficient to the continuance of the process. If we now consider these occasions as ideas in God's thinking—as we must, to grasp their reality—we will see the deeper reason why Edwards so cultivated the concept of "image": an image in consciousness is precisely the real but insufficient occasion of another idea it suggests.

Thus the second principle of historical order, as Edwards read it, is *typology:* it is "God's manner, to make inferior things shadows of the superior, and most excellent outward things shadows of spiritual, and all other things shadows of those things that are the end of all things."[79] Edwards' typologizing, so relentless that about Israel he insists that "their houses were typical houses, their magistrates typical magistrates, their clothes typical clothes,"[80] is not an arbitrary game or mere hangover from older exegetical method; since all things are thoughts in God's mind, their imaging references are precisely their objective connections. It would be gratifying if Edwards had explicitly said that imaging reference, as a principle of order, should best be understood as *musical* coherence, but he did not. I may, however, suggest that he could as well have.

II

THE CRITIQUE OF
RELIGION

> Those that go furthest in religion, that are in a natural condition, have no charity.
> —*Miscellanies,* 673

5

Justification by Faith

Jonathan Edwards' fame, and much of his theology, began in the same event with which began the most remarkable phenomenon of American religious history, the sequence of "revivals." This circumstance by itself would make Edwards a key figure for the understanding of our religious possibilities. The event in question is the "Awakening" at Northampton, kindled in 1734 by Edwards' sermons against "Arminianism," and on "justification by faith alone." Seldom have sermons had such consequence. Edwards' own celebrated account must be cited:

> About this time, began the great noise that was in this part of the country about Arminianism. . . . The friends of vital piety trembled for fear of the issue; but it seemed, contrary to their fear, strongly to be overruled for the promoting of religion. Many . . . [came] to inquire what was indeed the way in which they must come to be accepted with God. . . . Although great fault was found with meddling with the controversy in the pulpit . . . , yet it proved a word spoken in season . . . ; and was most evidently attended with a very remarkable blessing of heaven to the souls of the people in this town. . . . And then it was, in the latter part of December, that the Spirit of God began extraordinarily to . . . work amongst us. . . .[1]

But what was "Arminianism?"[2] In Edwards' use, and that of New England generally, it was not necessarily advocacy of the particular principles of the Dutch theologian Jacob Arminius, but rather a religious and theological mood of which Arminius had been the most notorious instance in Puritan memory. Broadly, "Arminianism" was New England's name for a kind of religion that appears in all times and places of the church, and has other times been known as "semi-Pelagianism," "synergism," etc. "Arminianism" is our inevitable self-serving interpretation of human responsibility over against God's mercy, according to which, if we are blessed it is at least partly because we have chosen and labored to be, while when we suffer God is suddenly invoked for our unilateral rescue. But what Edwards called "Arminianism" should also be seen as a somewhat more specific phenomenon, the peculiarly American form of this religion. What Edwards called "Arminianism" has perhaps never been more succinctly described than by Dietrich Bonhoeffer's phrase for American religion: "Protestantism without the Reformation."

Edwards' "Arminianism" was the Christian version—then there was no other—of the American culture-religion. It had and has many sects. The first to become theologically aware, whose dogma may perhaps be stated, "God never violates human personality," is that which rules "mainline" Protestantism and found its first self-conscious statement in the writings of such contemporaries of Edwards as Charles Chauncy, and which in the person of a neighboring pastor, William Rand, was apparently the occasion of the particular "great noise" to which Edwards refers.

Another sort of "Arminianism" ruled the experience of those in Edwards' congregation who eventually obtained his dismissal. This is the religion of achievers; since the Civil War its dogma has regularly been made explicit in the collocation of God and capitalism as defining "American individual freedom." At present, perhaps the most pervasive churchly Arminianism is that of those in all denominations who conceive faith on the model of therapy. Among those who intend to remain faithful to original American evangelical Christianity, it is regularly—a notable irony!—their version of revival that embodies yet another Arminianism. And where American religiosity is now entirely disencumbered of the gospel, there appears the distilled Arminianism of the religiously assisted quest for self-fulfillment. As Edwards said, "These principles are exceeding taking with corrupt nature, and are what young people, at least such as have not their hearts established with grace, are easily led away with."[3]

But what, univocally, was "Arminianism"? It was Protestantism without the Reformation. It was the assimilation of Protestant protest against spiritual bondage to Enlightenment protest against religious authority, that is, given the situation in the eighteenth century, against precisely the most specific elements of Christianity. "Arminianism" was Protestantism carried not by the Reformation's demand for greater fidelity to the gospel's radically upsetting promises, but by the exactly opposite concern, that the promises not upset bourgeois satisfaction. "Arminianism" was and is the religion whose first question over against the gospel of God's acts is, "But what is *our* part?" and over against the divine law that judges our acts is, "But surely God will not hold us so strictly accountable?" "Arminianism" was "Protestant principle" mustered not on behalf of threatened "catholic substance" but rather for the further mitigation of its offensive promises and demands.

The central objects of "Arminian" critique, as of all similar movements, were such politically and religiously upsetting doctrines as of "justification apart from works" or of "predestination." In Edwards' New England there was still no explicit attack on such hallowed teachings, though it would not be long until there was. What was in the wind was an increasing demand that God be *fair,* not only in apportioning worldly blessings but also in granting the experienced faith which for Puritanism was the sole basis of salvation.

The central event of human existence, for Puritanism as for all pietist Christianity, is the work of God's Spirit in the human soul, "regenerating" it, creating a new humanity whose mode of existence is called "faith." If the soul is thought to be self-conscious, it will also be taught, as Puritans did, that faith is normally a conscious experience, that if I live in it I know that I do. In fallen creatures, faith must have a beginning, "conversion"; and this too must normally be a self-conscious event. Finally, if a properly Augustinian doctrine of grace is maintained, it will be taught that the occurrence of conversion is strictly the gift and by the initiative of God. It is understandable that throughout Puritan history considerable anxiety was attracted precisely to this later point: Why does God give conversion to so-and-so rather than so-and-so? Specifically, what about me?

As Edwards encountered the demand for fair recognition of effort in his congregation, he quoted it in one of the anti-Arminian sermons: "God shows mercy to them that . . . have done a great deal worse than I."[4] A more archetypically American-religious protest cannot be imagined. Most of us, to be sure, no longer worry much about God's gift of conversion, but the application of the fairness standard to God remains a dogma of our culture-religion. Nor is the demand for universal fairness an accidental feature of our history. Fairness is the central Whig, bourgeois-revolutionary value; it was in a few years to overthrow British rule in the colonies. And this points to the chief nurseries of New England Arminianism: commercial prosperity and the relation between political and churchly righteousness. The impact of affluence is obvious and often noted. While Puritanism may promote entrepeneurial achievement, it is also plain that self-made persons, once they have had some success, will find a doctrine of total dependence on God's will uncongenial. The political connection perhaps requires further historical elucidation.

It is an old Christian problem: What is the relation between the righ-

teousness required by and in the polity and the righteousness granted in
the church to faith? In Puritan New England, the problem was exacerbated by the Puritan dream itself, of congregations of visible saints living
in "holy commonwealths." The problem was exacerbated also by the
"federal" theology, which made the notion of "covenant" between God
and created moral agents be the key systematic notion, and understood
the history of salvation and the structure of community as a system of
such covenants, each with its distinctive contractual arrangements.

The factors were cumulative. Puritans conceived the civil polity as
a circle concentric with the church, so that the public worship of the
church's God belonged to the righteousness requisite in the polity. Moreover, in the "federal" scheme, the civil polity was supposed to be founded
in the same "covenant of grace" for the rescue of fallen humankind, as
is the church. And while it was theoretically clear that the covenant itself,
and the "saving grace" it makes available in the church, are purely of
God's free will, it was equally clear that the righteousness established by
the same covenant in the civil polity is a matter of human will and works.
Since one belongs to the polity before belonging to the church, it was
hard under these circumstances to avoid the impression that the works of
civil righteousness are "preparatory" to the receiving of grace.

And then there was the matter of the "half-way covenant." New
England Puritans admitted to communicant membership only such as could
testify to the experience of conversion. This, of course, made a problem
about infant baptism. The federal theology reasoned that God's saving
covenant with experientially converted adults includes their children, so
that these can be baptized. It was then expected that at the right time God
would bring those baptized in infancy to their own experience of saving
faith, and so to communicant membership in the church. In disillusioning
numbers, this did not happen. The existence in New England of an ex-
tensively unconverted second generation was embarrassment enough; worse
was the problem about their children in turn. In view of the civil position
of the church, baptized but unconverted and so uncommunicant parents
nevertheless wanted their children baptized, as most Americans of this
sort still do. Every solution of the problem violated some Puritan conviction. After agonized debate, the standard solution from circa 1660 on was
that baptized parents who "owned" the outward covenant by which the
church existed as a visible society, who accepted the church's moral discipline and the objective truth of the church's creed, might have their
children baptized even though they themselves could not claim experience of faith and could not commune. By this regulation, a large and
unexpectedly self-perpetuating class arose of those who were precisely

"half-way" into the church—and who had arrived at this position quite apart from "saving grace," merely by doing what civil society regarded as righteous.

The half-way solution was unstable, and conscientious pastors regularly pressed one way or the other. Some tried to re-establish primal Puritan standards; it was his efforts on this line that were to undo Edwards at Northhampton. Others, most notably Edwards' own maternal grandfather and predecessor at Northampton, Solomon Stoddard, accepted the status of the New England congregations as mixed bodies of saints and experiential unbelievers. They dropped the half-way restriction and took into communicant membership all who "owned the covenant," proposing first to get them in and thereafter to work on their conversion. With or without acknowledgement, this has been the policy of the mainline American churches ever since.

The need of "revival" arose over against the "half-way" situation. American revivals have never been proclamations of the gospel to the straightforwardly heathen. They are attempts to bring those baptized or otherwise initiated for convention's sake the rest of the way. Such also were Edwards' "seasons"; the unexpected blessing on his anti-Arminian sermons was a burst of experiential religion on the part of persons who were in the meetinghouse to hear the sermons, but had heretofore been cold of heart.

II

So what did Edwards preach to his congregation of mostly half-way believers, that so shook them up? He realized the sermons had been important, and published them. It is hard for modern readers, with our brevity of attention, to believe that these dry and lengthy disquisitions can ever have provoked general excitement, but we must recognize that they did.[5]

In the multipart sermon on "justification," Edwards is concerned to make three chief points, all opposed to a "contrary scheme." The first is the central insistence of the Reformation: "that God, in the act of justification has no regard to any thing in the person justified, as godliness, or any goodness in him; but that nextly . . . before this act, God beholds him only as an ungodly or wicked creature; so that godliness in the person to be justified is not so antecedent to his justification as to be the ground of it."[6] There may indeed be many "that . . . have done a great deal worse than I," and no doubt this is in various connections laudable about me, but in his justifying judgment God takes no notice whatever of such circumstances. And God's justifying is indeed a making of judgments; Edwards knows that the language of "justification" is juridical language in Paul's use and in the use of the Reformation, and he adheres to the rules of the metaphor.[7] So also the justice given by God's justification is strictly an "imputed" justice, in the purest style of Melanchthonian and Calvinist teaching: God chooses to reckon Christ's righteousness to the sinner, and *so* the sinner is judged righteous.[8]

The anti-Arminian power of this doctrine is plain. It is the same doctrine that Augustine and the Reformers used against similar phenomena. Whatever I may "prepare" for, by diligent exercise of recommended religious means, and whatever I may get half-way or ninety-nine one-hundredths-way into by the works of human righteousness, I cannot anticipate that judgment of God on which my final worth depends. However in touch with my feelings I may be and in whatever order my relationships may be, God insists on granting me an affirmation to which all such credits are irrelevant. Here is an ultimate simplicity of the Christian faith, that is finally simply believed or not and by which a religiosity's claim to be Christian "stands or falls."

Readers of Edwards' sermons may well think that his own homiletical practice was not reliably consistent with this doctrine, for he regularly exhorts his hearers, both uncoverted and converted, morally and religiously to seek salvation. It was his repeated explicit doctrine: "If we would be saved, we must seek salvation. For although men do not obtain heaven of themselves, yet they do not go thither accidentally, or without any intention or endeavors of their own."[9] Yet it is not only in the justification sermon that he insists that the unconverted person can "never take a step" toward salvation,[10] that even if he/she does everything within his/her power, "in religion . . . , God is not obliged, by any covenant that he has entered into with man, to perform anything at all for him, respecting his saving benefit."[11]

We encounter here the Puritan problem about "preparatory" works, about the religious and moral endeavors of the not yet converted.[12] If nothing I do before the gift of faith and its righteousness "is regarded" by God in making that gift, it would seem that my unconverted behavior simply drops out of the evangelical story. But does the Christian preacher then have nothing to say to the unconverted? Is the preacher not to exhort them to "seek" salvation? To hear preaching and read Scripture and be sorry for sin? Those of other Christian traditions than the Calvinist may think the question itself a wrong one, but for the present I will merely report the ways in which Edwards dealt with it.

One way in which Edwards provided a rationale for "seeking" and for homiletic exhortation thereto is by the doctrine that while God often grants grace to seekers he rarely or never grants it to non-seekers.[13] One sees why he is driven to such an egocentric calculus. Nevertheless, were it an independent position within Edwards' thinking it would surely be quite an intolerable note to be sounded within Christian preaching.

I suggest, however, that the self-serving character of this calculation is the very reason Edwards can exhort the unconverted to make it. For there is also another way in which Edwards integrated "preparation" into the affirmation of grace, a way which takes us to the center of his critical understanding of religion. Edwards exhorts us to *seek* salvation; he does not suppose that seeking will ever *attain* salvation. His hearers, after all, are either converted or not. When the converted are exhorted to seek and do so, their seeking is simply the mode of life harmonious with the dependence on God to which grace has already brought them.[14] When the unconverted seek salvation, they embark on an enterprise which precisely by God's intent will eventuate in failure, and that is, in the undoing of the religious impulse of self-salvation from which it springs.[15] It remains, to be sure, that Edwards thought the self-serving calculus *true*.

Edwards' second insistence is that God's justifying imputation is not and must not be understood as leniency.[16] It belonged to "the scheme" of those "modern divines" here attacked, that what God has accomplished in Christ is to enable himself to accept as righteousness efforts on our part which would not in themselves be worthy of such regard. This "scheme" is very like the medieval scheme against which the sixteenth-century Reformers protested. Medieval theology of "grace" was concerned to locate our part in "the process" of salvation. It located our part in initial movements of charity and faith which are not by strict reckoning worthy of God's favorable verdict, but are nevertheless worthy by "appropriateness" to God's favorable verdict, should he choose so to regard them. All such reasonings Edwards regarded simply as absurd. For they remain within the order of law, and so reduce grace finally to leniency within that order; but a lenient law cannot truly be broken at all, since it allows in advance for the failures of those subject to it. If God's law is lenient, there is, strictly, no sin, and the project of justification is moot.[17]

In this part of his anti-Arminian polemic, Edwards sees very far. Its theme will become a main content of *Freedom of the Will*, a book that amounts to a description of late twentieth-century America, written two centuries in advance. For now so much may suffice: when the Christian gospel is made into a *mitigation* of the law, it is a spiritual poison of unequalled virulence. A community whose law allows in advance for its own breaking, is dissolving itself.

Third, Edwards is concerned to establish that "a believer's justification implies, not only remission of sin, or acquittance from the wrath due to it, but also an admittance to a title to that glory that is the reward of righteousness", in inseparable unity.[18] The part of the "adverse scheme" here countered is the teaching that Jesus back there took care of sin, and so removed the obstacles to the good life, so that we now must get on with it. In Edwards' description of this doctrine, what Christ "purchases" for us is "an opportunity to obtain heaven by our own obedience."[19] If we may judge by Edwards' allocation of time within his sermon, he was even more outraged by this sort of Arminianism than by the former two.

In both Edwards' and the Reformation's teaching, what is in Christ is not the mere possibility of becoming righteous, nor is it permission to become righteous that God imputes. What is in Christ and is imputed to us is simply our righteousness, all we will ever have or need. "To suppose that all that Christ does is only to make atonement for us by suffering, is . . . to rob him of half his glory. . . . For if so, all that he does is to deliver us from hell; he does not purchase heaven for us."[20] Edwards here insists on the doctrine of what Protestant scholasticism called Christ's "active obedience," his righteousness for us that is not merely a suffering of penalties but the positive achievement of a creatively obedient life.[21] What is at stake for him is his vision of human perfection, which is not first or last a vision of rescue, followed by self-achieved fulfillment, but of "heaven," of transfiguring absorption in Christ's "glory." The instant the sheer beauty of Christ, and that positive salvation which lies in our captivation by it, departs from the center of the church's life, Christianity becomes, to Edwards' contempt, a religious insurance scheme.

III

The technical doctrine of justification which Edwards—still in the sermon—develops to make these assaults on piety, is a radical version of standard old-Protestant theology. Only one feature must be noted here. The question is of course posed: Why is justification by faith "alone," and not also by love or hope or long-suffering? I brutally summarize Edwards' long and supple discussion.

Faith that justifies is faith in Christ, and such faith justifies because it "renders it a meet and suitable thing, in the sight of God, that the believer, rather than others, should have [Christ's righteousness] assigned to them."[22] In imputing Christ's righteousness to us, God treats Christ and us as one moral agent jointly, as Christ-for-us, and us-in-Christ. He can do so as he choses; and if he so chooses, Christ and we are in fact one moral agent, since every singular entity is such solely by God's regard. But if his regard in this matter alighted at random, this would be contrary to God's being, for God "delights in order and not in confusion." And so God ordains that something "real in the union between Christ and his people" should be "the foundation of what is legal" in it. "God sees it fit, that in order to a union's being established between two . . . persons, so as that they should be looked upon as one, there should be a mutual act of both, that each should receive the other, as actively joining themselves one to another."

Christ's act of union is analyzed by Edwards' doctrine of atonement, which I will discuss in its chapter. *Our* act is faith, that which on the believer's side "makes up this union between him and Christ." And *so* it is that "faith is the qualification in any person that renders it meet in the sight of God that he should be looked upon as having Christ's . . . righteousness belonging to him," while joy or love or hope are not.[23]

Three comments are needed. First, if we ask why then faith is not after all a work[24] that qualifies for the grant of righteousness, Edwards' answer is that if God's "constitutions" are as just described, the appropriateness of God's acceptance to our faith is not moral but *aesthetic;* God's wisdom in giving to faith the role he does is "in the fitness and beauty" of so doing.[25] That is, the connection between righteousness and faith occurs within that ultimate musical and trinitarian order which, according to Edwards' interpretation of reality, encompasses and transcends the moral order of merit and reward. Moreover, the occurrence of such faith is, as we will see in the next chapter, itself an unmediated event of God's own inner freedom.

Second, however strange this theory of justification may seem over against that either of Protestant scholasticism or of standard current liberalism, Edwards has with it reinvented the very doctrine of Martin Luther in a primary reforming tract, *The Freedom of the Christian.* There Luther taught that the marriage in faith of Christ and the soul makes the two so truly one, that in judging us righteous God does not impute a fiction but acknowledges a reality, a reality created by his own love.

Third, it must be admitted that there is a way in which this doctrine lacks something vital to the Reformation doctrine that Edwards otherwise followed. For Luther, the marriage of Christ and the soul is effected by

Christ's actually spoken marriage vow, by the gospel-promise which the church speaks as Christ's own word. The Reformation's doctrine of "justification" is not only about the believer's state and experience but was also and indeed primarily about the church's preaching and teaching. It is instruction to preachers, confessors and liturgical leaders: so speak of Christ and your hearers' righteousness that your words are the unconditional promise God's wedding vow must be. We encounter here an absence that we will note with increasing discontent as we follow Edwards' thinking and which is closely connected to the distressing features of his teaching about "preparation:" in Edwards' usual thinking, the gospel-*word* itself, as spoken in the church, lacks ontological weight.

The doctrine of justification by faith is now moribund in the American church, including especially the denominations officially committed to Reformation principle. Insofar as the church's moral agenda coincides with one or another version of the current American agenda, whether that is determined by liberal individualism or by concern for "traditional" communal values, our Christianity is straightforwardly legalistic; to be Christian is to "be open to" or to "uphold" something-or-other. But if the church is reminded by Scripture or tradition of imperatives and purposes not on a current American agenda, we suddenly remember also about "grace," denounce "legalism" and appeal to "the situation"; thus we show ourselves the very Arminians against whom Edwards directed also the second proposition above.

Perhaps an Enlightenment people *cannot* live by faith, unless there is displayed before them the beauty Christ has apart from his usefulness to us, unless we see around us not only the harmonies of nature and of social mechanisms and plans but the universal harmony of the specifically triune God. Perhaps here is the American church's presently urgent proclamatory and liturgical task.

IV

But however did such preaching—whose argument, though readers may find it hard to believe, I have much simplified—occasion a revival? It "awoke" its hearers by destroying their ability to proceed with their religious programs, with the means in which they trusted to put their lives right. The doctrine of justification destroyed Northampton's religious pragmatism. There are no salvific religious means, said Edwards; your religious program may have its virtues, but if you expect thereby to be brought to that godly destiny which is your only real hope, you are simply deluded.[26] Hearing this, his hearers could only ask, "But how then shall I be saved?" And they received the answer: only by the free choice of God. *That* is what produced the weeping. It is a fundamental and forgotten fact about America's Christian heritage: revival was not in its founding beginning a means to promote religion; it was the surprising result of a *critique* of religion.

The critique of religion began in general in the Enlightenment and, with the exception of Edwards, as itself a thoroughly religious enterprise. The normal Enlightenment criticized specifically Christian teaching by supposed general religious criteria, of utility in religion's public and private roles. In Europe, a long and circuitous history was needed before in the work of Karl Barth the functions were reversed, so that the critique of religion appeared as the gospel's own activity, as God's assault on antecedent religion, on that self-assertion which presumes to be justified otherwise than by faith. In the European development, first Friedrich Schleiermacher had to "overcome" the Enlightenment by securing "religion" itself as an autonomous necessity of human existence and by interpreting Christian faith as the fulfillment of this necessity. Then during a century of theology and piety founded on Schleiermacher's positions, the Enlightenment's critique had to reappear in such as Ludwig Feuerbach, Friedrich Nietzsche and Søren Kierkegaard, as an attack now precisely on Christianity thus self-interpreted as religion. Only then could Barth appropriate this critique as a function of the gospel itself. American theology once had an enormous advantage: it *started* from the point Barth reached, by the gift of one preacher. That we lost our start, and have not participated in the latter European movements, is what makes us "Protestants without Reformation."

A Faithful Narrative of the Surprising Work of God, printed in 1735, was the young pastor's account, still only incipiently thought through, of the amazing thing of which he had been an instrument. Just so it is an irreplaceable document of our religious foundations.

Converts, he tells us, "are first awakened with a sense of their miserable condition by nature, the danger they are in of perishing eternally, and that it is of great importance to them that they speedily . . . get into a better state."[27] These persons, we must remember, were mostly such as would now count as exemplary Christians; it was exactly conventional religiosity from which they were rescued. The first result was "earnest application" to the established means of salvation,[28] moral and religious reformation of a sort that again might now be regarded as extraordinary saintliness.[29] Yet all this was, in Edwards' diagnosis, mere "legal awakenings" and "legal convictions,"[30] intensified attempts at salvation by religious works. In Edwards' judgment, the spiritual content of such sincere searching is the opposite of what its subjects suppose. The Spirit is here engaged in "legal strivings" with natural religionists, wholly within the realm of that "common grace" without which no creature can live at all. The persons involved, moreover, regularly act "with a secret hope of appeasing God's anger";[31] and if they hear that they must rely instead on grace, set out to accomplish also this work, thereby continuing "the same thing under a new guise."[32]

What is "discovered" in "such exercizes," if the Spirit perseveres, is the "corruption of the heart."[33] If the Spirit perserveres, the outcome is "a conviction of their absolute dependence on [God's] sovereign power and grace . . . ; that they can in no wise help themselves, and that God would be wholly just . . . in rejecting them and all that they do."[34] In many, the break would then still be postponed; "they set themselves to walk more strictly, and confess their sins and perform many religious duties,"[35] but—again, if the Spirit continues—"as their attempts are multiplied, so are their disappointments."[36] And just then, when religion and irreligion are equally helpless, God either does or does not, and in any case in his own time and in whatever way he each time chooses,[37] reveal "the true remedy in a clearer knowledge"—and so not in an achievement but in the registering of fact!—"of Christ and his Gospel,"[38] "of the way of salvation, by free and sovereign grace, through the righteousness of Christ alone."[39] Conversion, according to Edwards, is the very undoing of religious fulfillment. We are justified by "faith." That is, we are justified by unity with Christ given or not given by God, and so *not* by the success of our religious project. "Arminianism" is religion in ignorance of this.

Finally, because conversion is precisely the undoing of religious fulfillment, Edwards' great concern in all his descriptions and defenses of the revival was to make it plain that there is no *method* of salvation, either for preachers or hearers. "There is an endless variety in the particular manner . . . in which persons are wrought on." "God is farther from . . . a particular method in his work on souls, then it may be some imagine." Succeeding events made him even more suspicious on this point.[40]

6

The Phenomenology of Religious Consciousness

I

Edwards' analytical examination of the religious phenomena he had helped set free proceeded step by step with his participation in them. A 1733 sermon, on "A Divine and Supernatural Light," had laid out the analysis of human personhood, and the chief critical norms, by which the examination would be conducted. I will use the sermon for the thread of this chapter.

Edwards' starting analysis of human personhood is that standard in western philosophy and theology since Augustine: as subjects, we exercise intellect on the one hand and will on the other; we know objects and choose objects. In Edwards' immediate environment, this analysis was often presented in a decidedly wooden form: as a psychology of two chief "faculties," substantialized dispositional properties of the soul, that supposedly "do" knowledge and volition.[1] Edwards' doctrine that an individual mind is simply a continuity of consciousness, constituted a continuity by the coherence of God's successive communications of contents, undoes such notions of "the" intellect or "the" will. What there is, is temporally extended consciousness, which is cognitive in that reality variously appears in it and is volitive in that it is drawn to or repelled by these appearances. Thus there is no "cognitive faculty" distinct from the appearance and concatenation of ideas, and no "will" distinct from the "affections," from consciousness' actual inclinations to or away from its ideas.[2]

Nevertheless, the sermon on "Divine Light" initially lays down the traditional distinction, without nuance: intellect deals with fact, the will with value, "excellence."[3] This does not mean that reason has no knowledge of the good, but that its knowledge is "merely speculative and notional . . . ;" it is not *perception* and does not grasp excellent things precisely in their excellence.[4] Therewith, Edwards encounters the continuing problem of the Western tradition's anthropology: value must

indeed be perceived to be pursued, and therefore the will cannot be a
mere faculty of spontaneous choice, of blind inclination and aversion.
Somehow the will must *know,* must be one with intellect; somehow, the
difference of will and intellect must be transcended.

Every competent western thinker has a nomination for this bridging
role; in our sermon, Edwards gives his. It is the key notion for all Edwards' analysis of human life; there is a sort of consciousness that "is a
sense of the *beauty,* amiableness or sweetness of a thing; so that the *heart*
is sensible of pleasure . . . in the presence of the idea." [my emphases]
"There is a difference between having a rational judgment that honey is
sweet, and having a sense of its sweetness."[5] Merely intellectual judgment that something is good, as Edwards calls it, "notional" knowledge
of value, does not grasp value as value.[6] Only "the sense of the heart"
does that. In notional knowledge of the good, "is exercized merely . . .
the understanding"; in the heart's sense of the good, "the will, or inclination . . . is mainly concerned."[7]

It will be useful to report here Edwards' fuller specification of merely
"notional" knowledge.[8] He notes that much of our thinking is not in fact
the interaction in consciousness of actual Lockean ideas of the things
known, but is a play of words loosed from the ideas they denote, or of
scraps of associated ideas used like words, as "signs". This thinking is,
he says, "a kind of mental reading," and "unless it is abused to an
indulgence of a slothful inattentive disposition, very well serves us."
Only when we seek new connections of ideas do we need to summon the
ideas themselves.

Since the ideas of "spiritual" reality, that is, the ideas of ideas, are
necessarily simply the ideas themselves re-enacted, thinking by signs is
both especially inevitable and especially inadequate in the case of spiritual knowledge. Moreover, even when the idea itself is re-enacted in
consciousness, there is a distance over against it given in the fact of its
re-enactment; and in that distance it may be grasped only in its being a
cognition of something and not in its being an object of the mind's attraction or repulsion. In our sermon and elsewhere in Edwards' writing,
both these modes are subsumed under "notional" knowledge.

Edwards' own analysis will perhaps seem still to remain within the
standard distinction of intellect and will, if we do not attend to Edwards'
careful choice of adverbs. Notional knowledge of value is said to be
"merely" an act of understanding, whereas the sense of excellence is
only "mainly" an act of will. For the sense of the heart is not mere
inclination to or away from a thing; it is precisely that the heart is "sensible of" its inclination. The sense of the heart belongs to that "one thing

wherein man differs from brute creatures," that "we are always present with ourselves, and have an immediate consciousness of our own actions";[9] it is a phenomenon of immediate self-awareness. Thus the sense of the heart is, after all, perception, indeed, "understanding" and "knowledge."[10] The heart's sense is precisely the knowledge given in that my inclinations are possessed by me as *mine*. Thus sense transcends the difference between knowing and willing.

Since, according to Edwards, the will simply is consciousness' inclination to or away from its own ideas, all acts of will are determined by the ideas that actually appear, that is, by knowledge.[11] And it is specifically the sense of the heart by which knowledge is thus mediated to inclination: "The will in all its determinations . . . is governed by its thoughts . . . of things with regard to those properties of the objects of its thoughts wherein the degree of the sense of the heart has a main influence."[12]

Vice versa, our apprehension of what is good is each time determined, besides by the inherent characteristics of our objects, by our "prior inclinations," by habits of consciousness established in the past. "The will always is as the greatest apparent good is,"[13] but the appearance of good is created not only by "what appears in the object viewed," but also by "the manner of the view, and the state and circumstances of the mind that views"; and this "particular temper" of the mind is the joint result of "nature" and education, custom and contingent circumstances.[14] It is the sense of the heart in which these hermeneutical tempers are located.[15]

Edwards was entirely deliberate in the synthetic position he assigned to sense. In his chief published work on religious phenomena, he wrote: in "spiritual understanding" there can be no "clear distinction made between the two faculties of understanding and will. . . . When the mind is sensible of the sweet beauty . . . of a thing, that implies a sensibleness of sweetness and delight in the presence of the idea of it. And this sensibleness . . . carries in the very notion of it, the sense of the heart; or an affect and impression the soul is the subject of, as . . . will."[16]

Edwards' doctrine lies in the main path of western thinking. "The good, the beautiful, and the true" have always been the three "transcendental" concepts by which we have regulated our interpretation of reality. Since the perennial problem has been the relation of the good and the true, assigning a unifying role to the beautiful would seem an obvious move. The clearest comparisons are with the German thinkers who at the turn of the eighteenth and nineteenth centuries inaugurated Europe's nineteenth-century effort to "overcome the Enlightenment," and in the process laid the foundations for specifically modern theology. The comparisons are with thinkers whom Edwards antedated by some sixty years. Material comparisons with Hegel would be stretched, but those with Kant and Schleiermacher are unavoidable.

Emmanuel Kant at once completed the Enlightenment and marked the general way thereafter taken by those dissatisfied with the original Enlightenment's inhumanity. His three "critiques" follow the three transcendentals, treating each as an inherent demand of personal existence. We are theoretically "rational," subsuming the world as it presents itself under inevitable unifying categories. We are "practically" rational, insisting that the world yield to our demand for order. And we are aesthetically rational, "judging" the extent to which the world seems antecedently amenable to these mandates of our personhood. Thus it is in aesthetic experience that theoretical and moral reason meet: here our moral demands upon the world are met with worldly facts, and the facts have personal value.

If Edwards had written after Kant, he would surely be regarded as one of those who with Schleiermacher gave Kant's analysis a particular content, and thereby saved "religion" from Enlightenment without denying the latter. Schleiermacher traced the Enlightenment's corrosive effect on religion to an assumption that religion must be either knowledge of God or a practical support for morality. Critique then discovers that specifically Christian religion depends too much on authority for its knowledge, and is often in fact threatening to conventional morality. But the disjunction of mere knowledge and mere choice is unreal, said Schleiermacher; in lived experience it is overcome in "sense" or "taste" for reality. And whereas neither knowledge nor choice separately can provide a center for my personhood, but rather set me over against the world and so sunder the totality in which God finds us, this "taste" unites me with myself and with the whole. If we understand that, and *then* judge Christianity, by the criteria appropriate to religion as sense, the judgment will be affirmative.

II

What, then, is religion, according to Edwards? Edwards uses the word itself, as everyone did before Schleiermacher, for all behavior directed to God. But his analysis mandates also a definition of *proper* religion. Properly, religion must be "a true sense of the divine excellency of the things revealed in the word of God," [17] more simply, a sense of "spiritual good,"[18] as against the sense of other goods. "There is a divine and superlative glory" in the vision communicated by the word of God. "He that is spiritually enlightened truly . . . sees it, or has a sense of it. He does not merely rationally believe that God is glorious, but he has a sense of the gloriousness of God in his heart."[19]

Just so, Edwards also has a definition of counterfeit religion: all religiosity from which the hearts' sense is missing. The possibility of such counterfeiting is given by the subsistence of other modes of consciousness over against, though not strictly *of,* spiritual good, and by the final unverifiability of the claim to have the true sense. For on Edwards' analysis, it must be possible, as a limiting case, for all the intellectual and linguistic phenomena of right knowledge and will toward God to be present, except what counts, the heart's sense. Since the directing unity of intellect and will is in this case absent, such true appearance must be, so far as the human subject is concerned, entirely at happenstance; but God, who may communicate such a complex of ideas if he chooses, will have his reasons. And while the sense of God must be a conscious experience, a particular conscious state's identification *as* the sense of God is something about which we may "be at a loss," as we may be about other such identifications.[20]

III

It is Edwards' chief contention about "this spiritual knowledge:" "God imparts [it] immediately, not making use of any intermediate causes."[21] In one way, this is within Edwards' metaphysics no remarkable assertion; *all* our ideas are directly communicated by God. But Edwards has provided an explicit definition for a narrower use of "immediate": that is immediately from God which appears in consciousness without causal connections to other finite objects.[22] It is not the intimate contact between God and the soul that is special about converting knowledge, but rather that the shining idea of God's beauty appears without rule-bound connections with its surrounding contents of consciousness. In communicating this idea, God thinks no lesser harmony than that of creation's total history, as he does in raising Jesus from the dead. Since that whole of ideas cannot as such be communicated to our finite spirits, the idea of God appears in our consciousness "uncaused," as a purely "Spiritual and Divine Light."[23] All the connections are displayed in a journal entry: Grace is "as much a communication of the Deity as light [is] . . . of the sun. Tis therefore fit that when it is bestowed, it should be . . . more immediately given'' and that God should "especially exercise his . . . free pleasure in bestowing it." [24]

"This spiritual light is not the suggesting of any new truths''; it is not even "every affecting view that men have of the things of religion.'' Notional truth, also in religious matters, and sincere conviction in knowledge of religious truth, are fully within the competence of "mere principles of nature." [25] This does not mean that illumination can accrue to just any set of religious ideas. The true sense of the heart has a specific object which alone has in fact the brilliance to light up the soul: it is "the things revealed in the word of God'' that have "a divine and superlative glory'' to which the heart's sense responds. There is nothing arbitrary about this. What makes the difference between illumined and natural religion is simply the difference between the brilliance which the true God has and other claimants must lack, as must all merely notional appearances of the true God. [26] The transforming power of a religious idea is not given by its notional content or its affect on us or even by the fact of the Spirit's agency in its appearance, but strictly by what there is "in the ideas themselves, which is holy and divine." [27]

The religious convictions and affections of "natural man'' are not therefore necessarily nationally incorrect or misdirected. Some persons have in any case "more . . . of an apprehension of truth than others.'' And this apprehension too is a "light'' and comes from the Spirit. It is the gift of "common grace," of that divine favor and assistance, decreed in the covenant of grace for the preservation of fallen humanity, without which the fall would have taken its course to universal destruction. Nor is there any reason why the truth apprehended by "natural men,'' and even passionately embraced by them should not nationally be that "revealed in the word of God"; indeed, the particular natural religionists Edwards set out to awaken were all of this sort. [28] The decisive line does not run between Christian and "other" religions. Where then?

The religious light given to natural religionists "is from the Spirit of God only as assisting natural principles. . . . Common grace differs from special, in that it influences only by assisting of nature; and not by . . . bestowing anything above nature," whereas the supernatural light "in the mind of a saint'' is the action of the Spirit "as an indwelling vital principle." The Spirit "unites himself with the mind of a saint . . . as a new supernatural principle of life and action." He "acts in a way of peculiar communication of himself'' to "the minds of the godly," so that he "operates" in them "by . . . exerting his own nature in the exercize of their faculties." [29] It is by a radicalized version of the Protestant doctrine about the indwelling of the Spirit, that Edwards draws the line between religion as a natural phenomenon of created existence and the awakened and enlightened consciousness of God's beauty.

But if the Spirit "exerts" *himself* in the activities of the saints' "faculties," is not he then in fact the agent of their deeds? Just this question is the knife edge between what American revivalism was in fact to become and what it could have been and might still be. If the Spirit and the saint are simply identified, this mystic identification must in practice mean that the convert's experience and agitations are taken as directly identical with the Spirit's presence. Just this identification has been revivalism's disaster. Such consequences do not in fact follow in Edwards' thought or evangelistic practice. But it is one of the historical fatalities with which his story is full, that his theological move at this point is among those which his death left hidden in unpublished drafts.

All our "ideas," we have seen, are directly communicated by God. But God, we must remember, is always for Edwards explicitly the *triune* God. And insofar as reality appears to us as the object of the heart's sense, this occurs by the Spirit's particular work, as over against that of the other trinitarian persons. The Spirit *must* do this work, in harmony with the inner-triune relations by which God *is* the Spirit: "Such . . . illumination . . . is the proper work of the Spirit of God. For the Spirit . . . is . . . the Author of our capacity of discerning or having a sense of heart of natural good or evil, for this really differs not from the faculty of man's will, and it was especially the work of the Spirit of God in creating . . . to infuse . . . this part of the natural image of god . . . who has [himself] understanding and will, which will is the same with the Holy Ghost, and therefore the assisting this principle . . . is proper to the Holy Ghost." [30] Even if, then, the good that with the Spirit appears to the heart's sense is in fact God himself, beyond mere "natural good," this is a perfectly intelligible event, when seen within the whole reality of created personhood and God's personhood. Further, if we are thus given a "glimpse of the moral and spiritual glory of God," it is unsurprising that it "inclines the soul . . . by an omnipotent power." [31]

Thus a systematically rational account can be given of supernatural illumination, as Edwards understands it. The Spirit lets "spiritual light . . . into the soul" simply "by . . . discovering the excellency of divine things." [32] The idea of God naturally *shines*. It is the particular trinitarian reality of the Spirit to reveal this idea in our consciousness as he does in God's own, and because of the trinitarian distinctions in God the distinction between God and our consciousness is preserved also by this illumination.

We may understand the matter so: the difference between natural religion and spiritual illumination is not in the nearness or intensity of God's presence, for God's intimacy to every created consciousness is unsurpassable. It is rather than in the life of saints God the Spirit chooses to play the same role that he does in God's own inner triune life. With saints, the inner dialectic of created consciousness and the triune dialectics of God's consciousness *mesh* differently than they do with others.

Finally, as to how the Spirit works such conversion, Edwards' account remained unexceptionally Puritan, until the last period of his life. The "means of grace" given the church—preaching and prayer, with baptism and the Supper—are occasional means only and not causes. The new light "only gives a due apprehension of the same truths that are revealed in the word of God" and would have nothing to illumine were biblical teaching absent; but of the light itself,[33] the "Word of God is no proper cause."[34] The word causes right notional knowledge of spiritual reality, but the sense of their divine excellence has no such "second causes" and is "produced by God immediately."[35]

The *Miscellanies* again carry us further. All that any "means" can do is "supply the soul" with matter for grace "to act upon when God shall be pleased to infuse it."[36] And a distinction between the community and the individual is decisive here. The word of God's promises, as promises "to his visible church" are promises of "blessing on his ordinances" of preaching, baptism and the Supper. In this mode they are "absolute promises"; if the ordinances are obeyed, blessings will follow to the visible church. But as promises to individuals within the church, they are only occasional means in the sense just described.[37]

Even admirers of Edwards may well be dissatisfied with his position at this point. If the key saving affection is immune to the word, why should the extra effort and emotional persuasion of revival preaching be undertaken? Why not simply provide "'notional' raw materials, as Puritan pastors did anyway, and wait? Edwards has an answer, but it is hardly convincing: "I think an . . . affectionate way of preaching about the great things of religion, has . . . a much greater tendency to beget true apprehension of them, than a moderate . . . , for this reason, that such a way . . . of speaking . . . does in fact more truly represent them."[38] This ingenious apology surely clashes with Edwards' continuous insistence that a right notional grasp of God is independent of the right sense of the heart. As to the argument that the gospel's promises are reliable, but only for the community and not for the individual, this depends on distinguishing individual and community in a way that accords ill with the place of communication in Edwards' understanding of being. We have in fact encountered the great systematic gap in Edwards' theology, the inefficacy of the word as he understood it. And we may call it a flaw with some confidence, for Edwards was to discover it himself.

IV

Since it is the light of the Spirit's new mode of presence that differentiates the saint from the still unawakened religionist, and since the presence of this light is never verifiable past counterfeiting, it would seem that conversion should be beyond empirical study. But in Edwards' phenomenology, the appearance of such a shining idea to the heart's sense must abidingly alter that "temper" of the mind by which all its inclinations and aversions are predisposed, for the heart is merely the complex of these "affections." And affections *are* describable. Edwards can analyze the change from the highest theological pitch: "The word *spirit . . .* is used . . . in two senses, either for a spiritual substance . . . or for the temper of the mind." Scripture's use, according to Edwards, is of the second sort. And therefore "whenever the Scripture speaks of the Spirit of God dwelling in us . . . it will signify much the same thing if it be said a divine temper . . . dwells in us." [39] Moreover, since a mind simply is the coherence of its contents, it can also be said that such a new temper is a new "nature" or "principle." [40]

Thus conversion is very directly a sanctification of the will, which is to say, it is communication of new affections. Spiritual illumination is a sanctification because it is the appearance of the idea of *God,* and the affection directly worked by it is inclination to God. "This light . . . only has its fruit in a universal holiness of life. No merely notional . . . understanding of the doctrines of religion will ever bring to this. But this light, as it reaches the bottom of the heart . . . , draws forth the heart in a sincere love to God." [41] Since the soul's nature *is* its inclinations, Edwards can say that the light thus "assimilates the [soul's] nature to the divine nature, and changes the soul into an image of the . . . glory that is beheld." [42] Indeed, our love to God is the same event as God's triune love to himself.

Spiritual illumination changes also the cognitive situation. The appearance of the idea of God is itself an access of overwhelming knowledge, bearing the certainty of immediate perception. [43] Moreover, there is a notional judgment that is here a direct accompaniment of perception: "A true sense of the divine excellence of the things of God's word doth

. . . directly . . . convince of the truth of them.''[44] Further, the new light ''sanctifies the reasoning faculty and assists it to see the clear evidence there is of the truth of religion in rational arguments.''[45] This last occurs in two ways. First, the evocation of a new complex of abiding predispositions means the overcoming of some previous complex, in sinful fact, ''the prejudices that are in the heart against the truth of divine things.'' And second, ''the attention of the mind'' is ''engaged,'' so that the mind has ''a clearer view'' of spiritual ideas and ''their mutual relations;'' thereby more cogent and productive reasoning on the subject is enabled.[46]

V

From 1735 to 1738, Edwards wrote a series of letters and other accounts of the revival, eventuating in the *Faithful Narrative*. By the time the *Narrative* was published, the Northampton revival was over; in 1740 a new and geographically wider revival began, chiefly carried by the Methodist—of sorts—George Whitefield. Edwards analyzed and defended also the new movement, amidst increasing controversy, with a 1741 speech at Yale published the same year, *The Distinguishing Marks of a Work of the Spirit of God.*

In that same year, James Davenport, a younger man than either Edwards or Whitefield, began an itinerant revival preaching which deliberately cultivated precisely what others regarded as the ''excesses'' of the movement. It was sectarian and ''enthusiastic'' and the future of revivalism would belong to it. By 1743, such phenomena had provided the occasion for a division of the New England church into two near-denominations, ''Old Lights'' and ''New Lights.'' Edwards attempted to promote balanced judgment by a new treatise, *Some Thoughts Concerning the Revival of Religion in New England.* This work expands the defense and criteria of the *Marks,* founds them more theologically, locates the revival in Edwards' scheme of salvation history and to its rebuke of revival's ''cold-hearted opposers'' adds an equal rebuke of fanatic revivalists. Appeals to balanced judgment proved vain. Edwards' meditation of the affair concluded in an analytical mode with *A Treatise Concerning Religious Affections* of 1746.

The sequence of these writings constitutes an unparalleled labor of religious description. Much of their contents belongs to later chapters. Here, I have to note Edwards' cautious attitude toward normative descriptions of religious experience and his defense of the revival against attacks in principle.

Edwards insisted from first to last that God neither was bound to nor in fact did follow any one sequence of experience in converting a natural religionist's affections. "The work of God" in Northampton, he thought, had been "glorious" precisely "in its variety."[47] He did indeed think he observed a general pattern. This is unsurprising. There are not a mere infinity of ways for a profound spiritual passage to be accomplished in the absence of an acknowledged rite of passage. Much the same pattern has appeared whenever within routinized Christian communities those with baptism already behind them have found themselves moved to "real" religion. Moreover, the pattern was that already described by Puritan theology of conversion; persons for the most part displayed the sequence they knew they were supposed to, which in no way suggests any inauthenticity of their experience.

As we have already noted, conversion, as Edwards observed and theologically described it, began with a merely natural conviction of sin and a merely religious attempt to achieve a better state, culminating, if the Spirit had his contrary way, with the sinner's "conviction of the justice of God in their condemnation."[48] With the appearance of this conviction, Edwards regularly observed a season of "calm." And "most frequently" he observed the calm informed by a "general hope" that God would grant the true faith whose lack penitents now acknowledged. Edwards thought that when this hope appeared, it was, despite appearances, itself already the hoped-for new life. "For as they are brought to see that God may damn them if he pleases, so they see that God may show them mercy if he pleases. A natural man is not convinced of either."[49] Finally came the explicit sense of God's excellence, not always identified as such by the persons who had it.[50]

Edwards took what must seem the considerable risk of describing persons who, in his judgment, had this latter sense. Above all, he instanced his own wife, whom he saw remain "for some considerable time together, in such views of the glory of the divine perfections . . . that the soul . . . has been . . . swallowed up with light and love."[51] This was attended by no esoteric phenomena, nor by any evident pride or disposition to neglect her secular calling.[52] Its apparent effects were an "increase of sweetness, rest and humility," and delight in singing.[53] Edwards' famous outburst must be cited: "If this be distraction, I pray God that the world of mankind may all be seized with this benign, meek, beneficent, beatifical, glorious distraction."[54]

From the start of the revival and increasingly in its later waves, these transformations of affections manifested themselves bodily. Young people especially fainted in groups.[55] Increasingly, more bizarre behavior appeared. Edwards found this unremarkable. Having deprived the mind/ matter difference of any final ontological weight, he thought it "easily accounted for from . . . the union between soul and body, how a right . . . sense . . . should have such effects on the body, even those . . . of the most extraordinary kind."[56] And no one, in his view, could really judge such manifestations.[57]

VI

It was precisely all this affection and its manifestation that disrecommended the revival to its critics. The revival's main literary opponent was Charles Chauncy, pastor of First Church in Boston and chief representative of a new sort of urbane New England pastor. His main charge against the revival was that the observable phenomena "savoured" of "enthusiasm,"[58] that by the revival's appeal to the emotions it removed religious life from the control of reason and deliberated choice.[59] Edwards joined the issue directly. "True religion," he asserted, "in great part, consists in holy affections";[60] indeed, the very "Spirit of God in those that have sound . . . religion," is simply a temper of "powerful holy affections."[61] Nothing "is more manifest in fact that that the things of religion take hold of men's souls no farther than they affect them."[62] It is just so in Scripture, which "represents true religion as being . . . comprehended in love, the chief . . . of all other affections."[63] "There are false affections and there are true. A man's having much affection don't prove that he has any true religion; but if he has no affection, it proves that he has no true religion."[64]

Edwards' assertions can hold only if the affections have in fact the place in consciousness he assigned to them. And in the absence of a functioning understanding of God as *triune*, that place, we have seen, is not to be found. The history of American religion after Edwards can be put in a very small nutshell: it has actualized Edwards' general interpretation of religious experience within an effectively unitarian religiosity, within which the affections could not be the bridge in consciousness they were for Edwards. That religious affections *grasp reality*, to be not only inclinations but also cognitions, cannot be established by the nature of affections in themselves, but only by the role played by the Spirit in God's consciousness and ours. Absent a decisively trinitarian worship of

God, human consciousness and its religious mode, as analyzed by Edwards, must fall apart again into knowledge on the one hand and will on the other, and the affections must either be identified with the will, which itself will then be understood as irrational, or must be relegated to the sidelines of consciousness, as mere "emotions."

That affectionate experience could have the place assigned it by Edwards was what neither enthusiasts of the revival nor its coldhearted opposers could conceive. The affections were seen by such proto-"mainline" sophisticates as Chauncy as opposed to reason and so needing to be overcome by will,[65] and by the enthusiasts as the place of blessed liberation from reason and will alike. Edwards saw the issue with his critics: "In their philosophy, the affections . . . are . . . not appertaining to the noblest part of the soul."[66]

According to Edwards, the affections, far from being irrational, are the very point where objective divine reality binds and controls consciousness. Thus the entire meaning of affections is in their "foundation out of self." When I discover the "deformity . . . and meanness" of my own religious affections this will, supposing that their object is the beauty of the true God, only "sweeten and heighten them."[67] And even when saints are given "assurance," the "sense of the safety of their own state," this is no great matter to them; the "supreme attention of their minds" is to something other than their state, "the glorious excellencies of God and Christ."[68]

The supposition of the irrational character of affections, the religious especially, has continued to determine American religion and theology. Charles Chauncy has many "liberal" descendants, for whom religious inclination simply as such is suspect, to be kept in a "private" sphere outside the body politic where reason and reasoned will must rule. And James Davenport has as many followers, by whom religious inclination, to whatever objects, is regarded as self-verifying and beyond public critique. It is remarkable how in practice the two sects have worked together, the first relegating all religion but Jefferson's to the for them irrelevant private sphere and the second rejoicing to be so relegated. Indeed, our very distinction between "public" and "private" has as its deepest motive the need to have it both ways: to banish religious commitment from the world whose public character compels reason in some measure to be obeyed, and yet to maintain a sphere of life where religious commitment can be indulged, and here indeed in irrational form. But what if Edwards was right?

VII

Edwards' posit of sense or taste as the point of unity of intellect and will, and so as the unity of consciousness with itself, and so as the home of religion, was remade in Europe by Kant and Schleiermacher, and became the basis of the nineteenth century's new piety and theology. Reimported into the United States it found great resonance with those who should have been Edwards' successors, and has played a vital role also in American religious life. Between Edwards' own teaching and that of Neoprotestantism there is, however, one crucial difference.

Edwards did not uncritically suppose religion to be a good thing. Kant, Schleiermacher and their successors, however they worked out the relation between religion sheerly as such and the actual religions, all supposed that being religious, all else being equal, was just as such good. Here Edwards was a true heir of the Reformation—*and* of the "critical" Enlightenment!—as those fathers of modern theology were not. For Edwards knew that if I lack that one gift which comes from the direction opposite to my religious reach, then it is precisely my religion that is my sin and my punishment, and that this is the more disastrously so as my religion is in itself more perfect. What I have in hand with my religion is always the attempt to use God to my purposes, from which only light from behind me can rescue. One more and last comparison cannot be excluded from this chapter: as Karl Barth inverted Neoprotestantism by bending all its critical passion to the critique also of religion itself, Jonathan Edwards obviated Neoprotestantism in advance, making its moves from the critical position in the first place.

If we are truly critical, we will not take "God" without further identification as the proper light and unity of the soul. It was such skepticism that Kant and the others lacked. For all their great and Christian insight, they prepared the ground for the nihilism that now ravages the Western church and civil community. Where God is left general and unspecific, where it is supposed that any "God" is a good thing, his location as created consciousness' unity with itself must sooner or later flip over into the dogma—now unchallenged in western religiosity—that we posit God by our own search for self-identity. And that doctrine must, in the fragmenting world of late-capitalist and socialist societies, where self-identity is not reliably available, become despair of God. For Edwards, however, God was always identified; that he is the Father of Jesus Christ belongs to his own triune self-identity. Therefore Edwards was able to make the transcendental move into faith, rather than out of it.

7

Love of Self and Love of God

I

In the terms of then standard theology and churchly ideology, it is remarkably difficult to state what divided the parties over the Awakening. Chauncy, prototype of the "liberal," "mainline" modern church, was no less vehement than Whitefield or Edwards that all must be miraculously and consciously born again; indeed he asserted it less cautiously and dialectically than did Edwards.[1] And Whitefield was no less concerned for rationality than were Chauncy and Edwards. With hindsight, we may say that the differences were made by where each located the miracle: Chauncy in the intellect,[2] Whitefield in the passions—*not* the "affections"—and Edwards behind both. It has been the differences rather than the agreements that became historically decisive.

Why did Edwards and Chauncy disagree at all about the Awakening, seeing how alike their principles of judgment were? Both were Calvinists, who taught that grace is an empirically ambiguous event, so that judgments of religious phenomena are always *judgments,* to be made cautiously and probabalistically. They even agreed about signs to look for in making such judgments.[3] The fact seems to be simply that Edwards was *hopeful* for the revival and Chauncy was not, so that what for Chauncy seemed "to have a dark aspect" for "the Work" was still for Edwards "no argument that a work is not from the Spirit of God."[4] Applying the agreed criteria to the actual revival, Chauncy had the better case: the revival Edwards justified was the revival that would have happened had Edwards remained dominant, as Chauncy did not fail to note.[5] But again: Why was Edwards hopeful and Chauncy not? Why did Edwards excuse phenomena that surely did "savour" of "enthusiasm," while Chauncy took them for veridical?

One cause, I suggest, was the clarity and exclusivity of the distinction Edwards made between natural religion and the Spirit's illumining. What was to become the churchly main line could think of conversion as "ordinarily" a *cooperative* work of "special grace" and religious "principles" antecedent to faith,[6] and of antecedent religion as exactly what grace was to perfect.[7] As we are now accustomed to put it, God "helps" "fulfill" what we in any case seek. Edwards, oppositely, understood conversion as a *struggle* between antecedent religion and the Spirit, and to Chauncy's alarm regarded a continuing such struggle as determining the life also of the saints. Therefore Edwards had to be profoundly ironic about actual religious phenomena; all are the joint product of grace and sin. "There is commonly . . . in high experiences, besides that which is spiritual . . . , natural . . . affections, and workings of the imagination, and a degree of . . . spiritual pride."[8] "Yea, the same persons may be the subjects of much of the influences of the devil . . . , and this be no more of a paradox than many other things that are true of real saints."[9] The reason is that the Spirit is in saints a new natural principle, and just therefore his "exercises are excited by means, in some measure as other natural principles are."[10] The irony breaks through: "We are to consider that the end for which God pours out his Spirit is to make men holy, and not to make them politicians."[11] Just in this irony, Edwards could be "forward" in judging by "charity."[12]

There are, according to Edwards' mature judgment in a late note, but two modes of human existence: life under "the predominancy of self-love" and life under "a contradictory principle" of "love to God."[13] "All mankind are in scriptures divided by these distinctions, and the Bible knows of no neuter or third sort."[14] It is necessarily so, for as final objects of the heart only two candidates present themselves: "the God that made" the created consciousness and the created consciousness itself with its world.[15] "Faith," Edwards loved to say, "is a *sensibleness* of what is real in the work of redemption";[16] and for Edwards this means finally, as we have seen, that faith is the sense simply for what is real. Regnant self-love is an opposite sense, and the only other possibility, since it is constituted by any and every loss of grasp on reality; as reality is in fact mutuality, so dominant self-love and every illusion are the same.[17]

II

Again and again, Edwards returned to the analyses of these two modes of life. As he once exclaimed, "They therefore who bring any addition of light to the great subject, the nature of true religion and its distinction from all counterfeits, should be accepted as doing the greatest possible service to the church of God."[18] What is it, exactly, that ails us human creatures? And how is the ailment related to our apparently ineradicable religiosity? It is, finally, the practiced answers to these questions that distinguish Protestantism with and without Reformation. Edwards' answers are unequivocal. What ails us—"original sin"—is self-love outside the context of love to God. And religion as a human propensity is precisely the highest actualization of this ailment, requiring the miracle of conversion to be bent to the love of God. Protestantism without Reformation answers oppositely. Sin is said to be insufficiency of religion; sin is failure to clarify our values, or fulfill our identity, or carry out our moral calling.

A *Miscellanies* entry lays out Edwards' starting analysis.[19] In a primary and most general sense, self-love "is a man's love of his own . . . happiness and hatred of his own misery." It would be nonsense to denigrate *this* self-love, since it is merely a conscious being's "capacity of enjoyment or suffering, for to say a man loves his own happiness . . . is only to say that he delights in what he delights [in] and to say that he hates his own misery is only to say that he is . . . afflicted in his own affliction." This self-love is simply self-consciousness with respect to consciousness' aspect as "sense." This self-love cannot compete with other loves, even to God, since it is given with and in them: if I love God, God is my good, and than to love God is to love my own good.

"But . . . ," now, "a person's good may be said to be his own good as 'tis his proper and separate good . . . , and [this] is what is ordinarily called self-love." This self-love too "arises simply and necessarily from the nature of a perceiving willing being." That is, self-love cannot remain a matter only of immediate self-consciousness, but insofar as I am conscious of myself as an object, as a "separate" something among other somethings, in what the Idealists would call "mediated" self-consciousness, self-love cannot but embrace also this object. And the love of myself as a separate entity can very well compete with love of other entities.

Indeed, all that is needed for "separate" self-love to turn all other loves into means of its own fulfillment, is that it be permitted to. Only God is an object of affection that can compete with self in drawing consciousness. All therefore depends on whether God in fact is the object of the heart's sense. Original sin is simply the absence of "the influence of God's Spirit whereby love to God . . . is kept up. . . . But this being gone . . . , self love governs alone. . . . There is nothing new put into the nature . . . , but only the same self love that necessarily belongs to the nature . . . , without regulation from that superior principle," without which "it naturally . . . breaks out into . . . pride, covetousness," etc.[20]

It is the dialectics of finite consciousness that Edwards here bluntly describes. If a finite consciousness does not love God, it will love only itself and hate all others. *That* is what ails us. And surely this is the truth, though Western reflection, including theology, has given millennial effort to evading it. We cannot, it seems plain, much longer continue the evasion; the curves of Western civilization's secularization and of its fall into a war of all against all plot each other too perfectly. It is not a social contract that overcomes Hobbs' "state of nature"; it is only the presence of God.

What enables the evasion is that we never quite arrive at a pure war of all against all. According to Edwards, what enables the evasion is, ironically, the remaining "common" influence of the Spirit. God does not *allow* self-love to attain its natural end. And now we must note: regnant self-love thus becomes in all actual finite consciousnesses a relation to God, a mode of participation in the Spirit.[21] The consequence is, that so long as we do not fall out of being altogether, we will exercise our self-love by being religious. Thus when Edwards discusses self-love concretely, it is always in fact "counterfeit" religion that is his theme.[22] Edwards does not mean that there is anything wrong with unconverted religion as religion; he means that all unconverted religion, the Christian included, is for ill and good a counterfeit of the illuminating work of the Spirit.

III

So how does the religion of self-love work? The Spirit's common work, as we have seen, is his "assisting natural principles"; this collobration, Edwards teaches, "gives no other notion to natural men of right and wrong but only as it suggests the relation . . . there is between such and such things and . . . being hated by others and having evil brought upon them. . . . The notion that natural conscience gives of wrong is not of something deformed and loathesome."[23] It is at this level that the Spirit promotes a "social contract," that he enables me to recognize the practical inseparability of your good from mine. But the egocentric predicament is not thereby broken, for the breakout can only occur at the *aesthetic* level, by a captivation of consciousness to reality other than itself and the converse sheer aversion to mutual "wrong." Short of indwelling as a new principle of life, the Spirit works consciousness of the worldly golden rule: "Conscience in natural men concerning the moral good and evil of their own actions, may be summed up in the dictate of their minds, concerning their treatment of others in this respect, viz. the acceptance they should give such treatment in case they were in the place and circumstances of their treatment."[24]

If now God is in any way present to consciousness, the egocentric social contract must instantly embrace him too and become religious; and were God not present, not even the social contract could be maintained. It is Luther's insight that here recurrs: that the soul once "turned in on itself" must "seek its own also in God." In Edwards' language: "There may, indeed, be . . . a great deal of what is called religion; but it is not . . . a seeking and serving God, but . . . a seeking and serving themselves."[25] The "principles" of such religion are exactly those of the social contract among creatures: "natural understanding and self-love."[26]

Where Christianity is the available religion, this seeking will be very Christian, and no less egocentric for that. It will then be the very benefits to *me* which God indeed promises in the gospel, for the sake of which I will attach to him; unconverted Christian religionists "allow God to be lovely" because "he has forgiven them, and accepted them, and loves them . . ., and has engaged to improve all his infinite power . . . in . . . exalting them, and will do for 'em just as they would have him." In this case, our "very lusts will make him seem lovely."[27] In epigrammatic contrast: the saints "don't first see that God loves them, and then see that he is lovely; but they first see that God is lovely . . . and then, consequentially, they see God's . . . great favor to them."[28] So Edwards told his congregation: "If your love to God has its first source from nothing else than a supposed . . . divine witness . . . that Christ died for you in particular, and that God loves you, it springs from self-love."[29]

With his implacable sense for reality, Edwards usually sees the matter from the negative side, from the natural fear of damnation. The "devils also . . . know assuredly that the gospel is true," but this involves no "sense of God's excellency but only of his greatness."[30] That is, their apprehension of God may be emotional but is nevertheless merely notional and not aesthetic. And unregenerate humans are in the same case. "Let us suppose a person who has been . . . in . . . terror through fear of hell; and is all at once delivered, by being firmly made to believe, through some delusion of Satan, that God has pardoned him, and accepts him as the object of his dear love. . . . It is easy to be accounted for, from mere principles of nature, that a person's heart, on such an occa-

sion, should be . . . filled with fervent affections, to that imaginary . . .
Redeemer."[31] The true propositions about forgiveness and acceptance
are "delusions of Satan" because entertained in the absence of the heart's
sense for God's beauty; the one limitation on the natural religionist's
"affecting sense" of God is that it does not sense "the beauty of . . .
[God's] moral attributes."[32]

IV

It is an infinite interiority of wheels within wheels into which Edwards
here plunges. Puritans were adepts of its depths; Edwards was among the
masters. Not all who entered found their way out again; one has frequent
fears also for Edwards. One example of his art will suffice. Having noted
that "There is a pretended great humiliation, and being dead to the law,
and emptied of self, which is one of the biggest and most elated things
in the world,"[33] Edwards probes: "examine again, whether or no you
don't think yourself better than others on this very account, because you
imagine you think so meanly of yourself. Haven't you a high opinion of
your humility? And if you answer again, 'No, I have not a high opinion
of my humility; it seems to be I am as proud as the devil,' yet examine
again, whether . . . on this very account that you think yourself as proud
as the devil, you don't think yourself to be very humble."[34]

The dialectic of human self-reflection is endless because of the contradiction at its heart: the same insight into the dependence of my good
on yours, which enables fallen creatures to live morally at all, also makes
self-love insatiable, since it depends on the common work of the Spirit
and so introduces self-love to the divine infinity. "There is no degree of
self advancement but what self love . . . will make men to seek for.
. . . [I]t will be contented with nothing short of the throne of God."[35]
Only make self-love love for *righteousness,* and you have a "disposition" whose strength is "inexpressible," as is what the person "will not
do and suffer, to . . . gratify . . ." it.[36]

How, in the life enabled by this contradiction, are we to tell light
from darkness? By the time Edwards, in the mature *Religious Affections,*
has finished listing ambiguous signs, it is hard to see what could be unambiguous. " 'Tis no sign" of religious affections' truth or falsity, that
they are intense, affect the body, enliven religious discourse, are not
willed by their subjects, are biblically in order, are emphatically loving,
are richly affectionate, follow the normal sequence of Christian experience, lead to increased religious practice, bring forth the praise of God,

are irresistibly convincing to their possessors, or seem right to the godly.[37] And the real "signs" of true affections which Edwards goes on to list, are not, on examination, *signs* of authenticity at all, but *analyses* thereof, factors of what makes "gracious" experience graceful.

Since the true saint is indwelt by the Spirit as a vital principle, and not merely worked on by him,[38] it follows, that "in those gracious affections which are wrought in the minds of the saints . . . , there is a new inward perception or sensation of their minds . . . , a new simple idea."[39] That is, the difference between egocentric and true religion is just the absence or presence in consciousness of God in his objective godhead, that is, in his beauty. Therefore one may also say that the difference between "gracious" and natural affections is simply the "amiable nature" of gracious affections' object, independently of the empirical character of the affections themselves.[40]

"Truly gracious affections" are therefore cognitive, both in themselves as sense of the heart and in associated notional illumination—though the later may be counterfeited by egocentric affections[41] and are all that empirically appear. Gracious affections are "attended with evangelical" as against "legal" convictions of sin and unworthiness, and the latter are "commonly" "bungling" imitations of the former—but only commonly.[42] As a new principle of "nature," they *last*[43]—but the temporary duration of egocentric affections may be a lifetime. Gracious affections are in "beautiful symmetry and proportion;"[44] and they make Christian moral practice the whole "business" of life[45]—which is just what egocentric religion is drawn to imitate.

The great virtuoso of Puritan spiritual scrutiny, who transformed it into a true phenomenology of religious experience, plainly has also run it into a dead end of its original purpose. On Edwards' results, strictly, the judgments "So-and-so has true/false conversion" or "I have true/false conversion" ought not merely be restricted to probabilities but cannot be made at all. What is really afoot with Edwards' "tests" appears most clearly in the four most interesting, which must next be considered.

"Those affections that are truly holy" are, Edwards writes, directed primarily to "the loveliness" of God's "moral excellency," rather than to his "natural excellency," that is, his omnipotence, omnipresence, and the like.[46] Edwards regards this as the great "test,"[47] and indeed it is a vital point not only of his phenomenology but of his theology. The division between these attributes that belong to God's nature but supposedly are morally neutral because independent of relations to other personal beings, and God's "moral" or "relative" attributes, is ancient and often disastrous in Western theology. Edwards here uses the distinction in a

new way: for the difference between God's presence in consciousness
with that *beauty* that draws consciousness out of itself and his presence
in that mere *utility* that entraps consciousness in itself. It is in God's
"natural" attributes that his "advantage" to us lies; just so these are our
religious temptation.[48]

Quite evidently, this distinction will not serve as a "test" of experience, since the way in which we will seek to take advantage of God's
utility is by counterfeiting captivation to his beauty, at least so long as
we are not utterly disencumbered of Christianity. Nor do the closely linked
other "tests" carry us outside this circle, though they again greatly increase our analytical understanding of it.[49] Since God's "moral" beauty
is manifested in *Christ,* gracious affections have *him* as their object. Since
they see sin's ugliness and not only its disadvantage, they "soften" the
heart for future affections;[50] indeed, "the higher they are raised, the more
is a spiritual appetite . . . increased," whereas "false affections rest
satisfied in themselves."[51] Gracious affections are christological and historical precisely because they are genuinely aesthetic, engrossed by God's
reality beyond themselves.

We have again encountered the place where Edwards' thinking runs
into antinomy within standard Puritanism. In his less irenic moments,
Edwards admits that in fact only God "challenges it as his prerogative to
try the hearts . . . of men";[52] especially in sermons it becomes apparent[53]
that so far as either observation or introspection can take us, false religion
and true are indistinguishable. But within Puritanism, where the spoken
godpel and the sacraments are held to be ambiguous, if the authenticity
of the experience of grace is not itself experienceable, grace disappears
from consciousness altogether. For any descendent of Augustinian faith,
this is disaster; as Edwards regularly used the axiom, it is "needful that
a person that is saved should be sensibly saved."[54]

On the side of the created consciousness, all Edwards' distinctions
of egocentric from gracious religion finally reduce to one: the former's
encapsulation in itself, its *reflexivity.* The "nourishment" of true experience is to view God, and that of "false experience is to view itself."[55]
Saints are "taken" with the beauty of God, other religionists with "the
beauty of their experiences" of God.[56] But surely this reflex must be
permanently invisible, since the very introspection that would search it
out is itself a reflexive mode of consciousness and so masks what it looks
for. Vice versa, if true religion is to be enraptured beyond myself by
God's beauty, then the very act of asking "Do I have true religion?" is
an abandonment of it. The egocentric predicament cannot be overcome
within standard Puritanism; it can only be driven to self-refutation.

It is a major triumph of European theology in the twentieth century, that it has worked through the antimony of finite consciousness' egocentricity, to what is, for hindsight, manifestly its only possible resolution: recognition of the ontological weight of *discourse*. Every *word*, every actual communication, is at once an external event and an event of my interiority. If I hearken to an actual *word* as God's word, I am at once fully self-aware and fully directed beyond myself. This had been worked through before in the faith's history; one of those times would be when Jonathan Edwards at the last overcame the experienced antimony of his own religion, a moment when American religion transcended itself. I am coming at the end to that.

V

Release from ego's curvature on itself is, then, in Edwards' reflection, affected by reversal of a transcendental principle, the aesthetic a priori or logic of "judgment." I have used Kant's language to characterize Edwards, but Edwards was more critical than Kant. Kant supposed without question that if the a priori principles of judgment—as of cognition or choice—could be uncovered, they would be the same for all times and places. The whole transcendental constitution of consciousness is, he presumed, ahistorical.

The impact of the gospel freed Edwards from this uncritical presumption. He did not doubt that the transcendental structures of intellect and choice are changeless, but precisely judgment, aesthetic taste, in which knowledge and choice are one and by which they are directed, is an historical variable. "The wicked at the day of judgment, will see everything else of Christ but his beauty."[57]

Edwards grasps the whole life of sanctification by two principles. I will present each by citing journal entries. The first: "holiness of heart doth of its own nature . . . keep men from errors in judgment about religion. . . . The reason is, that as the sanctified mind is let into the spiritual world . . . , it easily perceives what ideas are harmonious, and what are not . . . , the soul distinguishes *as a musical ear*" [my emphases].[58] The second: "The motives to believers to perform the commands of God, are not because salvation is [upon] the condition of doing them . . . , but the amiableness of God . . . , the loveliness of virtue, and its natural tendency to happiness."[59]

Thus all quantitative considerations are besides the point, in considering created holiness. All the saints' affections and works are ambiguous products of the Spirit and sin; how then does the love of God rule? "Tis from the nature of the object loved, rather than from the degree of the principle in the lover." We may understand it so: if there *is* love to God, God is loved above all, for only so can *God* be loved at all.[60] "If a man has any true love to God he must have a spirit to love God above all; because without seeing something of the divine glory there can be no true love to God, but if a man sees anything of divine glory he'll see that he is more glorious than any other."[61]

III

GOD AND CREATION

'Tis probable that the faculties of the man Christ Jesus, now in his glorified state, are so enlarged that he can, with a full and clear apprehension of mind, at the same time think on all the saints in the world, and be in the exercize of . . . a passionate love to all of them in particular.

—*Miscellanies,* 81

8

The Triune God

Whenever Protestant principle has undertaken its critique of catholic substance "without Reformation," it has become an attack on the religiously key points of Christian teaching. Doubtless most central of these for Edwards' experience was the doctrine of God's triunity. As we have had occasion to note in almost every chapter, the very template of his vision is that God as Triunity is "the supreme Harmony of all."[1] Edwards' reflective achievement, here as at other points, was to sustain Christian understanding as an Enlightened devotee of Newton and Locke, and by means of concepts won in reading them. Indeed, he did not merely maintain trinitarianism; he renewed it.

It is often and rightly said that Edwards' religion and theology are radically "theocentric": it is sheerly God's presence to consciousness which is in every connection decisive for our life as Edwards interprets it. Objectively all value and truth simply are God. In now turning to Edwards' more strictly dogmatic thinking, we therefore make the doctrine of God our prime rubric. But if we call Edwards' thinking theocentric and if we make the doctrine of God its comprehensive rubric, we must always remember that in Edwards' understanding it is only *because* God is triune that his reality can be morally and religiously decisive.[2] God is all in all as the supreme and inevitable aesthetic object: "God is God, and distinguished from all other beings, and exalted above 'em chiefly by his divine beauty. . . ."[3] And it is only in that he is in his own being a social harmony that he can be an aesthetic object at all: "[W]e have shown that one alone cannot be excellent; inasmuch as, in such a case, there can be no consent. Therefore if God is excellent, there must be a plurality in God; otherwise, there can be no consent in him."[4]

From the ancient church on, the root trinitarian assertion is that the history God has with us, as Jesus the Israelite with his "Father" in their Spirit, is not merely a manifestation or revelation of God but *is* God. In Edwards' language, to assert God's triunity is to assert that "the glorious things of the gospel," that is, the whole history narrated and promised in the message carried by the church, are what is "exalting" in God. Edwards' trinitarian assertions present the evangelical "things" as "in" God. Thus as an object of the aesthetic "view" they are the transcendent such object; and, vice versa, the Transcendent is thus the aesthetic—and so morally decisive—reality that it is.[5]

But the question has been: *Can* we entertain God's triunity after the Enlightenment? For the normal Enlightenment, "the doctrine of the Trinity" appeared as the single most implausible item of traditional teaching. Edwards, to his usual contrary, found understanding of the traditional doctrine exactly in his work with Newton and Locke.

II

The inherited dogma itself,[6] worked out at the councils of Nicea (325) and Constantinople (381) and by the "Cappadocian" thinkers in the intervening period, interprets the biblically proclaimed history between "Father," "Son," and "Spirit" as not only a history between God and us but as constitutive of God's own reality. But through the development of specifically Western theology, from Augustine on, there has been great pressure to restrict and mitigate this interpretation. The trinitarian doctrine explicated the biblical proclamation of a temporally participating and active God *against* ancient culture-religion's standard interpretation of deity, which made deity above all consist in immunity to time's activities and sufferings, in "impassibility." From Augustine on there has been, in effect, a counterattack by the culture-religion. The dogmatic formulations themselves, once fixed, could not be simply denied; insofar, therefore, as theology yielded to culture-religious pressure, the deed was done by a proliferation of mitigating distinctions.

On the one hand, there is, according to resultant standard Western teaching, the historical—"economic"—Trinity, the triune divine action between Jesus and his Father in their Spirit, which is the original concern of trinitarian faith; and on the other hand there is an "immanent" Trinity, the somehow-or-other triune structure of God "in himself." These are supposed to lie at fundamentally distinguished metaphysical levels. Of the "immanent" Trinity, standard doctrine says in the last analysis only *that* it obtains and that, however it obtains, it can introduce no "passibility" into God, no actual participation in time's stories and chances. The "historical" Trinity is supposed to be related to this "immanent" opacity as to its own transcendent condition, and as the revelation that but *not* how there does obtain such a condition.

Standard Western teaching thus undoes the original point of trinitarianism. The triunity of God himself becomes sheerly the necessarily postulated presupposition in God of the triune character of God's work, and is not itself to be further conceived. Thus insofar as God *is* conceived—and he will be somehow—the conception of God remains untouched by the triune gospel narrative. Our inability to think about God in a way appropriate to the gospel is then baptized by calling God's unthought triunity a "mystery"; the pious are to recite "God is one and three" but never to ask what this says. The triunity of God himself is thereby deprived of function in actual religious life; and it is unsurprising that trinitarian patterns of piety and interpretation gradually lost importance in medieval and most Reformation-era theology, finally to be explicitly renounced by the Enlightenment.

Remarkably, there is in Edwards' thought no trace of any of this. The standard mitigations and evasive distinctions are wholly absent. From his earliest reflections he supposed that the "Trinity would not be called a mystery for anything else, but because it was in a great measure concealed before Christ revealed it."[7] Instead, there reappear in his thought the patterns of the fourth-century Eastern theologians who created trinitarian doctrine in the first place, not to be a puzzle but to clear up puzzles. In Edwards as in them, the roles of Jesus and his Father and their Spirit in our history, and the roles of those three "persons" in God's own reality, intersect with each other to make but one divine history. Of a metaphysical break between God's triune history with us and God's "own" "immanent" being, Edwards knows nothing. I report two instances.

A sermon on "God Glorified in Man's Dependence" has the thesis: "The nature and contrivance of our redemption is such, that the redeemed . . . are dependent on [God] for all . . . and everyway. . . . [T]hey have all their good *of* him . . . , and . . . they have all *through* him . . . and . . . they have all *in* him." Edwards then argues how each of these triune dependencies is in itself complete: we have no other source of good than the Father, or mediator of good than the Son, or possession of good than the Spirit.[8] And yet, were any of these dependencies missing, our dependence would not be absolute, or what is the same, it would not be a dependence on *God*.[9] "Our having all of God shows the fulness of his power and grace; our having all through him shows the fulness of his merit and worthiness; and our having all in him demonstrates his fulness of beauty, love and happiness."[10]

For the second instance, an explicitly dogmatic reflection interweaves trinitarian discourse and discourse about atonement. "God is . . .

he of whom the purchase is made. God is the purchase and the price, and God is the thing purchased. . . . The great thing purchased by Jesus Christ for us, is communion with God, which is only in having the Spirit."[11] Note that the purchase is made by "Jesus Christ" and the thing purchased is the actual present life of the saints, and yet that the whole is a transaction among the persons of the "immanent" Trinity. Edwards states the principle: "As the persons of the Trinity are equal among themselves, so there seems [to be] an exact equality in each person's concern in the work or redemption," which "equality" is precisely that each has an equally vital "role" in their temporal "work."[12]

III

Two great conceptual problems are posed by all such authentically trinitarian understanding. Edwards masters both by means of his general conceptions of being and of consciousness, that is, by his own version of Enlightenment. The first is the relation between the immanent and historical triunities.

A late item in the *Miscellanies* states his principle. The Incarnation of the Son and the gift of the Spirit are the two ways, "manifesting" and "communicating," of God's "beaming forth of the infinite good" that he himself is. These two ways obtain because they "are agreeable to the two ways of the divine essence flowing out, or proceeding, from eternity within the Godhead, in the persons of the Son and the Holy Spirit: the one in an expression of his glory, in the idea or knowledge of it, the other the flowing out of the essence of love and joy. It is condecent that correspondent to these proceedings of the divinity *ad intra* . . . , God should also flow forth *ad extra*."[13]

The key notion with which Edwards here works, that the historical triunity is "agreeable" or "condecent" to the immanent triunity, is Edwards' version of a notion much used in trinitarian theory since Augustine: that it is, for example, "appropriate" for it to be the Son who *is sent* to be incarnate, rather than the Father, because within God it is the Father who gives deity actively and the Son who is gifted passively. But in standard teaching this notion serves to *shield* the "proceedings" in God from contamination by the temporality of his work *"ad extra,"* by insisting that the latter is as it is *only* "appropriately" to the structure of the former and not as reproducing it. Within Edwards' conceptuality the notion acquires exactly opposite force, since in Edwards' thinking mutual appropriateness is being itself.

There is one technical crux by which Edwards' difference from standard Western teaching, and agreement with original, Eastern patristic teaching can be shown. All orthodox trinitarianism has affirmed the axiom: "the Trinity's externally-directed works are undivided." The purpose of the maxim is plain: if the Son can do externally, that is on the creation, a work that is his work and not the Father's work, then he and the Father are two gods; and so for the Father and the Spirit. As the Greek-speaking fathers used the axiom, it meant that in every creative work of God the three persons have each their essential *role*. But as the Western fathers adopted the axiom, it meant that once the persons emerge into relationship with the creature, they are no longer "really" distinguishable. For the most notorious example: according to Western teaching, it was in fact and "appropriately" the Son who became incarnate, but it *could* have been the Father or the Spirit. Edwards choice between East and West is explicit: there is an "order constituted [immanently] among the persons of the Trinity with respect to their operations and actions *ad extra.*" Therefore the persons' indivisibility *ad extra* is that "all the persons of the Trinity do *concur* (my emphasis) in all acts *ad extra.*" [14]

Thus Edwards is able to draw rigorous conclusions back and forth between inner-trinitarian relations and the relations established in evangelical history, as standard Western theology could not. Not only can Edwards state the affirmative rule, that in the "work" of redemption "every distinct person has his distinct . . . offices . . ., agreeable to their distinct, personal . . . relations," but he can use negatives to make the correlations strict. [15] So for example, "It was not meet, that the redeemer should be God the Father; because he, in the divine economy of the Trinity, was the person that holds the rights of the Godhead, and so was the person offended." [16] Or again, "It was not fit that [the Mediator] . . . should be the Spirit, for . . . [in] being Mediator between the Father and the saints [the Mediator] is Mediator between the Father and the Spirit." [17] When Edwards begins "[T]he Holy Spirit is the harmony and excellency and beauty of the Deity," he can conclude by a straightforward "therefore": "Therefore 'twas his work to communicate beauty and harmony to the world." [18]

IV

The second conceptual problem of an authentic trinitarianism is the mutual distinction and relation of the "immanent" three in God. Again there is a principled entry in the *Miscellanies,*[19] this time amounting to a brief treatise.

Edwards begins, rather alarmingly: "I think that it is within the reach of naked reason to perceive certainly that there are three distinct in God, each of which is the same [God]." As the argument to which Edwards proceeds quickly shows, however, it is reason engaged in interpreting the particular God of the Bible which achieves—indeed without further help— these results. That this reason is "naked" means only that it does not argue by proof texts, and therein Edwards shows a correct understanding of the Trinity-doctrine's situation. For the doctrine did not in fact result from merely systematizing the Bible's discourse about God but from a rational effort to vindicate that discourse against alternatives and challenges arising in the faith's latter history. Thus at each step, Edwards *follows* conceptual argument with Scriptual exegesis, doing just what the Fathers had done before him.

"God," writes Edwards, "is infinitely happy from all eternity in . . . the perfect idea he has of himself. . . . The Almighty's knowledge is not so different from ours, but that . . . it is by an idea, as ours is, only infinitely perfect." In beginning with God's self-knowledge, Edwards follows a tradition stretching back at least to Origen. God, as personal, is a consciousness and just so necessarily a self-consciousness; thus he appears as his own idea. But in the tradition this way of beginning caused more trouble than it was worth, in that it was hard to identify this *idea* with either the personally existent Jesus of Nazareth or with God as such. Whereas within Edwards' super-Lockean interpretation of consciousness and denial of independent substances, there is instant insight. On that interpretation, "An absolutely perfect idea of a thing is the very thing, for it wants nothing that is in the thing, substance nor nothing else." Therefore God's perfect idea of himself "must be a substantial idea . . . , so that by God's reflecting on himself the Deity is begotten."

The connection of this argument to Edwards' general metaphysics is explicit: "It the more confirms me in it, that the perfect idea God has of himself is . . . properly God, that the existence of all corporeal beings is only ideas."[20] After a bit, he refined the argument, following another feature of his interpretation of consciousness: "Those ideas which we call ideas of reflection . . . , such as the ideas of thought, of choice, love, fear, etc. . . . , are not properly representations, but are indeed repetitions of the very thing. . . . Now if this be certain . . . , then . . . if God doth think of himself . . . with perfect clearness . . . that idea he hath of himself is absolutely himself again."[21] Or he can vary the argument, exploiting yet other features of his system: "God loves infinitely.

. . . Thus there must have been an object from all eternity, which God infinitely loves. But we have showed, that all love arises from the perception . . . of consent to being. . . . But we have shown, that consent to being and consent to God are the same. . . . [T]he object, which God infinitely loves, must be infinitely perfectly consenting . . . to him: but that which infinitely and perfectly agrees is the very same essence."[22] We should not be surprised that the dialectics of Edwards' interpretation of Locke prove so flexible of trinitarian insight; as may by now be apparent, it was a trinitarian critique of Locke's position by which Edwards conceived his interpretation in the first place.

Edwards' treatment of the Spirit's procession is parallel to his treatment of the Son. "The Holy Spirit is the act of God between the Father and the Son infinitely loving and delighting in each other. . . . This is certainly distinct from the other two; the delight and energy that is begotten in us by an idea, is distinct from the idea. . . . [A]nd yet it is God, for the pure . . . act of God is God, because God is pure act."[23] The notion of "act," here used by Edwards for a quick proof, is central in the tradition, but is not well integrated in Edwards' system. Other entries make *his* point better. God's eternal "exercize," he writes in "The Mind," is "in infinitely loving and delighting in himself, in the mutual love of the Father and the Son. This makes the third, the personal Holy Spirit or the holiness of God, which is his infinite beauty, and this is God's infinite consent to being in general."[24] The Holy Spirit once thus interpreted, his identity as a "person" of God easily follows within the warrants of Edwards' system. As yet another journal item has it: "The word 'spirit,' most commonly in Scripture, is put for affections of the mind; but there is no other affection in God essentially . . . but love and delight—and that in himself."[25]

V

We cannot pretend that Edwards worked out a complete doctrine of triunity, covering the agenda of the classical systems. Most notably missing is any use of the concept which had become central to all successfully developed trinitarianism and which one would have expected to be immediately congenial to Edwards: of ontologically foundational relations. What trinitarian questions and solutions would have appeared in his full systemactic theology, in its "entire new method," we do not know.[26] He set down the forming principle: "All that Christ does in this great affair as mediator . . . : but also what the Father, or the Holy Ghost, have

done, as united or confederated in this design of redeeming sinful men
. . . : is all but one work, one design.''[27]

What he did find time and reflection to work out was those parts of
trinitarian theory most vital to his vision—or perhaps we should say,
audition—of God. God is a consciousness, centered in and by his taste
or affections, as is every consciousness. He is absolute in that in him the
elements of the consciousness make a communal Harmony in themselves;
thus he can both delight in his own beauty within himself and open to
include other consciousnesses. We ''live and move *in* him'' not only as
we are brought to ''salvation;'' *all* other consciousnesses than God exist
and exist as they do in that they are included in him. As we have seen,
the difference between saints and sinners obtains only in the different
ways our affections mesh in the absolute Community.

It is inescapable how decidedly catholic and very little Protestant *this*
theocentrism is. Edwards thought himself as anti-Catholic as any Puritan,
and indeed he was in his understanding of history and the church. Yet
one of the most striking features of his thought, in the present connection
especially, is how congenial it is to many strands of medieval piety and
reflection. It is doubtful, for example, that Edwards and the first Francis-
can school could have found much about which to dispute. At a level
below confessional anathemas and precisely at its heart, Edwards' theology was grandly ecumenical.

In his own time, the recovered catholicity of Edwards' central theological vision could hardly have been noted, even by himself. But America is no longer a denominationally Protestant country, even insofar as it
is still a Christian country. And more centrally to the concerns of this
book, insofar as our Christianity, including that of most denominational
Roman Catholics, continues to be determined by what the Enlightenment
did to Puritanism, it is precisely the structuring dogmas of ''catholic substance'' we have need of. For if our Protestantism is to recoup its missed-
out Reformation, this can, paradoxically, only be done by a recovery of
catholicity. But the great catholic doctrines must be appropriated with and
by Enlightenment—just as Edwards did.

9

The Offense of God's Actuality

I

Edward calls to the adoration of *God*. That is to say, about this reader of the Bible and believer in Jesus's resurrection, that he calls to the adoration of an actual someone. Edwards' God is an other than you or me, who has his own sense of the heart and whose sense comprises the true idea and the decisive choice. Such divine actuality is irremediably offensive to "Arminianism." What it meant for Edwards to believe in God may perhaps be expeditiously displayed by citing his letter of July 1750 to Thomas Gillespie, just after his dismissal from Northampton: "I desire your prayers that I may take a suitable notice of the frowns of heaven on me and this people . . . in the bringing to pass such a separation between us; and that these troubles may be sanctified to me, that God would over-rule this event to his own glory . . . that God would open a door for my future usefulness, and provide for me and my numerous family." [1] No Protestant without Reformation can believe in this way; the question again is whether we can now at all believe in any other way.

Throughout Christian theological history, it is the linked doctrines of providence and election by which God's actuality is insisted upon. To know that all things, and particularly human creatures' destinies, happen within the will of God, and to believe that there is indeed and in fact God, are obviously the same thing exactly—at least, if with "God" we refer to anything like what the Bible refers to with that word. The assertion is no Calvinist speciality; it is equally essential to the faith of a Thomas Aquinas or a Martin Luther. Thus it is the doctrines of providence and election in which also the offense of God's actuality is most immediate.

That "predestination" should be a common Christian topic is always a shock to American Christians when we hear of it; we suppose it an old "Presbyterian" tenet, which they too have now wisely abandoned. The standard Enlightenment's theory and practice of human existence, "liberalism,'' cannot tolerate an actively sovereign God; and this ideology penetrates also the church, also or even especially its "conservative" parts. Jean-Paul Sartre only perfected modernity's understanding with his rule that even if there were God it would be necessary to disinvent him. Two lines of reflection will suffice for our purpose.

We may begin by noting the unanimity of all American political parties in the great liberal doctrines. The two American parties have always been what elsewhere would have been two factions of one party. We are all, to use the old terminology, Whigs. That is, we live by three convictions: (1) that we inhabit a history which is supposed in the long run to progress toward the good, whatever the good is from time to time taken to be; (2) that the envisioners of this good and the agents of this history are human individuals; and (3) that therefore communal entities are instrumental to antecedent individual purposes. American political wings differ only about the nature of communal entities' instrumentality. A genuinely conservative party, that located primary historical agency not in individuals at all but in natural communities—families, neighborhoods or guilds—we have not had; the Republican "conservatives" are nothing of the sort. Nor have we had, except as an interesting oddity, a socialist party, that located agency in the *post*-individualist solidarity of the working class.

The biblical God, however, is precisely the Agent of history. If he is real, the liberal doctrines are delusions. We may say, as all Christian theology has, that God's historical agency is effective "in, with and under" the agency of creatures. And we may even come to the insight that God's sovereign freedom and our created freedom do not compete and just therefore also cannot infringe each other. But then we have repented the liberal claim.

Liberalism's refusal to regard communities as primary historical agencies, and its need to keep God out of the action, are closely linked phenomena. Communal entities are in any case agents only by the presence of a spirit who embraces the individuals belonging to the group and yet is other than their mere average interest. Communal entities can, therefore, meaningfully regard themselves as the masks and missionaries of God the Spirit's agency. Such claims are full of danger, as history richly teaches, but they are also the only carriers of historical promise. The liberal attempt to make individuals simply as such the makers of history is incompatible with the reality of God.

On a second line we note the absence of *suffering* from the liberal understanding of human agency; and we must here mention that Edwards observed and delineated the nature and error of the absence.[2] Previous and more realistic societies acknowledged that humanity's location in history is constituted in "action" *and* "passion," in doing *and* being done to. That we propose and something else disposes is obvious and not finally obscurable even by the most potent ideology or technological superstition. The only question is whether Someone or No-one disposes; our final options, other than bad faith, are hope in God or historical nihilism.

The truth is: we live in history not only by agency but also by patience. It is good to try to "do something," but what when our trying is for naught? Is that merely bad? Is there nothing in evil but a challenge to our effort?

It is death that both sets the question inescapably and tests all answers. In history we both act and suffer now and sooner or later will only suffer. What are we to hope about that? The correlation of death and God, as enemies to each other but allies against our illusions, has always been a center of Christian understanding. Liberal doctrine is the refusal to acknowledge that when we finally *must* be still, it is to learn "that I am God," to learn who in fact rules history.

All the above acknowledged, it would nevertheless be neither faithful nor plausible simply to assert "God's" sovereignty against liberal illusions. Once the Enlightenment's truth is experienced, we indeed must defend ourselves against most gods' claim to sovereignty. To stay with the American deities, to attribute active rule to the god of the polity's deism would indeed make us "into puppets," whereas the gods of the private "religious" sphere are too private and eccentric to be trusted with much power. Everything really depends on *which* God we adore as Lord or, what is the same thing, how God's lordship is effective.

Edwards is remembered by Americans—where he is remembered at all—for his uncompromising homiletical assertion of God's free choice, whether in its determination of our final destiny or in its determination of the penultimate course of events. This may be illustrated at near random from his preaching. "God, therefore, as it is his design to manifest his own glory, will and does exercise his sovereignty toward men, over their souls and bodies, even in this most important matter of their eternal salvation. He has mercy on whom he will have mercy, and whom he wills he hardens."[3] I will cite the famous "Sinners in the Hands of an Angry God" just this once; "There is nothing that keeps wicked men at any one moment out of hell, but the mere pleasure of God," his "mere arbitrary will, and . . . unobliged forebearance."[4] But therein is nothing distinctive to Edwards. Edwards' thought was bent not upon the assertion of some divine sovereignty or other, but upon identification of *which* God

is sovereign, specifically, upon a trinitarian and christological understanding of the great "decrees." It may also be said in advance that such
a doctrine as Edwards' works very differently than the strawfigure "predestination" Arminianism is accustomed to set up and denounce.

II

The will of God as proclaimed in Scripture can be described under a
plurality of rubrics: God chooses to create, to allow sin, to save from
sin, to save by the Son's death and resurrection, to save Jones (and not
Smith?). Puritans devoted much thought to finding the appropriate rubrics
for these "covenants" and "decrees," and to sorting out their various
priorities and dependencies. The effort was by no means simply scholastic. For central example, it determines our whole interpretation of God,
whether we think he "decreed" our creation in order to have an object
to redeem by the Son's death and resurrection, or decreed redemption as
emergency repair for a creation itself otherwise motivated.

Edwards was a typical Puritan in his devotion to these questions.
But all his reflection had a single and radical goal: to work out how all
"the work of God is but one. Tis . . . but . . . one scheme, one contrivance."[5] We have already noted the one goal by which the "scheme"
becomes one: "God created the world to provide a spouse and a kingdom
for his Son. And the setting up of [this] kingdom . . . is what the whole
creation labours . . . to bring to pass. This work of redemption is so
much the greatest of all the works of God, that all other works are . . .
parts of it, or appendages to it, or are some way reducible to it; and so
all the decrees of God do some way . . . belong to that eternal covenant
of redemption which was between the Father and the Son before the
foundation of the world.[6] Every decree of God is . . . reducible to that
covenant." As paradoxically as possible: "the giving being to the world
[is] from mercy to God's church."[7]

Edwards works out the dependencies within God's one "scheme"
with his usual rationalism. Priorities among God's decrees, as among
those of any coherent consciousness, are, he analyzes, of two sorts. There
is the priority of a willed end to the possible means of its achieving. And
to some means, there is the priority of those givens by which those means
are in fact possible means to the end. That God will glorify himself in
the redemption of creatures is within God's decreeing the only prior decree in the first sense; as we have seen, the glorification of God and the

happiness of creatures turn out to be the same thing. The existence of creatures and the permission of sin are means to this end; that they are means thereto depends, however, only on their own possibility, so that in God's will they are consequent only to the choice to redeem. Finally, that God will redeem by the particular way of unmerited mercy and punitive justice, is consequent on the fact of sin, since only supposing sin are these means of redemption.[8]

But all this talk of "schemes" and "decrees" can easily give a wrong impression: of God deciding in advance what is to happen and then causing it to come to pass. Two points must be adduced here.

First, what Edwards here discusses in standard Puritan terms is the same event we earlier heard him describe as the emanation and return of God's glory. A late *Miscellanies* entry is analysis of this event.[9] God's goodness, which is his will that others be happy and holy, is one thing. His desire to have beings other than himself, to whom to be good, is another thing, for God's goodness is in itself fully exercised within the triune life, whereas to "desire new beings to communicate happiness to 'em" is "the disposition that is in the infinite fountain of good and of glory and of excellency, to . . . flow out; which . . . is called God's 'glory' in Sacred Scripture." Thus in making creatures blessed God does not merely *exercise* some of his attributes, notably his goodness, but God himself and so all his attributes are *communicated*. Finally, those two "dispositions, of exalting himself and communicating himself, may be reduced to one, viz. a disposition to . . . exert himself to an effect," which effect is "the communication of himself ad extra." And it is *this* unitary "disposition," and so *not* any plan to achieve some "result" or other, which is God's will to his own "glory." "God's glory, as it is . . . the end of all God's works, is in one word the *emanation* of that fullness of God that is from eternity in God . . . towards those creatures that are capable of being sensible and active objects of such an emanation."[10]

Second, in Edwards' full metaphysics, it cannot be thought that God plans in advance and then works to achieve his plan, since for God, to conceive as actual is to make to be actual. Therefore, "the decrees of God are no other than his eternal doing what is done . . . by him in time." His "acts themselves in executing" are simply "decrees for a present effect," and "this act of will that now is, cannot be . . . really different from that act of will that was in him . . . from eternity, in decreeing that this thing should be at this time." In effect, the "eternal decrees" are simply the reality in God of his history with us. "The de-

crees of God must be conceived of in the same order, and as antecedent
to and consequent on one another in the same manner, as God's acts in
execution of those decrees." [11]

Edwards has, in fact, overcome the whole notion of God "predestining" events in a temporal reality from which God is himself removed.
According to Edwards, all events, "historical" and "natural," occur by
the immediate presence of God. In the language of the texts just now
before us, God "exercizes" and "communicates" his own self, and *so*
there are destinies other than himself yet encompassed in his self-chosen
purpose. God, we may say in the language of much recent theology,
above all *lives;* and his rule is but the sovereignty of his life.

III

Since God's decreeing is his life, it is a *triune* event. We already have
the proposition before us: the prior decree of redemption is an "eternal
covenant . . . between the father and the Son." God's primal covenant
about us is not *with* us, but triunely with himself. We may note in pass-
ing that this is Edwards' explanation of how the covenant of redemption
contains no conditions for us to fulfill: we are not among its contracting
parties. [12] "All God's eternal decrees [are] comprehended in that eternal
transaction that there was between the Father and the Son, even the covenant of redemption." [13] Yet more drastically: the work of redemption
manifests the "mutual relations . . . and . . . economy there is established amongst [the trinitarian persons] in the eternal covenant these divine persons entered into about this work and in the several offices . . .
each one bears in it, and how they are therein connected one with another." [14]

There is in Edwards' thinking at this point a remarkable interplay
between what the triune God chooses and what he simply is. Christ is
conceived, at this level of reflection, as universal mediator, as between
God and all creatures, so also within the triune life and within the world
of creatures, and in both connections as mediator both of what is separated by evil and of what is separated merely by nature. [15] Thus the Son's
role in the triune life makes him also "the only fit person of all persons,
whether created or uncreated," to carry out the other mediatorial roles. [16]

The inner-triune covenant stipulates the Son's redeeming mission,
and the roles of the Father and the Spirit therein. Thus the eternal "decree" of "predestination," in Edwards' understanding, determines first
and foremost the fact and destiny of the incarnate Christ. It is not pri-

mally a decree about which of the rest of us shall and shall not be "saved;" it is primarily abut the destiny of Christ-with-his spouse the church. The goods to which the great decree predestines are all promised only to "Christ mystical . . . , as a public person . . . , virtually containing the whole future church that he had taken . . . on his heart." [17]

The eternal covenant is to be christologically understood both as to its subject and as to its object, both "as the accomplishment of the decrees was wholly committed to [Christ] . . . and also as the man Jesus is . . . the first of the elect, the Head of the elect body." [18] On the first line, Edwards' position is unambiguous and consistent through his career. All determinants of his teaching come together paradigmatically in this sermonic passage: "Seeing there is one of the persons of the Trinity united to the human nature, God [note well, the *Trinity*] chooses in all his transactions with mankind, to transact by him. He did so of old . . . when, although Christ was not actually incarnate, yet he was so in design . . . , in the covenant of redemption. . . . And since the incarnation . . . , God governs both the church and the world by Christ." [19]

We have traced much of the other line: all is for the sake of Christ. He is the "elect" creature. [20] What God "determined" was "to exalt one of the creatures so high that he should be one person with God and should have communion with God and glory in all respects answerable, and so should be the head of all other elect creatures that they might be united to God and glorified in him." "Christ's election is the foundation of ours." [21]

Also for this doctrine there is a late journal entry that amounts to a full draft systematic analysis. [22] He proceeds by steps. First, "all things that God ever decreed, he decreed for the sake of his beloved Son." Second, "That which more especially was God's end . . . was to procure a spouse or a mystical body for his Son." The "decree in appointing the individual creatures that were chosen to be members of his body" is thus merely analytical within this "procuring." Third, "As God determined . . . [that] his Son . . . have an object . . . of his infinite grace and love, so God determined that this object should be one. . . . Therefore the many individual persons were chosen, yet they were chosen to receive God's love in union as one body, one spouse, all united in one head." It is again merely analytical within *this* decree that those chosen to be one with Christ are thereby chosen to "the holiness and happiness of the head"; and "after this is the consideration of the circumstances of the individual chosen members" that they are "sinful, miserable, etc." so that the "particular way they should come to participate with the Head" should be "by Christ's satisfaction." And last, fourth, in choosing a body of creatures for his love, God chose a head creature in that body, who is just so "head of the whole creation" and is "to be strictly united to him." Thus Christ's human nature is "the head of election. All are elected only as his members." A comparison intrudes itself also in this chapter. Edwards' doctrine of election anticipates at most key points the justly praised "christological" doctrine of election developed by Karl Barth. Barth convicted the tradition of abstraction at a disastrous point: just when doctrine comes to speak of the volitional actuality of God, it forgets that its God is God in Christ, and speaks of the predestining God as of a monadic Majesty determining events from an abstract timelessness. In his determination to understand God in *Christ* as the predestining God Barth found only Luther as a predecessor; Edwards is really closer to Barth's particular doctrine.

The linked doctrines of providence and predestination state the offense an actual God must be to all standard religion. Just therefore, it is vital that they state the actual offense of God and do not obscure it with extraneous offenses. It is the monadic Majesty of traditional predestinarianism who at the great dissolution went off by itself to become the God of Deism. But this abstract sovereignty then could not be born. It was contained by restricting it to the past tense: according to Jefferson, it was safely before history that we were "endowed" by the Creator with all our blessings. Now, it is up to us to use them, without interference by any continuing actuality of God. It was not least among the purposes of Barth's doctrine of election to free western societies from the liberal politics practiced under this moot Creator. There is the same connection in Edwards.

IV

Edwards overcame the functionally unitarian vision of God that has appeared in standard descriptions of "predestination" and "providence" and that has made this language offensive in false and unnecessary ways. The predestining God is the *Trinity;* his predestining is simply that he *lives* one way instead of another; and what he predestines is *Christ.* But thereby the essential offenses of God's actuality are only the more starkly presented. There are two; readers have surely already felt both. The one: if God is sovereign, then we are not. The other: if God rules *this* world, than his rule is morally opaque in ways the standard Enlightenment cannot acknowledge. I will pose the offenses in order.

Even if there are territories of reality where God is not sovereign, our claim to them remains preposterous; then no one is sovereign there. But just that preposterous human claim to a piece of creation wherein we are autonomous is a main impulse of modern Western history. The demonisms that come to inhabit our assertion of autonomy have surely been demonstrated to sufficiency; foreign policies based on deterrence with communicidal weapons are only the most appalling of them. It is a great experiment of the modern West, to try if our moral will may not remain sound and if the expedition of our will may not remain beneficial, also without assumption of God. The results of the experiment are in. It turns out that individual decisions and individual action may indeed be well done *etsi deus non daretur,* "as if God were not a given" but history so lived becomes the more ferocious the longer it continues.

Whether the shared civil posit of an actual God is now possible for America, is outside the scope of this chapter. But the *church,* to be faithful to itself and useful to the polity, is required to offend the presumption of autonomy and the denatured talk of God that accompanies the presumption's religious versions. The church, to continue the example, is required to say: the "security" of the United States is not really in our hands; therefore we must presume that all means of defense that require us to arrogate absolute value to our own nation will be turned against us. The American church has resisted hearing of the offensive sovereignty of God from such foreigners as Barth. Perhaps we may heed one of our own.

If we acknowledge God's sovereignty we may well come to deny his goodness; we arrive at the second offense of God's actuality. Edwards reflects at length here; my description also will be more extended.

Edwards wastes no time trying to get God off the moral hook for the fact of sin and evil in his creation. The pusillanimous atheism which reassures sufferers that "God is not responsible" does not appear in his thought even to be rebutted. Plainly, a God such as the one asserted in the gospel could have created a world in which sin and evil had no role; and since no such world exists, either this God is not or he is finally accountable for sin and evil, even if he does not "cause" or "do" them. Edwards does not even spend much time on the truly terrible question thus posed. He faces it and registers the lack of a solution: "'Tis evident by experience that great evil, both moral and natural, abounds in the world . . . : great injustice . . . and extreme cruelty to the innocent . . . , as well as innumerable extreme sufferings. . . . That it should be so ordered *or* [my emphasis] permitted, in a world absolutely . . . under the . . . government of an infinitely . . . good God, has a seeming repugnance to reason, that few, if any, have been able fully to remove."[23] The favorite device of Edwards' time was the defense of God's justice by reference to our "free will"; in the late finished work on *Original Sin,* he demolishes it in four paragraphs: whether we are created with a propensity to sin, or created "able" to remain righteous but in a world in which none have so far succeeded, comes morally to exactly the same thing and makes no difference at all to God's responsibility.[24]

Edwards' reflection is devoted rather to the *role* played in God's "scheme" by his permitting sin and evil. "Even sin and wickedness . . . comes to pass because God has a use for it."[25] We have already seen that according to Edwards our fulfillment as not merely happy creatures but as the "spouse" in the triune life depends on our being rescued not merely from immaturity but from sin.[26] "[T]he sin, in general, of the saints is for their good . . . in this respect . . . that it . . . will issue in a high advancement of their eternal happiness . . . beyond what they would have had, if they never had been fallen creatures."[27] Edwards discusses three aspects of evil's role.

The one is stated in Puritan language about successive "covenants." In the historical working-out of the primal "covenant of redemption" there have appeared first the "covenant of works" and then the "covenant of grace." In both, according to Edwards, humankind has appeared as a corporate whole, and our destiny has depended on a head of the whole. Had Adam "stood," he would have "obtained eternal happiness" for the race, but it would necessarily have been the happiness appropriate to be earned by a human for other humans: the "happiness of man" and of "earth that is the habitation of men." But when Adam fell, and for our rescue only a "covenant of grace," mediated by God himself, could then suffice, Christ became our new corporate head, "one that properly belongs to heaven." The happiness he wins for us is that appropriate to him; but this is "the very happiness of God himself . . ." which we will have as inhabitants of "his country, even heaven."[28] The "righteousness" that would have been imputed to us from Adam would have been "human" and the imputation would have been by "natural . . . derivation"; Christ's righteousness is "human-divine" and its imputation is by "faith," a "spiritual active union."[29] "Gospel holiness differs greatly from the holiness of man in innocency. Man had the Holy Ghost then as the Spirit of God, but now he must have it as the Spirit of the Son of God."[30]

A second aspect is stated by Edwards' doctrine of God's self-manifestation. "The terribleness of God is part of his glory," and so a "sense of it" must belong to our vision of God and so to our "perfect and becoming and answerable joy and happiness."[31] In terms of the "manifestation'' itself: "It is . . . proper that the effulgent glory of God should answer his real excellency.'' Therefore it is "necessary'' that his self-revelation should reveal "God's awful majesty, his authority and dreadful greatness, justice and holiness. . . . But this could not be except sin and punishment were decreed.'' [32]

The third aspect of evil's role appears, as an explicit doctrine, most fleetingly of the three, but is perhaps nevertheless the most deeply anchored in Edward's system. Human creatures are to be admitted to nothing less than personal intimacy in God's life, "to the kisses of his mouth.'' Just this is the reason why we must be first humiliated in being rescued from failure, lest our elevation blur our consciousness of the difference between us as creatures and God. [33] To appreciate the point, we remember that in Edward's interpretation of reality, consciousness is all, and that a creature is what I am and so must remain if *I* am to be exalted.

Not only God's sheer permission of evil must offend, but also the freedom with which he manages and rescues from it. Edwards was a proper Calvinist, who taught that whom God "procures'' to belong to the Spouse is finally determined only by his uninfluenced decision. [34] "[I]t is from the mere mercy of God that the benefits of Christ are applied to such and such particular persons.'' [35] That the persons chosen are only some of humankind, that God leaves other persons to be damned, does not, to be sure, necessarily follow from the Calvinist principle; Edwards taught it because he supposed it was a simple teaching of Scripture. But even if we followed the "universalist'' strain in Christian history, that would not remove the offense. For even if God inflicts final loss on no one, his penultimate inflictions are quite enough to make his goodness mysterious. Edwards made just this point with his usual cool: the Arminians' plea that God would surely leave no one to eternal suffering is, he said, refuted by "plain fact, for if there be any meaning in the objection, this is supposed in it, that all misery of the creature, whether just or unjust, is . . . contrary to the nature of God . . . which we see to be contrary to fact, for we see that God in his providence, doth indeed inflict very great calamities on mankind even in this life.'' [36]

The first offense of God's actuality is to our claim of autonomy. Acceptance of the offense is good, in that it frees us from the demons that come with the claim. We must now ask: From what can the second offense, as Edwards evokes it, free us?

The proclamation that God is sovereign in *this* world breaks us out of merely moral reality as defined by bourgeois insight. It evokes the cracks in the merely moral order, and the abyss in the ordering God. It— to use traditional concepts—opens a supernature that is not simply the extension or even perfection of nature, but can be also a threat and an outrage.

The twentieth century must surely make us hear such teaching. The "heavenly city of the eighteenth-century philosophers" has broken walls and fallen gates, and monsters come through the breaches. If we will not believe that the monsters too are in God's hand, we must turn from God to other assurances. Edwards' God may be hard to trust, but "after Auschwitz" the merely moral universe and its gentlemanly God are simply and trivially implausible.

Given the creation that is, either there is no God or he is far deeper and quite otherwise hidden than we have conceived. Either there is no God or there is one who can decree evil in order to turn it to good beyond our fathoming. Edwards could not entertain the atheist alternative, for he *perceived* God in that he perceived God's mystery. We must now perhaps entertain atheism more actually, partly because we so rarely transcend mere "notional" knowledge of God but also because we have gone through history that Edwards was spared.

Only by seeing nothing but the "natural" order can we go on our liberal way. But how are we to do that, now? Surely only by endless stratagems of avoidance, which must eventually generate both a politics and a religion of illusion—and, indeed, we have gone far on that way. If we escape from it, it will either be to see only the monsters, in such spasms of pure communal nihilism as in Europe have been called "fascism," or to see even the horrors as somehow, in whatever agony, God's own. It would be a transmogrified but perhaps also fulfilled liberalism that risked the latter vision.

10

Christ

I

Since Christianity is intrinsically a missionary faith, Christian teaching about God consists always in the reinterpretation of some antecedent apprehension of God by what happens with Israel's Jesus and in his church. "Naturally" the antecedent religion, whatever at a time and place it is, resists the intrusion; whence arises "natural theology." The kind of discourse that appears in theological systems under the heading "christology" has the function of delegitimizing this resistance.

Defending our unevangelized theology we plead: "But could God himself really have walked with Adam or lunched with Abraham?" "Can it really be, as an ecumenical council of 553 decided, that 'one of the Trinity died?' " "Mary is surely Jesus' mother, but can anybody be 'the Mother of God?' " "What sort of God would let his body be broken and pushed around on our altars?" "How can you limit God?" The questions are intended to be rhetorical; they have their force from what "everyone" knows "of course" to be true of God.

Christology is the analysis interior to getting over such self-evidencies. The heart of the conflict is between the universally antecedent dogma that God must be "impassible," immune to time's challenges and fatalities, and the involvement of Jesus' "Father" with Jesus' life and fate, that is, with time, death and bodies. Particular christological propositions are more or less adequate as they more or less ingeniously and permanently outrage what we all "of course" know about God.

To whatever extent an antecedent interpretation of God is not just rejected when it encounters the gospel, there will be in the new Christian interpretation a body of belief about God shared by believers with the culture's antecedent religion. In the Western theological tradition, for which the antecedent interpretation is that of Socrates and his inheritors, the body of shared belief has been extensive. Western theology has accounted for this shared knowledge by crediting its acquisition to humanity's "natural" powers, which belong to all, believing and not. And since in modern Western countries believers and unbelievers together make the public sphere of polity and economy, it has been tempting to put the public sphere under the rule of God "naturally" known and restrict the gospel's theological import to one or another inwardness. We have noted how decisive this temptation has been for American religion.

Some rehearsal of history is probably needed here. In the actual development that has led to our situation, the first stage of christological struggle ended with the Nicene-Constantinopolitan dogma of 381. Second and third century theology had come to denote Jesus' identity with God by the myth/concept "Logos" ("Word"): in Jesus, it was said, God's Logos has appeared. Thereupon the culture-religion's questions were promptly pressed: "How can the Logos be God, since he sleeps like a human and weeps and suffers?" At Nicea and Constantinople, the gospel asserted itself against this question, by the doctrine of triunity, which makes the logos a "person" of God's being, suffer though he may. But the pressure thereupon only shifted one metaphysical notch—and christology proper began. Now the self-evidency was stated so: "How—if, as is now agreed, the Logos *is* God—can Jesus be the Logos, since Jesus sleeps and weeps and suffers?" Surely the Logos must be *somehow* otherwise related to the man Jesus than by identity? Perhaps the Logos *inhabits* Jesus or *communes* with him? Or is *reflected* in him? Or . . . ?

The two great theological schools which disputed christology through the fifth and succeeding centuries can neither of them be said to have fully carried out the needed debunking of antecedent certainties, for neither had any longer the intellectual energy simply to deny that God must be "impassible." The school of Antioch by and large capitulated, and practically left Jesus as one thing and God-the-Logos as another. The school of Alexandria pressed the attack harder, insisting that the impassible Logos and the mortal Jesus are but one actual entity. It must be factually true that "God the Logos died" or that "Jesus rules." But whatever can such insistences *mean?* Alexandria purchased its profundity at an intolerable price of paradox.

Our Latin fathers understood the Antiochenes and never understood the Alexandrians. This has shaped the whole history of Western christology. Western thinking perhaps moved more simple-mindedly in the Antiochene track than had the Antiochenes themselves. Thus the brilliant analytical christologies of medieval Western scholasticism had meager matter to analyze. It would be caricature to speak of "the scholastic" christology. Still, the following positions are common and suffice for my purpose. The "personal being" of any real thing is understood as so different a metaphysical factor from the "nature" *of* which it is the person, that the person of the Logos can be said to become the person of

Jesus without positing any direct consequences for either the Logos or Jesus. Thus the assertion of a "personal" or "hypostatic" union of God and this man in Christ can be taken as a purely logical assertion: that *somehow* such biblical and traditional sentences as "Jesus rules" or "God died" are true. *How* they are true is then to be stipulated by a different doctrinal complex, of the "communion of attributes."

Under that heading we learn that there is no "real" sharing of attributes between Christ's deity and his humanity, but only a sharing "in (true) words." That is, propositions of the sort "The Logos dies" or "Jesus rules" are true, but they do not structurally reflect the reality that verifies them; structural congruence is achieved only by the longer propositions "Jesus (who is hypostatically one with the Logos) dies" or "The Logos (who is hypostatically one with Jesus) rules." Finally, the pair of these doctrines is saved from vacuous circularity by the doctrine that Jesus' humanity is gifted with created extraordinary attributes that *reflect* the Logos' divine attributes.

One may well wonder how believers can have been satisfied with this christology, which after all the maneuvering is over leaves God himself quite uninterpreted by what happens with Jesus. I suggest: the West could get along without positing a "real" mutual interpretation of God and the human Christ because the Western church's own mighty reality substituted for the missing christological reality. The church's own reality served to assert the identity of God in himself and God in Jesus, and so to maintain the interpretive action of the latter on the former.

The most famous instance of this matter is provided by the western church's problem with the doctrine of Eucharistic "real presence": How can these objects on our altars be God's body for us? The scholastic christology could provide no understanding of this marvel; Christ as body is where he rose and ascended to, he is in one place at a time, like any real body. The Eucharistic presence was therefore finally classified as a sheer unanalyzable supernatural event, of "transubstantiation," occurring anew at each celebration. But a Eucharistic miracle has to be a predictable miracle; as we participate in the Eucharist we cannot be left wondering if this time it is happening. Thus the church's own ministerium acquired the role of authorized miracle-invokers, empowered to say "This is my body" and have it be true because they say it. That is, the power of the priesthood substituted for feeble christology.

The Reformers, who rejected such roles for churchly institutions, had only two moves open. Calvinists and other "Reformed" theologians sacrificed the ancient identity of the loaf and cup, the body on the altar, with God; the Lutherans, determined to maintain that identity, had to work on a christology that would do so in itself, without churchly miracles additional to those of Incarnation and Resurrection. The Lutherans developed a radical doctrine of the "communion of attributes." The human Jesus, they said, "really" shares in such divine prerogatives as omnipresence, and so can be wherever he promises to be. But whatever would an omnipresent body be? The Lutherans recovered the line of Alexandria, and like Alexandria purchased their profundity by unintelligibility.

By a different route, we have again come to note the unmediated tension in the vision of God which Calvinist Christianity brought to this continent. We noted earlier the former role of the medieval church. Now we may put it so: the existence of the church did what pusillanimous Western christology could not. By the church's reality as a natural and political administration—of inner communion, as an impassible impersonal institution—of suffering love, as an empire beyond empires—to subject us to the Crucified, the church mediated the christologically unmediated polarities of Western Christianity's vision of God. Take away the institution and leave the christology as it was, and you have the Calvinism that Puritans brought to this country. Puritan theology was in the present respect a compendium of unresolved tensions: between God as utter Despot and God as familiar Friend, between God as pure and distant Reason and God as inexplicably forgiving Presence, between the God who finally can condescend to no "means" and the God of a passionate Eucharistic piety—finally, between "God" flat-out and Jesus.

No one could live with these tensions, and New England Puritanism, taking advantage of its primeval position, ameliorated them by putting the commonwealth where the church had been. The New England towns as such, by their inseparably spiritual and public entity, substituted for the papal church and were again to mediate the two halves of Western Christendom's vision of God. The attempt was undone by its own difficulties—consider only the "half-way covenant"—and by polity-making cooperation with Deists.

When Deists and Puritans clashed, they agreed on ground rules: the dispute was always about whether and for what "fidelity" to Christ is needed *besides* due honor to the distant world-Ground. It was the Deists who were the engineers of our polity. The polity-machine they created, their mill of the greatest good for the greatest number, was a public realm made expressly for the endowing and not interfering "Creator," a realm from which christological "religion" was explicitly excluded. Insofar as the Puritans connived in the society so arranged, Calvinism's tensions were finally sundered.

We have, as noted before, two national religions. Our political and economic life is under the aegis of a late-antique Deity released from and now immunized against reinterpretation by the gospel. And we have a smorgasbord of Jefferson's banished "religions," free to do everything but make any difference. Insofar as Jesus is one of these offerings, we cannot be grasped by him as by God, and grasp him instead as teacher, example, personal savior, or whatever. Protestantism without Reformation is constituted by the defeat of christology.

II

Finally we may turn to Edwards. The labor of his life may be described also in terms of this history. He perceived, with great clarity, the sundering of Calvinism. What he called "Arminianism" may here be characterized as the split of the Christian relation to God into "deistical" notions of God on the one hand and a sentimental affiliation to Jesus on the other. In his grandfather's settlement of the relation between church and society he saw the communal correlate of Arminianism, however Calvinist Stoddard himself surely was. Plainly, the theological assignment laid before him was centrally an assignment of christology; it is yet another of our disasters that what he achieved remained mostly unpublished.

Readers who come to Edwards' drafts from the traditional discussions must first be struck that this Calvinist teaches a "real" communication of God's divine attributes to the human reality of Christ that might have seemed a bit unguarded even to Cyril of Alexandria or Martin Luther. We can choose instances to span the history of salvation.

In drafts for his planned antideist apology,[1] Edwards isolated *creating* as the pre-eminently "distinguishing" work of the "one only Jehovah," that is, of the God whose reality Deists and Puritans presumed they together affirmed. But the reason for the analysis was to give full shock value to the proposition that "the man, Christ Jesus . . . , a creature" is the one who "created all things visible and invisible." All the Johannine and Deutero-Pauline discourse about creation "in" or "by" Christ is taken directly of the man Jesus. So straightforwardly does Edwards understand all this, that it makes a problem for him about the creation of the man Jesus, since it can hardly be "that he makes himself."[2]

The continuing upholding and governance of the universe is Christ's work also, and that precisely during his time of weakness and limitations. Moreover, it is his "ordinary operation and care" as the particular creature he is.[3] The miracles of the historic Christ can be spoken of so:"[N]or was the *man* [all emphases mine] Christ Jesus lifted up with pride with all those . . . *divine* works that he wrought . . . in his own name and *of his own will as* the *God* of nature."[4]

The difference between Christ's prophecies and those of other prophets is that christ prophecied "what he himself would bring to pass."[5] And of Jesus' total existence as Redeemer, Edwards taught, in the one direction: "[T]he love the human nature had to mankind, and by which he was prompted to undergo so much, it had only by virtue of its union with the Logos; 'twas all derived from the love of the Logos, or else they would not be one person";[6] and in the other: "[T]he love of the man Christ Jesus [for the Father] was in some sort infinite. . . . He had [before the dereliction] actually been infinitely happy in the enjoyment of the Father's love."[7]

Perhaps most astonishing of all are Edwards' evocations of the End. It will be "the beam" of Christ's bodily glory "shining on the dead that shall raise them . . . " and that shall "change the living."[8] "[T]he light of heaven . . . will be the light . . . of Christ's glorious body."[9] Then all heaven will have its "life and beauty and being from that luminary."[10] And in that the saints look upon this "luminary," they "may see God with their bodily eyes, as well as by an intellectual view"; they will see Christ's human body, "that appears with that transcendent visible majesty, glory and beauty that is exceeding expressive of the divine goodness, holiness and grace."[11] A metaphysical point should be remembered here: in Edwards' vision each person's body simply *is* an expression of the spirit that person is, so that it is no miracle that the risen Christ's "external glory" should manifest his "spiritual glory." But human spiritual glory in Christ's case has become "divine," enabling the saints' "pleasure from external perception" to "have God for its object."[12]

Edwards did publish one longer essay in christology, the sermon "On the Exellency of Christ." The effort of the sermon is to evoke a christological vision that is at once and in itself of God, of the human Christ and of the rest of us.

Christ's "excellency," according to the sermon, is his worthiness to be adored. This latter consists in "an admirable conjunction of divine excellencies."[13] Three sets of admirably—that is, both surprisingly and beautifully—conjoined attributes are then discussed.

Christ has, first, divine excellencies that are "unlikely in one subject," that is here, in the same God. Here the remarkable "conjunction" characterizes the oddity, over against antecedent self-evidencies, of the

Christian interpretation of God as such. Edwards explicitly mentions two pairs: "infinite highness" with "infinite condescension" and "infinite justice" with "infinite grace." [14] We should note about "condescension" that precisely as condescension to creaturely others it is for Edwards a *divine* attribute of Christ. [15]

Christ has, second, excellencies whose conjunction would otherwise be *impossible* in the same subject but which are conjoined in this subject because he is both God and man. Seven pairs of such attributes are discussed in what at first seems more or less traditional fashion. But several are attributes which the divine or human nature would not have at all apart from conjunction with the other, that are not brought into the union but are created by it. Thus "dominion" is earned for christ's divine nature by his human suffering, and "obedience" is a human manifestation of the trinitarian being-begotten. [16]

And Christ has, third, excellencies "expressed in him towards men, that otherwise would have seemed impossible to be exercised towards the same object; as particularly . . . justice, mercy and truth." Here is the point where the "admirable conjunction" is soteriological; in Edwards' discussion all the former polarities function here together in a rich dialectic to overcome the seeming impossibility, to free God in Christ from Deity's seeming necessary separation from us. [17]

A second part of the sermon then describes how the conjunction "appears in Christ's acts," as narrated in the second article of the usual creeds. Here the restraints of traditional Western christology and Edwards' Calvinist tradition are entirely abandoned; attributes are shared and crossbred in bewildering interchange. Thus, for example, divine "condescension" and human "humility" *together* veil divine "majesty," which nevertheless manifests itself in human "authority" and in the miracles, "which were evidently divine works" done by "the man" Jesus. [18] Or again, Christ's sacrificial death is "the greatest degree of [human] humiliation," the assent to which is the "most glorious" of Christ's acts of divine majesty. [19] Finally, in a discussion of the exaltation and return, all depends for Edwards on christological attributions that are plain instances of a "real" human exercise of divine power: "the man Christ Jesus," *in* his human humility, rules the universe by *"his* [my emphasis] divine majesty and power." [20]

Throughout the sermon, not only does Christ's reality as God the Logos determine what it means for him to be the human that he is, but his reality as this particular human determines what it means that there is the God he is. Throughout the Alexandrian and Lutheran tradition it was always asked: Does not the sharing go both ways? Does not Jesus' spe-

cifically human reality characterize God? Neither Cyril or Luther dared
say straight out that it does, for the foundational reality that would thus
be communicated to God the Logos would necessarily be *passibility,*
openness to be affected by time's events. Even Edwards is cautious. But
the Sermon is not compatible with the standard positions; and the *Miscellanies* hold the following sublime passage from early in his work,
which once read illumines all Edwards' thought: God's love "as it is in
the divine nature, is not a passion, is not such love as we feel, but by
the Incarnation [God the Logos] is really [!] become passionate to his
own, so that he loves them with such a sort of love as we have to him,
or to those we most dearly love. . . . So that now when we delight
ourselves at the thought of God's loving us, we need not have that allay
of our pleasure . . . that though he loved us yet we could not conceive
of that love."[21] The Incarnation, he later writes, is so that our love of
God may be not only "adoration of a glorious being," but "friendship"
with a "companion."[22]

III

Edwards taught the doctrine just described in order to grasp the unity of
Christ's one reality for and enveloping us. It is essential to everything
that he believed and valued that in "closing" with the man Jesus we,
without qualification or further mediation, are closed with God.

As we have seen, conversion saves, according to Edwards, not because it elevates our religious life but because it initiates a specific personal identity of Jesus and the believer. Reality is composed of hearts in
community; community is constituted in the cognitive affections, and
centrally in that total affection he calls the heart's sense. Now the unity
of hearts in affection is varied and complex; and what counts as one
entity in this field need not always be one heart. There is no a priori
reason why the unity of two hearts cannot in one or another respect be
such that for some purposes they must count as one being. Particularly,
the "excellency," of Christ may really become the excellency of the
believer; Jesus may be so united to us that we "may be justly looked
upon as the same. Now there is no other way of different spirits being
thus united than by love."[23]

Edwards' doctrine of justification analyzes the conditions of such an
affectionate unification on the believer's side; when we come to his doctrine of atonement we will find that it is an analysis of the conditions on
Christ's side. For now, we note only that such unity by affection must

be between metaphysically like hearts: it is the human Jesus with whom believers can "close."[24] But if our unity with the human Jesus made only his human excellence ours, this could suffice for our forgiveness before God, but not for the purpose of forgiveness, which is participation in God's own triune life. "Closing'" with the human Jesus must in and of itself be closing with God, or be frustrated of its meaning. By Christ's atoning love for us and our faith in him, we are passionately united to a human heart that is a divine heart and God is united to us as a divine heart that is passionately human. The matter can be taken very far indeed: "Christ has an human nature as well as we. . . . The inclination which in us is turned to the other sex, in him is turned to the church, which is his spouse."[25]

With these reflections we touch what seems to me the deepest reason for Edwards' christological hardihood. If it is the one and only true *God* with whom the believer closes in Christ, then the one and only true God *is that one* with whom the believer closes in Christ. Edwards needs above all the latter statement; it is demanded by the universality of his vision. Ideologically, politically and socially, God-as-such and the object of Christian piety were being divided around Edwards. He could not acquiesce; he could not abandon the wide world to another God than Jesus. And he could expect no extra-christological help.

Each period in the church's history compels theology to particular pursuits. The modern situation of the church within the larger community, pioneered by and exacerbated in America, compels us both to affirm our new social position as one sect among many and to assert the God of our gospel as the one true God who creates and rules all, in whose obedience alone the public world can be right with itself. This labor is a christological labor.

IV

Edwards was neither an Alexandrian nor a Lutheran. His technical christological achievement, and the possible importance of his christology for American systematic theology, is that he achieved an "Alexandrian" mutual interpretation of God and Jesus in part by classically Puritan means, by the doctrine of the Spirit, and in part by his Enlightenment interpretation of personal being.

There is in the *Miscellanies* a fully developed draft that lays out his program.[26] First is the proposal: "As the union of believers with Christ be by the indwelling of the Spirit of Christ in them, so it may be worthy to be considered whether or not the union of the divine with the human nature of Christ ben't by the Spirit of the Logos dwelling in him after a peculiar manner and without measure. Perhaps there is no other way of God's dwelling in a creature but by his Spirit. The Spirit of Christ's dwelling in men causes a union so that in many respects [they are] looked upon as one. Perhaps the Spirit of the Logos may dwell in a creature after such a manner that [the] creature may become one person [with the Logos] and may be looked upon . . . as such.''

Later, Edwards would come back to argue what he here asserts.[27] In Scripture it is plain that, for example, Christ's knowledge is both ''by the Spirit'' and his own natural achievement: ''Christ . . . revealed the Father as one that knew of himself without a revelation. And yet the knowledge of divine things that the human nature had was by the Spirit.'' This is coherent only if the Spirit is the *bond* of the personal union, if the Spirit of the Logos is so the spirit of the man Jesus that the Logos and the man are the same subject.

In the larger draft,[28] there then follows an analysis of *how* the indwelling of the Spirit may effect full personal identity. There are, in Edwards' account, two sides to the matter. ''The man Christ is united to the Logos . . . 1st by the regard which God hath to this human nature. God . . . loveth him as his own Son; this man hath communion with the Logos in the love which the Father hath to him as his only begotten Son. Now the love of God is the Holy Spirit.'' ''The man Christ is united to the Logos . . . 2ndly, by what is inherent in this man whereby he becomes one person [with the Logos], which is only by the communion of understanding and communion of will, inclination, spirit or temper . . . such that there is the same consciousness. Thus the man Christ Jesus was conscious of the glory and blessedness the Logos had in the knowledge and enjoyment of the Father before the world was, as remembering of it, John 17:5, and he has the same Spirit or disposition towards the Father [as does the Logos]. . . . He is disposed towards the Father as being his own Father in the manner that he is the Father of the Logos.''

Edwards, we remember, acknowledged two severally necessary and jointly sufficient conditions of personal continuity. The one was a radicalized version of Locke's: continuity of memory. Two different consciousnesses could not have the same contents, for how would they then be two? Expressly to our present concern, one mind cannot completely know another without ''union of personality,'' for there is nothing to view of another mind but its ''ideas and exercises,'' so that ''to have an immediate view of the ideas and exercizes of any mind . . . is the same as to have an immediate perception, sense, or feeling of them *as* they pass . . . in that mind.''[29] The other condition applied his theological understanding of substantiality: a self-identical consciousness would still not be a self-identical person if God did not so regard it, for all continuing individual things are constituted such as a sequence of God's thoughts.

The first unity of God with the Logos, stated above, satisfies the theological criterion of personal identity, and the second satisfies the Lockean criterion. The first unity is perhaps relatively unproblematical. But neither the speculative vigor nor the exegetical difficulty of Edwards' assertion that Jesus *remembers* the innertrinitarian life of the Logos can be missed. The Jesus with this memory is the Johannine Jesus but would be hard to find in the Synoptic Gospels. Moreover, traditional teaching— in West *and* East—escaped this problem because identity of "person" did not, in the metaphysically technical use of the word, necessarily involve consciousness. But once Edwards had denied that consciousness is a property of something else, of some spiritual "substance," the traditional metaphysical analysis of the "person" was no longer conceivable. And it may well be that on *any* modern understanding of personhood Jesus' union with the Logos must be, as Edwards supposes, "doubtless . . . some union of the faculties of his soul.''[30]

However such particular difficulties may be reckoned, more important is to notice the remarkable move Edwards has made. He has in effect reabsorbed christology back into the doctrine of the Trinity. Jesus and the Logos, according to him, simply and directly satisfy the normal criteria of personal identity. Thus Jesus and the Logos are not two entities problematically become one; they simply are the same person. And a person is what each *is*. Therefore the question for Edwards is in fact no longer how two can be one, but how Jesus himself can be a member of the Trinity, how Jesus can be rightly called "the Logos."

Jesus, says Edwards, is a second person in the Trinity because he is a perfectly mirroring consciousness over against the Father, which we call the "Logos," and because he is regarded by God with that innertriune regard that is the Spirit. Jesus is the "Logos" by his own relations to the Father and the Spirit; he is not somehow ontologically pasted together with a metaphysical extra entity of that name, that independently has the necessary relations to the Father and the Spirit. The tone of my analysis will have betrayed that I think this is the only traversible path of understanding under the conditions of post-Enlightenment reflection. I would say that Edwards' is a profoundly "demythologized" christology, were the word not burdened with irrelevant controversy.

Those of various theological traditions will doubtless think that one or another of Edwards' christological devices cannot be the best. Those

who like myself descend from the Lutheran branch of the Reformation
may prefer to pursue a radically christological interpretation of God by
trying metaphysically to clarify and use old Lutheranism's paradoxes. But
Edwards' daring must be the model for all: what we must find how to
say is that the Jesus who was born, taught, worked, died and rose is
himself "one of the Trinity," that God is not God without him. And it
may be that Edwards' peculiar Calvinist and Enlightened way of conceiving this, by the doctrine of the Spirit and by a super-Lockean doctrine of
personality, is the right way for an American speculation.

Nature and Supernature

Throughout our investigation of Jonathan Edwards' thought, we have traced and filled in an apprehension of reality as encompassing harmony. God is the Harmony of Father, Son and Spirit. And in the space opened by the Son's harmony with the Father, the Son too wills to unite a plurality, so that other and created spirits join the melody. What is real? A community of consciousnesses in their love of one another's beauty, which is to say, of one another's participation in the community.

In the history of Christian thought, Edwards is by no means the first adorer of unity. All that strain of Greek patristic contemplation which stems from Origen has shown the same passion, as have medieval Franciscans, late medieval mystics, or many a Lutheran pietist or speculator. The passion is, moreover, clearly an authentic part of faith. The theme has sounded from Ignatius of Antioch on: "As the Lord did nothing without the Father, with whom he is one," so the very life of believers is the cultivation of unity. "You must all come together as into one temple of God, as on one altar, one Christ Jesus, who came forth from the one Father and who exists and moves about that same One." [1]

But while the passion is faithful, the systems that carry it out have proven tricky. Perennially, the theological apprehension of universal unity in God has been unable to accommodate essential matters of the gospel. First, Christian monists have often had to hear, sometimes from far lesser minds, that they have "insufficiently considered the gravity of sin." And faith must consider sin gravely, since its object is sin's overcoming. Then, believers cannot help noting that those who do not yet believe the gospel have nevertheless their own modes and practices of ultimate concern, that there is the plurality of "the religions." And while it will not do merely to consign other religions to error, the Christian envisioners of oneness have commonly too quickly assumed that "all religions" are at heart one, thus violating both the phenomena and the gospel, which proposes to free us precisely from the gods. Next, it is perhaps the central problem of Christian reflection, to state how the coming Kingdom is to be at once the overcoming and the fulfillment of the history we now live. Christian monists have generally thought of the Kingdom under the rubric of reform, rather than of revolution, and have in consequence not been able to articulate the radical novelty of the reality promised by the gospel. And finally, there is the related problem: What about the history of Israel before the coming of Christ? How does it prepare the great event?

The massive monism of the standard Enlightenment has made all these temptations endemic in America's Christianity, and in very plain form. No one who had "sufficiently considered the gravity of sin" could propose to *cure* it or to banish it by a mere accession of religion; nevertheless, it is the common understanding of the mainline American denominations that the gospel is a means of therapy and of "evangelicalism" that one need only become more committed to be saved. That all religions are going to the same place has, despite its intrinsic implausibility, become so much a part of our religious common sense that when we are reminded that the Bible takes a different view, we react not with argument but with incomprehension. And we are the West's virtuosos at identification of our nation and ideologies with the interest of the gospel, uninterrupted even by such protests as have sometimes momentarily sobered other parts of the church. The question about Edwards must be: Was his particular audition of harmony cast in faithfulness to the breaks and novelties which the gospel evokes? Can Edwards show us how both to adore wholeness and honor discontinuity?[2] I will take up the subjects just noted, in the same arbitrary order.

II

It is clear from the start that Edwards' doctrine of atonement is of different tendency than that which often appears in the central tradition, and notably among Edwards' successor revivalists. Those who—rightly—weigh sin heavily regularly so proclaim Christ's "sacrifice" as to rip reality apart, confronting fallen creatures with an alienated God the Father whom the Son can only and just barely reunite with us by answering alienation. Edwards too knows of God's wrath—indeed, he is notorious for his knowledge of it—but for Edwards, God's righteous rejection of sin is God's own problem, since he is antecedently determined to be merciful. Thus Christ's atoning suffering is God's own anguish suffered in the historically actual achieving of mercy.

The constant tenor of Edwards' reflection on sin and atonement is therefore praise of God's reconciling wisdom: for example, "It was wisely contrived that he that is . . . the first born of every creature, the head of all, should perform the most eminent obedience, as Christ did by his sufferings. . . . It was wise . . . that the head of all the creatures should be in some peculiar . . . manner united into God, that so the creatures who are as his body should be united by him."[3] And the constant theme is love: it is precisely the pain of actually loving *us* that is the divine sacrifice.[4] If faith is how we "close" with the human Christ and so with God, Edwards' doctrine of atonement describes how the human Christ closes with us while remaining God-the-Logos. Edwards' doctrine of atonement takes sin as weightily as may be, but is not therefore an account of divine emergency measures to deal with a contingent fall. The doctrine of atonement is rather the center of Edwards' unifying construal of reality: all things are one harmony, *because* of Christ's reconciling life and death.

Atonement, according to Edwards, occurs in that Jesus is so united to us that we "may be justly looked upon as the same. Now there is no other way of different spirits being thus united but by love." The union is complete if the love is complete, that is, if it is love unto death.[5] If we pose the ancient question, "Why did Jesus die?" Edwards' answer is that only "love that is sufficient to put the lover in the beloved's stead even in the total loss of himself . . . may be looked upon as perfectly uniting."[6] And that in this case the total loss of self is in fact demanded, is what sin does to this love, for Christ's uniting with sinful man would be a mere condoning of sin, and so precisely an abandoning of love, unless he took upon himself the suffering consequent on our unwillingness to be loved.[7]

Edwards left also on this matter the draft chapter of a mature systematic treatment.[8] In it, he begins with the classic concept of "merit," to designate what Christ obtains for us by his life and death. But he instantly provides a definition of the concept which amounts to its replacement by a new one: "merit" is "anything . . . in any person . . . which appearing in the view of another is a recommendation of him to that other's regard, esteem and affection." Thus the set of relations considered by atonement doctrine is removed from the realm of abstract credits to be balanced by a judicial calculus, and located in the universal community of hearts. There, what appeared arbitrary and mysterious becomes obvious and natural: "'Tis not unreasonable, or against nature . . . that respect should be shown to one on account of his . . . connexion with another." In fact, it is the most ordinary occurrence of life in community, that in this fashion the "merit" of one is "imputed" to another, *that is,* that what "recommends" person A to person C should also recommend B, A's "connexion," to C.

Leaping to a crude preliminary statement of Edwards' point: the atonement worked by Jesus' life and death is achieved by such a community of him and us that if the Father loves the Son he must love us also. Edwards' whole doctrine is a drastic generalization of the old Calvinist doctrine of Christ's *intercession* for us with God.[9] Edwards proceeds more analytically. That Christ comes in this way to stand in for us sinners is a particular case of a general principle—though we will eventually note that the principle holds only because of this case. Edwards narrows his considerations step by step.

Surely, thinks Edwards, if someone "that is very dear to any person, and of great merit in [his] eyes . . . , not only stands in a strict union with another, but also does particularly express a great desire of that other's welfare . . . , it is agreeable to nature, that the welfare of the person united to him should be regarded" by the friend "as if it were his own." And, moving a step, this will be the more so "when the way in which this person . . . seeks . . . the client's welfare . . . is by suffering and being at expense of his own." And yet more if the patron applies directly to his friend, and the "expense" is for what "his friend regards as his own interest"—as the Father regards both the salvation of his creatures and the rejection of sin. And yet another step more "if the merit of the patron . . . especially appear" in the pains he takes "for the client's welfare." And finally, when the merit *consists* in the pain, the expended natural good is equal to the merit, that is, is itself a *moral* good: "the worthiness of the patron and the value expended are offered both together in one, as the price of the welfare of the client."

Even these minutely distinguished accounts do not yet balance. What is needed to make it "fit" that a "client" and his "patron" be looked on as "completely one," is "when the patron's heart is so united to the client, that when the client is destroyed, he from love is willing to take the destruction on himself," when "his love to the client is such . . . as to . . . swallow up his [own] whole interest." Moreover, if "the person that needs favor be . . . unworthy, then . . . the union of the patron with his client, and his undertaking to seek favor for him" must so occur as not to infringe his own merit. And there must "be a sufficiency in the patron and his relation to the client, to answer to such a degree of favor as is proposed to be obtained for him."

Plainly, Christ as patron, we as clients, and God the Father as friend satisfy all these requirements. There is in this case "everything requisite in order to the fitness of the acceptance of the client on account of the patron, and his receiving such favour from the patron's friend, as is requisite to all that pertains to the client's welfare. So that such acceptance and such favor shall be in all respects proper, according to the nature of things and [the] common sense of intelligent beings.''

I have reported Edwards' analysis of atonement in some detail not only for its own sake but also because it provides such a fine instance of this chapter's general point. That Christ's life and death unite sinners with God is not, in his understanding, a breach of the ordinary way of things; it is no miracle, in the vulgar acceptation of that term. It is wholly ''fit'' according to ''nature'' and the standards of judgment appropriate to such matters. And yet it is a marvel, the central event of the universal blaze of glory. Just so are ''nature'' and ''grace'' related throughout Edwards' thought.

III

What then of the religions? Edwards' analysis is complex, using several crossing distinctions whose relation is nowhere explicitly stated. It will be best to list these at the beginning, and let evidence for the listing emerge as we then go. Central in Edwards thinking is the now familiar difference between ''natural'' religion based on ''common grace,'' and ''saving'' or ''supernatural'' religion, the religion of ''special grace.'' But in his consideration of the religions also a distinction of ''natural'' from ''revealed'' religion plays a great role, which does *not* coincide with the first. Nor does either coincide with the distinction between heathen and Christian religion.

Natural religion, where ''natural'' is opposed to ''revealed,'' is, says Edwards, that appropriate to our situation with God as our Creator, Preserver and Judge. God's provision for the knowledge requisite to appropriate worship in this situation is ''reason.'' But if humanity falls, if we disobey the mandate of reason, and if God then nevertheless embarks on ''salvation from sin and its evil consequences,'' if, that is, the ''covenant of grace'' occurs, then God ''sustains a relation entirely new, and distinct from the natural relation of a Creator. . . . And we have a new concern of God, and a new dependence on him, entirely distinct from that which is by nature . . . , which renders a new . . . sort of religion proper and becoming,'' the religion Edwards calls ''the religion of sinners.'' In these new relations we cannot find our way by reason, for the new situation is created by a free disposition of God's wisdom among the ends of his

infinitely many perfections, and so can no more be predicted by finite
minds than creation could have been. If now we are to have appropriate
worship and dependence, "divine revelation" must occur. And it does
occur; indeed, its occurrence is identical with God's action to establish
and maintain the new situation; in this new "display" of God's perfections is "founded" a new way of adoring God, "a new religion." [10]

Revealed religion is not necessarily supernatural or saving; for it
may remain "notional," the sense of the heart may not be kindled. Nor
is it identical with the revelation to Israel and the church. Since revelation
is the communication of the covenant of grace, and since the continuance
of fallen humanity is enabled only by that covenant, revealed religion
must be God's initial gift to fallen humanity as a whole. Edwards can
state the matter as a conclusion from evidence: "[I]f we look over all the
accounts we have of the several nations of the earth, and consider everything that has been advanced by . . . the philosophers; we can meet with
nothing to induce us to think, that the first religion of the world was
introduced by the use . . . of mere natural reason. But on the other hand
all history, both sacred and profane, offers us various arguments to prove
that God revealed to men in the first ages, how he would be worshipped." [11] He can also deduce the original revelation as a necessity of
the preservation included in the covenant of grace: "'Tis manifest that it
was agreeable to the Creator's design, that there should be some moral
government . . . maintained among men . . . , in nations, provinces,
towns or families . . . , [otherwise] the world of mankind would destroy
itself"; [12] but revelation belongs to the very notion of moral government
in the fallen situation. [13]

Insofar, therefore, as the nations' plural religions teach *falsely* of
God, Edwards must understand this as historical declension. On the side
of humanity, the declension has occurred as "men, instead of adhering
to what had been revealed, came to lean on their own understanding." [14]
On God's side, it is ordained by a usual principle of his providence: "As
[Israel] were separated to be God's peculiar people, so all other people
. . . were . . . given over to Heathenism. This . . . was only to prepare the way for the more glorious . . . victory . . . of Christ's power
over the . . . world, and that Christ's salvation of the world of mankind
might become the more sensible." [15] The specific revelation to Israel can
thus itself be understood as an "extraordinary interposition of Providence" to re-establish "true religion" after "the church . . . that had
been upheld in the line of Abraham's ancestors" had been "already con-
siderably corrupted." [16] The revelation to Israel in Christ is what "was

plainly wanting . . . to recover mankind out of their universally degen-
erate state,'' as the ''best and wisest'' heathen have themselves acknowledged.[17]

Thus Edwards, far from being distressed by similarities between
heathen and biblical teaching, as these were in his time beginning to be
collected, was delighted with every one he could learn of—in ''ancient
Chinese books,'' the religion of the Indians, or wherever.[18] He was of
course thoroughly familiar with the philosophically reflected religion of
classical antiquity, and found much truth in it.[19] So far as he was concerned, ''Socrates, that great Gentile philosopher, who worshipped the
true God, as he was led by the light of nature, might pray to God and be
attending his duty when he did so.''[20] Indeed, Edwards supposed that
Plato and others were inspired by the Holy Spirit to say ''such wonderful
things concerning the Trinity, the Messiah, etc.,'' since inspiration belongs to common rather than special grace.[21] Edwards goes so far on this
line, that so far as appears in his notes and publications the only thing
Christian religion teaches that paganism *could* not is the personal identity
of the Messiah, that he is in fact Jesus of Nazareth. *Perhaps* Edwards
was not even always sure that the Spirit never indwells pagan religionists
also in a saving way.[22]

Insofar as the religions are false, Edwards calls them ''frail.'' Reason and the surviving tradition of primal revelation, even with preserving
and correcting inspiration by the Spirit's common mercies, do not suffice
to prevent disastrous error. Also this frailty is important to Edwards, as
showing the need of renewed revelation through Israel's history and finally in Christ.[23] Nor is Israel's distinction that she is not frail. On the
contrary, Israel's equal or greater frailty belongs to her position: ''Tis of
itself a great proof of revealed religion, that the Jews should for so many
ages retain the knowledge of the true God, and notions of him . . .
agreeable to the most refined reason; when all the nations about 'em . . .
were sunk . . . in the grossest idolatry. It was not owing to anything
peculiar in the genius of that people, any distinguishing taste for learning,
beyond other nations. They were unacquainted with the sciences that were
in vogue in Greece and Rome, and seem to have been as prone to idolatry, in themselves, as other nations.''[24]

It cannot be said that Edwards' understanding of the relation between the religions and the gospel is adequate, whether by the standards
of the comparative and historical knowledge that has since been gained
or by the standards of his own most penetrating theological insight. The
hypothesis of historical derivation of the religions from one primal reli-

gion cannot be confirmed; and the relation between *any* religion and the gospel must be more dialectical, by Edwards' own lights, than here appears. But certain features should nevertheless be attentively noted.

First among these is the incongruence between his distinctions of "natural" from "revealed" and of "natural" from "supernatural." It has been assumed by much recent theology that revealed knowledge of God must be saving, but clearly this is a prejudice. Edwards' position is subtle. All actual religion, according to him, depends on revelation, and is *not* therefore necessarily true nor, insofar as it is true, necessarily insofar "saving." That is, revelation itself is to be understood as a factor in a complex *history* of religion, the goal of which is certain and blessed but the course of which must be empirically ascertained. Moreover, *all* religion is historical; "natural" religion that is not revealed is a merely theoretical construct, since the covenant of grace in which the fall is allowed and preservation decreed is in fact the beginning of all things.

That Edwards then understands the joint truth of the religions' history as given in a unanimous *Beginning,* and religious history as thereafter only a history of sundering, is his great failure in this matter. For surely it would have been more "fit" to his grasp of reality to have located the truth of the religions in a joint *Outcome,* and to have understood the history of the religions as God's way to a *final* universal Unity. Doubtless here is a point at which Edwards simply did not transcend either the normal Enlightenment or standard theology. But we may also point to a systematic cause. If the Outcome—rather than the Beginning—is to interpret the present, it must somehow be itself a present reality. But the present reality of the future is the *word;* and through nearly all of Edwards' work the word has no ontological weight. We have arrived again at a deficiency previously reached.

IV

We have begun to talk of eschatology. In that department Edwards was a "millennialist"; he expected a period, the thousand years of the Revelation, of "the church's great prosperity," located between what we now experience as history and the final Kingdom of God. This provides the starting point and theme for our discussion of the way in which Edwards related history and the Kingdom, since in a millennial conception the millennium simply *is* that relation, an actual hinge between this age and the Eschaton.

Whether *Revelation* was itself in fact millennialist is disputed, but that need not detain us. There has anyway on the basis of *Revelation* been a recurrent millennialist strain in the church. But also, it has been a minority strain; the catholic tradition, including mainline Calvinism and Lutheranism, has rejected expectation of the thousand years. In this matter, Edwards was sectarian, as were other New England Puritans.

I must begin by reporting Edwards' description of the millennial event and condition.[25] The millennium will be inaugurated by the destruction of one great component of fallen history, "Satan's visible kingdom." Edwards has no developmental or otherwise merely optimistic expectations of history. God's spiritual initiative "will not affect the overthrow of Satan's visible kingdom, till there has first been a violent . . . opposition made," "a mighty struggle . . . by external force" between actual human governments.

The event will be an event of this age; it "will not be accomplished all at once . . . but . . . is a work which will be accomplished by . . . use of the ordinary means of grace," made savingly effective by a decisive "outpouring" of the Spirit "for the wonderful revival and propagation of religion." "Heresies, and infidelity and superstition" in the church "will then be abolished." The "kingdom of Antichrist," that is, the papacy, "shall be utterly overthrown." The "other great kingdom which Satan has set up in opposition to the . . . church, viz., his Mahometan kingdom, shall be utterly overthrown." The oppression of the Jews will cease and they "in all their dispersion . . . shall wonderfully have their hearts changed . . . and . . . flow together to . . . Jesus." And thereupon finally "one nation shall be enlightened . . . after another, one false religion . . . exploded after another."

The millennium itself is characterized by Edwards in detail[26] which I shall much abridge. In the place of Satan's visible kingdom, a visible Christian "kingdom" will be "set up . . . everywhere through the . . . habitable globe." This "kingdom" will have political character; from unpublished notes we learn that each nation will have its own form of government, but none tyrannical.[27] "It will be a time of great light and knowledge" shared over the whole earth and especially noteworthy among races now thought inferior. "It shall be a time when religion shall in every respect be uppermost in the world. . . . The saints have hitherto . . . been kept under. . . . But now they shall be uppermost." "There shall be universal peace. . . . Then shall all the world be united in one amicable society." "It will be a time of excellent order in the church of Christ." It "will be a time of the greatest temporal prosperity."

By "Satan's visible kingdom," whose destruction will begin the millennium, Edwards denoted a straightforwardly historical entity, a counterpart and opponent of the church. In this age, the church is observably oppressed by actual historical agents; with Edwards, such observation is in itself theological, since he acknowledges no secondary causes between God's mind and created history. Thus since the historical record shows that Islam established itself by military destruction of fully half the then extant Christian community, Edwards just therefore identifies Islam as a realm of the Opponent.

The identification of the papacy—not the believers under it—as the main province of Satan's visible kingdom, as the "kingdom of Antichrist," doubtless needs more extended explication. There is again an historical record: the papacy did indeed seek to repress the Reformation by all available force, and we should remember that this Counter-Reformation was still in full swing in Edwards' time. It was also not unreasonable for Puritans to see the alliance of Stuart absolutism with Laudean episcopalianism, which had driven them from their homes, as belonging to the same phenomenon.[28] But since this conflict occurred within the "visible" church, Edwards' judgment includes a theological judgment that cannot itself be simply read from the record.

From well before the Reformation, churchly radicals of many sorts had seen the papacy in *Revelation*'s figure of Antichrist; Puritans continued the tradition. It is Edwards' *particular* judgment which we must note. His grievance against the papacy was double. First, the papacy was the protecter of the church from Reformation, the institutionalization of a recrudescence of standard corrupted religion within the religion supposed to be purified by revelation. And second, insofar as the church was nevertheless reformed, the papacy persecuted it.[29] Now we may well doubt that the parties to the great division of the Western church can be sorted quite so neatly or that even justified ecclesiastical anathemas reach quite so deeply; and in any case, precisely the historical record has continued and taken new turns. The theological *standard* by which Edwards identifies "Antichrist" within the church is nonetheless worth noting.

But now, in reading history in this directly theological way, did not Edwards go beyond what he could validate by his own standard of authority, which is, after all, the Bible? Where in Scripture do we read about Muhammud? He has an answer: "There are two ways wherein the Scriptures gives account of the events by which the work of redemption is carried on: one is by history, and another is by prophecy: and in the one or the other of these ways we have . . . an account . . . from the beginning to the end."[30] The doings of "God's providence" are, Edwards is bound to think, "related in human histories"; by the mutual interpretation of these and inspired prophecy, the ways of providence must be identifiable.[31] Throughout his career, therefore, Edwards labored and relabored at the interpretation of the apocalyptic portions of Scripture, and especially of the one complete apocalypse to have entered the canon, the *Revelation*. In this labor, it was his determination to correlate every symbolic prediction with an event on the record or yet to be expected.[32]

There is surely no other feature of Edwards' thinking quite so foreign to me and most of those likely to read this study, as the complex just sketched. Some, however, of the strangeness can be overcome. For the present chapter, we may gain some understanding on the following lines.[33]

Though millennialism has become strange to "mainline" American Christians, this is a recent development. Until well after the Civil War, also America's major Protestant bodies expected the thousand years. And the doctrine has deeply marked American attitudes, in ways which still persist and the noting of which may uncover our closeness to Edwards. The millennium is not the Kingdom of God, it is to occur in this world. It can therefore be an object of political and moral, and not merely religious expectations: *this world* may yet become a realm of peace and justice and true religion. If we look again at Edwards' description of the millennium, we will see that it is a catalogue for the great campaigns of revival and reform which from Edwards' day almost to ours have been the history of American Christianity and the moral history of the American nation. When Puritan reality was sundered, and evangelical religion created its second, volunteer public arena, it was the millennial hope which could and did provide it with an appropriate program.

We may well ask: After all, what would America be without the hope that even in this world a better world is possible? A world "better" precisely by the standard of the Bible's vision of the Kingdom? What indeed would Christianity itself be with no touch of such a hope? Without, as Karl Barth once put it, "a pinch of millennialism?" There is, of course, a theological problem: Can a millennium, which is an anticipation of God's Kingdom, be an object of *our* political and religious striving? The question brings us to the last matter of this section.

Edwards was not only a millennialist when Protestant orthodoxy was not, he was a "postmillennialist" when most other millennialists favored "premillennialism." Also in this most American Protestantism followed him until after the Civil War.[34] We call Edwards "postmillennialist" because, following what were in his time new exegetical proposals, he taught that Christ's visible advent would follow and not, as was standard millennial teaching, precede the thousand years. Picking up the narrative of *The History of Redemption* where I interrupted it: at the end of the thousand years, "there will be a very great apostasy. . . ." The renewed "wickedness of the world will remarkably call for Christ's immediate appearing."[35] Only then, after the millennium and after a great recrudescence of Satan's kingdom, "Christ will appear in the glory of his Father" and "that new heaven and new earth . . . , which had been building up ever since Christ's resurrection, be completely finished."[36]

One should carefully consider what this doctrine does. The great discontinuity, God's decisive revolution, comes between the millennium and the End, not between us and the millennium. Thus on the near side, the millennium is continuous with penultimate history; it will be brought, as Edwards said, by the "ordinary means" of religious and moral reformation, by collaboration between the graceful work of the Spirit and nature with its common "light" of religious and cultural progress.[37]

Moreover, these means are now put in believers' hands to be used. For Edwards, the main thing we can do to bring the millennium is prayer. He interpreted prophecy to say that the immediate precurser of the thousand years will be that "there shall be given much of a spirit of prayer to God's people . . . , unitedly to pray to God in an extraordinary manner, that he would . . . pour out his Spirit . . . , and advance his spiritual kingdom in the world."[38] At one point he attempted actually to organize the project.[39] Americans after Edwards have often preferred other means than prayer, but postmillennianism is very easily thus secularized.

On the far side, the millennium is separated from the Kingdom not only by the final advent of Christ but by the greatest of all Satan's earthly eruptions. The millennium is not the Kingdom and cannot become the Kingdom by anything within its own dynamism. It is—Edwards' favorite word again!—"fit" that the millennium should end with a final apostasy, an apostasy enabled by the technological and moral progress of the millennium, to show the "insufficiency even of such means and advantages" without special grace.[40] There will be a better world in this world; and even it will be saved only through death and new creation.

The postmillennialist conception is not nearly so bizarre as may first appear. A bit of demythologizing yields the teaching that there can be a better future in this world; that this will occur by virtue of the promise of the Kingdom; that believers are to hope and work for such betterment; and that whatever is achieved will enter the Kingdom only by death and new creation. Constructive conceptualization of such teaching is well beyond the bonds of this study. But I may register the opinion that the teaching is true, and also that some such metaphysical interpretation as

Edwards' audition of universal harmony must provide the context of its reflection.

Referring back to earlier observations, the millennium is needed in Edwards' system in order that the whole of history may be at once "means" and "image" of the great spiritual reversal. The light that shines also in fallen history must once triumph within it, if grace, for which history as a whole is the necessary typological occasion, is to predominate in the eternal balance. That in the millennium, "Nor will that be true, that few shall be saved,"[41] is the inner-historical image of the final triumph of grace, as are the present sufferings and failures of the church the image of what grace overcomes.

V

Thus it is created history as one whole occurrence, *with* all its religious and secular necessities and achievements and revelations, that is bracketed and transfigured by the miracle of mutual love, by the great alternative to the self-love which is the dynamism of the "natural" order. We have seen how self-love as such is the inevitable act of a finite consciousness and is morally neutral, yet in lived actuality is always the self-love which destroys community; just so, "nature" and its morality and religion are in themselves good, or would be if they ever appeared in themselves, but in actual history appear only as mutual oppression and the "religion of sinners." We have also seen what the love is that transcends self-love; it is simply the triune life, in which we are embraced. It is this participation, and nothing else, that is the "grace" that transcends "nature."

There is in this interpretation only one actual order of reality, the triunely plotted divine life as it opens to posit and embrace other lives. The orders of nature and of sinful and preserved nature are but abstractions from reality. Sinful yet preserved nature is an enacted abstraction; it subsists because some actual lives indeed abstract themselves from the triune life by and in which they nevertheless live. Yet even this enacted abstraction occurs only as it belongs to the plot of the one triune life. Nature as such is an unenacted abstraction; it has the reality only of what might have been had not created lives been so plotted in the divine life as they in fact are; also this "might have been" belongs to the plot of grace.

Within history, Edwards works out the relation of God's devices by a complicated and subtle version of the Puritan doctrine of successive "covenants." The foundation of all history is the "covenant of redemption," the purely inner-triune concert which allows reality other than God. On it, two inner-historical covenants with us are based.[42]

The one, "the covenant of works," was made between God and Adam, and in him with his descendents;[43] it promised merely creaturely salvation on the condition of obedience to God's commands.[44] Within Edwards' thought as a whole, this covenant was made to be broken. And in Edwards' discussion of actual history, this covenant appears only as a factor in its successor, "the covenant of grace."

The covenant of grace is the "marriage covenant" between Christ and the church. All the Father's promises to believers are made to "Christ mystical . . . as a public person . . . virtually containing the whole future church that he had taken . . . on his heart" in the eternal covenant of redemption. The covenant of mercy is made when Christ first opens this heart to us. It's one condition on our side is faith.[45]

And now it is vital to Edwards' conception that the covenant with *Israel* is the covenant of grace, Christ's marriage with his church. The historical steps, from the supposed first gospel-promise to Adam and Eve on through Christ's resurrection, are not distinct covenants but successive "dispensations" of *one* covenant.[46] In both Israel and the present church, the "same salvation" is given; in both, the incarnate Christ is the Mediator; in both, the Spirit "is the applyer, and in the same way;" in both, faith as "the entire unition of the heart to Christ," is our side of the covenant; in both the "means of the application" are in general the same, that is, the word of God and the ordinances of religion; and in both all this is sufficiently revealed.[47]

The differences between the two dispensations come down to a dialectic which before Christ's resurrection remains between the sense of the covenant and its outward "exhibition." There is a double "covering" over grace, before Christ: the covenant of works, with its laws proposed as conditions of salvation, remains as the ordained "means"; and the covenant is an exclusive national covenant and so again "outward." Accordingly, all revelation is within old Israel subject to a dialectic between the "letter," the external sense, and the "spirit," its final meaning. Edwards exemplifies this dialectic on the first commandment: "Thus these words 'Thou shalt love the Lord thy God' . . . may be taken . . . either for a perfect love to God . . . as the price of his favor," and so as an exhibition of the covenant of works, or as "the sincere and certain acceptance of our hearts of God and Christ, graciously offering themselves," and so as a description of faith and its covenant of grace.[48]

It is in virtue of this dialectic that the dispensation to Israel is itself an historical "means" of a succeeding dispensation, that its actuality is that of an image, of "types." "[T]he whole nation . . . was, as it were, constituted in a typical state."[49] "[By] the journey of the children of Israel through the wilderness . . . all the various steps of the redemption of the church by Christ were represented."[50] The Exodus was "the greatest type of Christ's redemption."[51] The Temple "was the house where Christ dwellt, till he came to dwell in the temple of . . . his human nature, which was the antitype."[52] And the sacrifices prepared for an atonement.[53]

Undoubtedly, Edwards thus sees an "advance" from old Israel to the New Testament church. But this advance is not from nature to grace or from law to gospel. The miracle that is the union of Christ with the soul is in both dispensations; the advance from one to the other is reflection *in* history of the relation *of* history to its bracketing transfiguration. It is, to conclude this matter, worth noting that Edwards was enabled by this doctrine to take a far different view of Judaism than has to this day been customary among Christians. The miracle of the Jewish nation's preservation in worship of the true God, when all around idolatry triumphed and "in spite of their circumstances, endowment, and history," still continues in their "in many respects yet more wonderful" preservation "as a distinct nation" in the terrible circumstances of the dispersion.[54]

VI

What is "above" or "beyond" nature is not, according to Edwards, *something* other than nature; it is the miracle of nature's musicality. What is supernatural in the atonement is the harmonization of the whole precisely by our dissonance. Revealed and unrevealed religion are phenomena of one history; what is supernatural is that this history is saving. Neither the church's failure nor its millennial success are more than phenomena of that same history; both are fulfilled by Christ's new love. And within that church, the line between Israel and the Christians is not a line between nature and grace. Yet none of these discontinuities is in itself denied or mitigated.

IV

COMMUNITY

Tis evident that man was intended for society . . . and if in subservient interests, surely most of all in the great happiness for which he was created.
—*Miscellanies*, 99

12

Community and Personhood

I

"Cur deus homo?" "Why did God become man?" The final answer in Edwards' sense must be: in order for the triune Community and the created community to make one. The "happiness of society," he wrote in an early journal entry, consists "in the mutual communication of each other's happiness; neither does it satisfy . . . only to receive the other's happiness, without also communicating [one's] own." Apparently, however, creatures cannot communicate happiness to God, since he is always perfectly happy; then his society and ours must remain forever separate. "But in the gospel God is come down to us, and the person of God may receive communication of happiness from us. The man Christ Jesus loves us so much, that he is really the happier for our delight . . . in him." [1] It will be seen that Edwards' whole discussion of Christ and his work merely explicates the assertions of this entry.

The crowning proposition of Edwards' early and foundational metaphysics was: to be is to pertain to the community of consciousnesses. I have used this proposition as an axiom in all my interpretations of his thinking. It is now time to turn again to the notion of community, for itself.

God's own "happiness," wrote Edwards, consists "in communion, as well as the creature's." [2] The whole creation is so arranged as finally to achieve the happiness of both. And this must consist in mutuality, in the sharing of *different* and just so shareable happiness. Accordingly, also the created community, as Edwards is passionate to construe it, is a metaphysically diverse community of angels, saints in heaven, and probationary saints on earth, perfected as community by inverse relations between natural or achieved worth and God-given status. Angels appear with unexpected frequency in Edwards reflections, primarily to provide another kind and level of created consciousness beside humanity. And then we find an even more unexpected switch: "God is pleased to make goodness

141

the end of greatness, [to] make that in the creature which is properly belonging to the nature of the creature subordinate to that which is . . . communication of the divine nature . . . ; and accordingly has he . . . made . . . saints the end of angels.''[3] So it is exactly Jesus Christ, the "God-man," who is lord also of the angels, and it is by their service of his service to humankind that they have "obtained eternal life."[4] As to the "saints in heaven," their "happiness . . . consists very much in beholding the works of God relating to man's redemption wrought here below."[5]

Edwards thus describes, as the being of beings, a metaphysical community to which would be "appropriate" political and economic communities very different from those envisioned by the usual Enlightenment. The basic assumption of liberalism's political maxims is that political and economic persons are in those capacities interchangeable and irreducible. Each is an atom in the public space, with an atom's characteristics. Each is, as public agent, fully describable by quantifying laws and condition statements that equally well apply to any other such atom; just so, each is impermeably an "individual." In a community perfected on these lines, there would be no natural hierarchy; and as events nevertheless came to rank us, status would be a reward exactly proportioned to achievement. Just such a community, according to Edwards, is the one God does not intend.

Liberalism's mechanistic ideology does not necessarily follow from the great political idea of freedom, shared with equal passion by Puritans and Deists. That we are to be equal and free meant in Puritan and revolutionary understanding that we are to be equally at home in the polity, in the community's arena of moral deliberation. It does not follow that we all have the same role or the same kind or degree of authority in the communal discourse, or that we all contribute equivalently to its maintenance. Nor does it follow that there is anything wrong with this, that we *should* be merely equivalent in any of these ways.

In the living discourse of any actual community, the speakers, whether these are few as in most polities or many as in Western modernity's ideal polities, do not all have the same word or the same sort of words to speak. Gifts and authorities of different sort and equal weight, and of the same sort and unequal weight establish the community's freedom by their mutual interplay. In the eighteenth century, it was at least only about the polity and economy that mechanistic metaphysics caused this to be forgotten; that it is true of family and church and guild was assumed. It is one of the twentieth century's terrors that the forgetfulness is spreading, that, for random examples, spouses claim "equal rights" over against each other and clergy protest any "double standard" of their behavior.

II

Edwards did not leave a developed doctrine of created society. Even about the church, he wrote only on particular topics; and his remarks on the civil community are sparse, if vigorous and characteristic. But the three major works of his maturity, the only parts of his projected synthesis to be published, are in fact extended and radical analyses of fundamental political concepts, conceived, moreover, in explicit confrontation with liberal ideology. *Original sin*[6] attacks the rigid distinction of individuality from community, as well as the great liberal program of human self-perfecting; *Freedom of the Will* diagnoses in advance the pathology of any society in which freedom becomes freedom *from* the community; and *True Virtue* has public virtue as its object. The first of these works will be the chief text of this chapter, and each of the others of a following chapter. In all three, Edwards diametrically dissents from standard liberalism as this was being born in his time, and on a basis at least as Enlightened as is that of the commoner opinions.

Edwards' dissent is apparent in the little social criticism he left. Of the free-market mechanism coming to dominance around him, he disapproved, as a collective sin against the command not to steal. When goods are sold for a higher price than would be necessary to provide reasonable income to the merchant, this is, by Edwards' lights, fraud;[7] or when "the necessity of poor indigent people is the very thing whence others take occasion to raise the price of provisions," it is extortion.[8] The blessings of affluence, he preached, are those "riches God commonly . . . gives . . . those whom he . . . despises most."[9] The millennial program—to be realized, we must remember, in this world—is for a society in which the "merchants of the earth shall trade for Christ more than for themselves, and their merchandise and their hire . . . shall not be . . . laid up for posterity, but shall be for them that dwell before the Lord, to eat sufficiently, and for durable clothing . . . and to make the [church] glorious."[10]

Also for the famous walls of separation, footings of which were being set in place around him, Edwards had no use. It seemed to him "evident . . . by natural reason" that any lively community, "whose welfare most especially depends on a communication with one another," can be united in the requisite sort of "common interest" only by a common "Object of their worship."[11] Accordingly, in the one direction he affirmed the "authority of councils" and the "power of the civil magistrate in matters of religion"—even after one such council had undone him at Northampton.[12] And in the other direction, he could regard it as a chief evidence of the Northampton revivals' authenticity, that it had brought the civil township to settle a longstanding dispute about its public lands.[13]

III

So to the big book on *Original Sin*. The rising bourgeoisie found the notion of original sin the single greatest religious offense to its ideology and aspirations. As Edwards defined the doctrine in the first paragraph of his treatise, it has two parts: the assertion that we are all in the same disastrous situation before God, characterized by "inate sinful depravity of the heart," and the doctrine of "the imputation of Adam's first sin."[14] Each part is an independent offense. The new bourgeoisie were committed precisely to the transcendent value of social differences, differences produced not by organic place in the whole but by the individual's ability to free himself from the organic whole, by individual initiative. As for "imputation" of Adam's sin to his descendents, a God who could do such a thing would be supremely *unfair,* and so unworthy of worship by any liberal lights.

It was the writings of a renegade British Presbyterian, John Taylor, in which Edwards found a convenient formulation of the mood and ideology he deplored. Taylor's *Scripture-Doctrine of Original Sin,* published in 1738 or 1740, had found immediate resonance in a New England which, with or without literary help from abroad, was increasingly discontent with the rough old Calvinist doctrine.[15] Edwards worked over his reading and his reflections for a decade, before publishing *Original Sin* in what turned out to be his death-year, 1758.

Edwards' method in this book is first to establish a prima facie case for an Augustinian doctrine of original sin, from Scripture and experience, and then to consider modern objections, chiefly as brought by Taylor. It is the latter effort that transforms the essay from a strictly dogmatic defense of received theology into a critical examination of soon to be received political dogma. Edwards makes "the corruption of nature" the thread of his argument, and uses and defends the doctrine of imputation as he goes.

According to Edwards, "original" sin is a "disposition" or "tendency''; and the way we establish that such a thing obtains is, here as otherwise, ''by observing what is constant or general in events; especially under a great variety of circumstances: and above all, when the effect . . . continues the same through great and various oppositions.'' [16] Proof of original sin will therefore consist in showing that humankind ''universally run themselves into . . . perdition, as being finally accused of God . . . through sin,'' from which it may be inferred ''that the natural state of the mind of man is attended with a propensity . . . to such an issue; and that therefore their nature is corrupt and depraved with a moral depravity.'' [17] Edwards insists on one preliminary ''consideration'': if sin is interrupted by ''interposition'' of divine grace, this must be excepted from the ''circumstances'' relevant to testing ''the natural or innate disposition of man's heart.'' [18]

That sin is in fact universal, Edwards establishes both from Scripture and from the general human record, therein emulating the creator of the doctrine, Augustine. By Edwards' announced program, he must first use Scripture as a repository of reliable information about the fact of general sinfulness. But he also exegetes the standard passages which have been taken directly to teach or to count against the doctrine of original sin; [19] and he derives further argument from Scriptural witness about the nature of redemption itself. [20] For our purposes, I need not take us through the somewhat tangled thicket of Edwards' citations and analyses. Edwards' biblical exegeses are almost always faithful to the texts, within the limits of then available information, in stark contrast to those of his opponents.

Before marshalling the evidence, Edwards stipulates what the argument usually slides over: the orthodox contention is not that humans have a tendency always to sin but that they always have a tendency to sin. [21] Thus an argument cannot be mounted against the doctrine by claiming that we sometimes do good, or even that we do more good than evil. Nor can it be adduced that the doctrine is unbiblically gloomy or takes an empirically unwarranted pessimistic view of human potential or achievement; the doctrine could as well be true if the history of the race were mostly upward and onward—as, indeed, Edwards expected the millennial history to be! Edwards observes that Arminian assertions at this point are often like argument ''that the state of that ship is good, to cross the Atlantick Ocean in, that . . . will infallibly flounder . . . by the way; under a notion that it may probably . . . sail above water more hours than it will be sinking.'' [22]

But if some of us may perhaps err little and do much good, and if in the millennium this will be true of most or all, how can the race be judged ''perverse'' and ''depraved?'' How can such a life be regarded as "sinking?" Here it becomes apparent that Edwards' doctrine, like all classic doctrines of sin, is a theological doctrine and not a disinterested assessment of human tendencies. What is to be judged, indeed by the evidence, is which of *these* two states the human person "preponderates to, in the frame of his heart": "a state of . . . favor with God; or a state of . . . abhorrence in the sight of God."[23] Sin is failure of "regard" to *God* and *his* will,[24] and of this failure must it not be agreed "that even in the least instance it perfectly swallows up all the value of the sinner's supposed good deeds, let 'em be ever so many?" Edwards' metaphor of the ship must, to be fully appropriate, be changed for a personal metaphor: Arminian reckonings are like insisting that "the domestic of a prince was not a bad servant, because . . . he did not spit in his master's face so often as he performed acts of service."[25]

The *theological* moral question is: How does the sense of *God's* heart grasp *us?* And that is the question from which Protestantism without Reformation abstracts, casting its moral balances first without reference to God, and only then invoking him to "reward" or "punish." It is apparent that so soon as a more genial moral sense appears, to which rewarding and punishing are not so essential, God must disappear from this moralism altogether. Already this early in his case, Edwards thus confronts the modern-Western line of thought. And a second preliminary analysis comes to yet closer grips.

Edwards supposes the objection, that "though it be evident that there is a tendency . . . to this general event, that all mankind should fail of perfect obedience . . . and incur a demerit of eternal ruin . . . yet it may not lie in man's nature, but in the general constitution and frame of this world, into which men are born."[26] To this, Edwards has a reply furnished directly by his metaphysics:[27] "It alters not the case as to this question. . . . That part of the system is not good, which is not good in its place in the system: and those inherent qualities of that part of the system, which are not good . . . in that place, are justly looked upon as evil inherent qualities. That propensity is truly esteemed to belong to the nature of any being . . . that is the necessary consequence of its nature, considered together in its proper situation in the universal system of existence."[28] Thus to account for human corruption by instancing, for instance, "bad example," is "accounting for the thing by the thing itself. It is accounting for the corruption of the world by the corruption of the world."[29]

Rousseau's myth, which lies at the heart of liberal moralism, also in its churchly versions, is thus exposed for the sophistic myth it is. Edwards is surely right: it is perfectly empty to say that I am good in myself but corrupted by society, for I am intended for society, and if I am not good there I am not good in what I am intended for—which amounts simply to my "corruption," in any useful sense of the word. With what may be called the Officer-Krupke syndrome, the next chapter will be more concerned, but we may note here: in no healthy community would it count as a *mitigation* to plead that "We're depraved because we're deprived," true though it may be.

It is against the social doctrine which makes such mitigations specious that Edwards' book on original sin is in fact directed. The assertion that we are originally both corrupt and culpable is an assertion about precisely the social entities that we are, in the actually existing societies. The doctrine of original sin, at least in Edwards' version, allows the deprived to be as responsible for their deeds as are the privileged, and reveals the successful in a captivity as wretched and self-inflicted as is that of those they look down on. The budding capitalists of Northampton were not disposed to abide such teaching, but it might have been their political and otherwise communal salvation to have done so. As for the underclass which was coming simultaneously into being, it is surely one of its chief curses that the elites dehumanize it by denying its members the personal responsibility they claim for themselves.

Edwards does then hold, again from Scripture and the general record, that all humans in fact sin as soon as they are moral agents, and continue thereafter to "sin continually and progressively";[30] and that they in fact show more sin "than righteousness," taking "sin" in its proper theological sense.[31] He particularly notes humankind's "extreme folly and stupidity in matters of religion," despite both reason and revelation;[32] the predominance in history of plainly wicked persons;[33] and the small fruit of the impressive means God employs to maintain righteousness, whether common or spiritual.[34] All of which, Edwards thinks, "clearly determine the point, concerning the tendency of man's nature to wickedness; if we may be allowed to proceed according to such rules . . . of reasoning, as are univerally made use of . . . in experimental philosophy."[35] In view of the position established to begin, these arguments have a quality of overkill; we will understand their use if we remember that simple optimism was a large part of the ideology Edwards set out to counter.

The chief Arminian arguments, as Edwards found them in Taylor, are then three. First, "that to suppose men's being born in sin, without their choice . . . is to suppose what is inconsistent with the nature of sin."[36] Second, "that to suppose men receive their first existence in sin, is to make him who is the author of their being, the author of their depravity."[37] Third, the "great objection against the imputation of Adam's sin to his posterity . . . that such imputation is unjust and unreasonable, for as much as Adam and his posterity are not one and the same."[38]

Edwards' response to the first objection will be considered in the next chapter. His response to the second is an instance of his general doctrine of nature and supernature: whether with Adam, us, or the whole we make together,[39] "In order to account for a . . . native depravity of the heart of man, there is not the least need of supposing any evil quality . . . *wrought* into the nature of man, by any *positive* cause . . . either from God or the creature."[40] All that is needed is for the supernatural presence of the Spirit not to be given, for created nature, following its own inevitabilities, to undo itself.[41] "The inferior principles of self-love and natural appetite . . . , being . . . left to themselves, of course became reigning principles. . . . The immediate consequence of which was . . . a turning of all things upside down. . . . Man did immediately set up himself, and the objects of his private affections . . . , as supreme; and so they took the place of God."[42] Edwards knows that this argument, which relieves God of *authorship* of evil, does not finally *excuse* God for the reality of evil; he only thinks, as we have already seen, that all theologies are in an equally bad case at that point.[43]

IV

The third objection is the "great" argument,[44] and Edwards' response to it the great point of this chapter. He begins by stating the fact as he conceives it according to Scripture: "God, in each step of proceeding with Adam, in relation to the covenant . . . established with him, looked on his posterity as being one with him. . . . And though he dealt more immediately with Adam, yet it was as the head of the whole body, and the root of the whole tree. . . . From which it will follow, that both guilt . . . and also depravity of heart, came upon Adam's posterity just as they came upon him, as much as if he and they had all coexisted, like a tree with many branches."[45] Within Edwards's system, the *possibility* of it happening so is plain: all that is needed is that God, on Adam's sin, withdraw special grace from Adam and create his posterity without it. It is the "propriety" of God's so "proceeding" that is Edwards' matter here.[46]

The case is not, according to Edwards,[47] that Adam sinned for himself, that God thereupon withdrew special grace, and that we have somehow "inherited" sinfulness from this situation of our ancestor. According to Edwards, Adam's case and ours are not sequential but parallel, in every respect but one. Both with Adam and with us, the first appearance of an "evil disposition" and the "first act of sin" are the same event, in that sin is a turn of the heart's sense away from God. Both Adam and we become guilty by this dispositional emergence. And, both with Adam and with us, that the evil disposition, once present, remains "as a confirmed principle" is the punishment of the first transgression, produced by God's withdrawal of special grace.

The difference between Adam and us is that Adam's sin proceeded from a state of grace and occasioned the withdrawal of grace, while we are created lacking grace, so that we inevitably enact an evil disposition so soon as we are moral agents. On Adam's side, this makes the possibility of his initial sin a mystery—which Edwards elsewhere labored to illumine, without notably greater success than has been usual on the point.[48] On our side, it means that the initial appearance of an evil disposition is not in the full sense an *act* of ours, in that we do not by it become different than we were before; by his withdrawal of grace, God "constitutes" us as doers of Adam's sin.

Our initial sin is therefore a "participation of Adam's"; more concretely stated, the "first being of an evil disposition in the heart of a child of Adam" is that "he is disposed to *approve* of the sin of his first father, as fully as [Adam] himself approved of it when he committed it."[49] It belongs to Edwards' interpretation of human existence, that no "external" act *belongs* to a person "otherwise . . . than as his heart was in it."[50] But all our hearts incline to Adam's external act, so that if we ask *whose* act it is, the true answer is that it is all humankind's act. Thus according to Edwards, the historical totality of humankind makes in this matter "one moral whole," which so far as agency and responsibility are concerned are in the same case as if we had temporally *"co*existed"[51] as an active community.

The central insight here proposed and operative, though sometimes obscured by the polemical situation, is that universal human history constitutes the life of a natural community. As a family is indeed "one complex moral person," so is humankind, and "by the law of union" of such actual community, there is "a *communion* and *coexistence* in acts and affections: all jointly participating, and all concurring, as one whole, in the disposition and actions of the head."[52] In the case of the total human community, "Adam" is the name of this "head." Or rather, "Adam" is *that* head of the community by whom it acts in its past-tense solidarity, in the solidarity of that mysterious act *from* which God's redemptive providence is taking us.

This drastic affirmation of human commonality is problematic in two ways. First it is an unwelcome moral challenge to us. The doctrine demands that I accept responsibility for human history's total act as my act, even though the standard Enlightenment's entire anthropology is an elaborated refusal to do any such thing. By hindsight, it is not, to be sure, hard to see that the standard Enlightenment's doctrine has been morally corrosive. If I cannot take responsibility for humankind's act, how can I take it for that of my nation? If not for my nation's act, how for that of my family? On the Arminian principle we must eventually arrive exactly where we have arrived: with a society in which no community has any but an arbitrary and temporary reality.

But though modernity's course has been disastrous it may nevertheless be true to humanity's case. Indeed, modernity's course surely must be true unless there is God. For, to argue in a way beloved of Edwards, if we affirm a common spirit of all human history, "we say the same" as those who affirm God, whatever linguistic prejudice we may obey. Edwards can demand a moral course opposite to that of usual modernity because he affirms "God's wise constitution," by which "root and branches" are so united that "the case in fact is, that by virtue of this oneness, answerable changes . . . through all the branches coexist with the changes in the root." [53] And that brings us to the second way in which such universal human solidarity is problematic, and also back to that "great argument" which is the matter of this section: "But now the grand objection is against the reasonableness of such a constitution." [54]

If there is God, he can treat humankind as one agent, but ought he? That is, does he? In Taylor's view, such a proceeding would be in "contradiction to the true nature of things," [55] as established, after all, by God, according to which "Adam and his posterity are not one, but entirely distinct agents." [56] We come to the deepest bite of Edwards' dissent from the common political wisdom: this objection, he says, is "founded on a . . . wrong notion of what we call *sameness* or *oneness*, among created things." [57]

V

Edwards laid it down most bluntly in a journal entry: "[A]ll created identity is arbitrary." [58] It is a very modern and even postmodern point; its two adepts so far have been Edwards and Jean-Paul Sartre. It may well be hard to see why "we should be guilty of Adam's first sin," as Edwards' wrote in one of the first *Miscellanies,* but this "is no more unreasonable . . . than that we should be guilty of our own that we have been guilty of in time's past.'' For, as Edwards continues in a passage that could as well have been written by Sartre, save for one word, ''we are not the same we were in times past, any other way than only as we please to call ourselves the same. For we are anew created every moment; and that that is caused to be this moment, is not the same that was caused to be last moment, only as there is such a relation between this existence now and a certain existence in time past as we call sameness; such as remembrance, consciousness, love, likeness, a continuation of being both as to time and place without interval, *etc.* [last emphasis mine].''[59]

If we could assume the substantiality of material things, as Edwards thinks we cannot, we could make a start by saying that ''my'' acts are all those performed by ''my body.'' But the Enlightenment rightly insists on excusing me from responsibility for much of what my body does. Once exceptions are granted, there is no halt before the nihilism Sartre explored, in which there are no guarantees that a lobster's claw will not be ''my'' hand, or that I am ''my'' mother's child. To halt the slide, we may perhaps assert a ''transcendental unity of apperception'' itself, a sheer self-unifying power of consciousness; but idealism's device turned out either to make each consciousness God—an implausible result—or to reestablish the encompassing God from whom we were departing.

''All created identity is arbitrary.'' Then all depends on whose arbitration we have in mind. It is surely true and all modernity has made us know it: we are ''the same we were in times past . . . only as we please to call ourselves the same.'' We can stop there with Sartre. Or we can continue with Edwards to characterize the relations ''between this existence now and a certain existence in time past,'' which ''we call sameness,'' as ''relations the sovereign God has constituted stated conditions'' of personal identity.[60] It is true and the Enlightenment had eventually to learn it: we are whom we are chosen to be. As to who makes the choice, it can finally only be each of us for him/herself, or God for all; it is a sovereign free choice in either case.

If we allow that the arbitration is God's, then we must also allow that ''what relations he will constitute'' to be ''stated conditions of derivations of guilt,'' is ''entirely at his will and pleasure.'' There is no more in the nature of things against our being ''guilty of Adam's first sin'' than of our being ''guilty of our own . . . in times past.''[61] There is only the question of what God in fact chooses; nothing can be laid down a priori from the creature's side. ''What insight I have of the nature of minds,'' Edwards noted a little later, ''I am convinced that there is no guessing what kind of union and mixtion, by consciousness or otherwise, there may be between them."[62]

In *Original Sin* itself, Edwards' argument is more cumbersome.[63] Its chief drift is that there is nothing in the phenomenon of any momentary existent, and particularly of a momentary consciousness, that necessarily involves identity with any other momentary existence: *identity* is never itself a phenomenon. If then I am the same as yesterday's person, this derives from beyond the phenomena. And why then shall I not, for certain purposes, be the same as Adam?

The first step of the argument is that God's act of preserving creatures in any moment is exactly the same sort of act as the creature's "initial" creation.[64] God creates "things out of nothing at each moment of their existence."[65] This doctrine has regularly appeared through Christian history, since it so clearly is that of the Bible. Yet the main line of theology has resisted it, because the outcome has been anticipated to which Edwards drives it: that creatures thus have in themselves no ground of their self-identity across time. For, as Edwards continues, any two momentary existences are then simply independent "effects" of one "cause";[66] and if any one is so related to predecessors as to be "the same" as they, this is solely because the cause, "God," so constitutes the matter, "by communicating to them like properties, relations, and circumstances; and so, leads us to regard and treat them as one."[67] In no way does any momentary existent so depend on its predecessor as would be the case if their identity lay in anything they were in themselves.[68]

In consequence, there can be and are as many "various kinds of identity . . . found among created things." as there are divine purposes.[69] One such purpose is that there be creatures to whom "personal identity," and in our present particular "guilt from past wickedness" pertains. And if God establishes such continuity in the matter of Adam's sin and ours, that is then the reality.[70] We have only to inquire into the "wisdom," that is, the "analogy and harmony" of his choice.[71] On *that* basis, "That men's hearts should be deeply affected with grief and humiliation before God, for the pollution and guilt which they bring into the world with them . . . is not in the least unreasonable."[72]

VI

Where is the line between individual and community? Between me and thee? It is, finally, wherever in a particular matter serves God's creative purpose for humankind; and there is no one such line. So, at least, Edwards interpreted the matter. A society that lived by this truth, even as brokenly as societies generally live by what they take for truth, would be greatly liberated. It would be able to guard civil rights without abolishing civic duty. It would be able to pursue equality without egalitarian myths. It could be faithful to the Enlightenment's dream of liberty without corroding community's organic actuality.

America's communal entity has been undone by the practiced supposition that we can be free only by treating one another and regarding ourselves as inertial masses, bouncing merely causally against each other in public space. But this intrinsically preposterous metaphysics does not necessarily follow from the Enlightenment's vision of freedom. Quite another interpretation of community is equally Enlightened. Therewith, Edwards has brought us to his fiercest passion. The book on original sin disposes of errors. The truth is freedom.

Community and Freedom

13

The American nation was created by the Enlightenment's passion for liberty. Apart from revolution there would have been no such nation at all; and the institutions by which a nation was thereupon structured were carefully crafted, by the Enlightenment's best receipts, to preserve the freedom once won. Nor have we ever ceased to conceive ourselves as the archetypical instance of the free nation.

The American nation has therefore also been especially troubled by the inner antinomy of the Enlightenment's dream of freedom, an antinomy related to that of Western Christianity's interpretation of God, but not congruent with it. On the one hand, freedom has meant for us what it meant for the Greek and medieval free cities, for the towns and township communities of the colonies, and for the governing class of the colonial state authorities: access to the forum where the community deliberates and decides its own good, participation in the polity. Taken of the community as such, this freedom is then the community's ability to conduct such deliberation for itself. On the other hand freedom has meant for us what it means in mechanistic political theory: freedom *from* the community's deciding of the good, the existence of a space where I, as we have come with great accuracy to state it, can do my own thing. The two conceptions can at best uneasily coexist, since the one calls me into the community and the other calls me out of it.

It is the first, classic liberty which animated the idealism of our revolution and nation-building. The freedom of a citizen of a Connecticut town or a Virginia township was that of responsible participation in communal affairs. When Thomas Jefferson wrote of "life, liberty and the pursuit of happiness," it was the pattern of his own life, as local magnate and eligible representative to the House of Burgesses, that emotively defined "liberty." British government was opposed as tyrannical precisely because Americans could not be elected to Westminster. America was to be a free nation; that is, America was to be its own polity and was to extend access to the polity's life as widely as could be appropriate.

The revolutionary and constitutional fathers' political *theory,* however, often proposed quite a different liberty. If the polity is a mechanism, then freedom can not be the polity's own predicate. At most, the polity can be constructed for the preservation and promotion of freedom located elsewhere; indeed, liberty must then be that there *is* a realm outside the polity. It is the most remarkable single event of American political history: no sooner had ''liberty'' been achieved by the creation of a sovereign polity within our own shores, then this polity was itself perceived as the great threat to ''liberty.''

What secretly happens in the standard Enlightenment's political theory is that the polity is assimilated to the economy. Those Enlightenment twins, the Marxist and capitalist ideologies, agree perfectly on the decisive proposition: that political events and relations are but the secondary effects of economic events and relations. But what can freedom be in a community constituted by its economy, that is, precisely by its deterministic aspect? It can only be what again capitalists and Marxists agree in proclaiming: freedom *from* the community, an arena of choice not determined by the communal mechanism. When an American says, ''It's a free country, isn't it?'' the meaning is that in this nation he/she disposes of a very large area outside the polity. And when a Marxist denies the truth of the American's claim and asserts that only socialist nations are on the way to freedom, the meaning is that any space outside the community is yet an illusion and that freedom will be established only by the final complete abolition of communal mechanisms.

We must inquire: Where did this second notion of freedom come from? It is with this question that the connection to theology appears, and to Edwards' book on *Freedom of the Will.* For the Enlightenment drew here on an ancient concept of western theological and philosophical reflection: the concept of *liberum arbitrium,* of ''the free will.'' The concept was inveterately troublesome but, in some analogy to the concept of 'substance,'' had been kept in check within the West's pre-Enlightenment affirmation of history and personhood. Transferred to the world of achievers and their victims, the demand for ''free will'' drove all other considerations before it.

The foregoing quotation marks around *free will* are to a point: Western theology's classic affirmation of *liberum arbitrium* is *not* identical with the straightforward affirmation that some or all of our willed acts are freely done. Many of our most lucid thinkers simultaneously and with easy consistency have denied that humans possess *liberum arbitrium* and wholeheartedly maintained the commonsensical affirmation of freedom, of such propositions as that I arose this morning at seven because I chose to, so that my arising then was a free act. Assertion of "the free will" is rather a particular *explanation* of practical freedom: "the free will" is an alleged entitive capacity my possession of which is to be the ground of my acts' freedom. It seems a possible question: How *can* my arising at seven have been free as it evidently was? The standard theological-philosophical answer has been: Because you possess a free will.

One should carefully note the diction surrounding "free will," as the previous paragraph displays it. "The free will" is supposed to be a *something* which I *possess*. Since my possession of this thing is to be the explanation of my free behavior, my possession of it must be antecedent to my dealings with other persons, for it is above all the freedom or unfreedom of those dealings that are to be explained. That is, "the free will" is precisely a feature of the *individual* in the very sense of mechanistic political theory, and it is mine prior to all communal relations. "God has given his human creatures free will" was the one proposition of traditional dogmatics which "Protestantism without Reformation" could adopt with unfettered enthusiasm.

Edwards planned and executed the *Inquiry into the Modern Prevailing Notion of that Freedom of the Will Which is Supposed to be Essential to Moral Agency* as his major entry into "the Arminian controversy." He regarded the Arminian reassertion of "the free will" as the root error among all the eighteenth century's departures from original Calvinism.[1] Thus he planned a major study of the matter from at least as early as 1747;[2] the work finally appeared in 1754.

Freedom of the Will is the most methodical of Edwards' writings. He begins by a lengthy fixing of the terms and positions of the controversy. He then conducts a direct philosophical attack on the Arminian position, arguing a negative answer to the question, "[W]hether there is, or can be any such sort of freedom of will, as that wherein Arminians place the essence of the liberty of all moral agents."[3] The Arminian challenge is then taken up in its own sense; it is this effort which transforms also this work from a dogmatic and philosophical defense of Calvinism into a work of political prophecy and diagnosis. For the Arminian gravamen against Calvinism was that its denial of *liberum arbitrium* must, if taken into practice, undo moral responsibility and disorder the community. It was the same claim made by Erasmus against Luther; Luther's reply, *On the Bondage of the Will,* is the most notable predecessor and parallel to Edwards' book. But whereas Luther was inclined to let society fall, if the truth had that result, Edwards turned the Arminian charge against itself and denounced the delusion of "the free will" as the great solvent of modern communities.

II

The first part[4] of *Freedom of the Will* is a piece of what would now be called ordinary-language analysis. All parties agreed that humans are willing agents; that their agency is, at least sometimes, free; and that God is sovereign. How then can a controversy arise? In Edwards' view, because "philosophers" do not use the terminology of "will," "cause," "necessity" and "liberty" in its ordinary-language senses, but create "philosophical" uses detached from the ordinary uses, and then do not consistently remember that they have done so, continuing sometimes to use the words by their old rules.

Edwards begins with "will." His opening sentence sets the whole tone of the book: "It may possibly be thought that there is no great need of going about to define or describe the 'will,' this word being generally as well understood as any other words we can use to explain it: and so perhaps it would be, had not philosophers, metaphysicians and polemic divines brought the matter into obscurity."[5] In the "general and more natural notions of men, according to which language is formed," a person's "willing" something is simply that person's "choosing, liking best, or being best pleased" with it. "Volition" does not denote another event than "preference,"[6] and it is then nonsense to talk of will where there is no "inclination of the soul."[7]

Questions about what "determines" the will, Edwards therefore regards with suspicion, but "if the phrase be used with any meaning," the question must be about what causes a person to choose one thing rather than another.[8] And if *that* question is kept clearly in focus, Edwards think its answer is obvious: the will is "determined" by "that motive, which, as it stands in the view of the mind, is the strongest."[9]

But even this plain answer is likely to cause confusion unless certain points are observed. A "motive" is not to be considered apart from the total situation in which choice is to be made;[10] and the term must be taken of "the direct and immediate object of the act of volition."[11] Moreover, in many contexts two qualifications are necessary. The first qualification is, that it is more precise to say "that the will *is* as the greatest apparent good . . . is, than to say that the will is *determined* by the greatest apparent good . . . because an appearing more agreeable . . . to the mind, and the mind's professing and choosing, seem hardly to be properly . . . distinct." Edwards allows himself to be insofar philosophical as to distinguish between the "voluntary action which is the immediate consequence . . . of the mind's choice," which is "determined'' by the greatest apparent good, and the choice itself, which is "determined" by the object's dispositional property to appear as the greatest good.[12] The other qualification is that this potential of the object to appear "agreeable" is constituted both by "what appears in the object viewed" and by "the manner of the view,"[13] the later involving both reasonings and the established tempers of the heart.[14]

"The words 'necessary,' 'impossible,' etc. are,'' Edwards notes, "abundantly used in controversies about free will"[15] and are an abundant source of confusion.[16] In "common speech," he says, all these terms are relative to the notion of effort by an agent. What is "necessary" is what someone or everyone cannot help, what "is, or will be, notwithstanding all supposable opposition."[17] What is "impossible" is what no agent could bring to pass. And to speak of "inability" is to speak of the agent's situation in such cases. Finally, "Anything is said to be 'contingent,' or to come to pass by chance or accident, in the original meaning of such words, when its connection with its causes or antecedents, according to the established course of things, is not discerned," so that the thing is unpredictable.[18]

Philosophers, however, often use all these words "in a sense quite diverse from this common use . . . , for they apply them to many cases in which no opposition is supposed."[19] The new use of "contingent" is perhaps especially remote from its common use; philosophically, "contingent" "is abundantly used . . . for something which has absolutely no previous ground or reason."[20] The creation of philosophical uses is not in Edwards' view necessarily an evil, but it becomes one if we continue to "apply the words" by the "habitual connections of ideas" involved in the ordinary uses[21]—which is what Edwards thinks regularly happens.

If we suppose, as Edwards does, that for some purposes we do need the philosophical uses of this complex of language, and if we are careful *not* to bring along those connections of ideas which the philosophical uses were created by leaving behind, then "philosophical necessity is nothing different from certainty." "Certainty" is here not subjective conviction but whatever is in any case "the ground of the infallibility of the proposition" that states that case.[22] It is in the philosophical sense, hoping to avoid its pitfalls, that Edwards himself proposes to use "necessity" when he sets out to prove that necessity "is not inconsistent with liberty."[23]

Edwards here attempts analytic clarity about matters whose clarification would in fact be the agonizingly slow labor of his and the following two centuries, and are still in large part controversial. He distinguishes three sorts of "philosophical" certainty. The first is relatively straightforward: that is certain which it would be logically absurd to deny, as that God (supposing he is) is infinite, or that "two and two should be four." [24] His stipulation of the second class is less lucid: "a proposition, which affirms the existence of something, may be . . . certain, because the existence of that thing is already come to pass." [25] It is not immediately apparent what Edwards here means by "the existence of something," but if we consider of what he in fact speaks in this connection, the existents in question turn out to be willed acts, motivations etc., that is, *events* rather than substances. So if we take "Caesar crossed the Rubicon," or "Caesar's crossing of the Rubicon occurred," as an instance, his point is that if this proposition is ever true, it cannot get to be not true. Finally, Edwards says that if there are any necessarily true propositions other than those of these two sorts, they must be derivable from propositions of those sorts.

Edwards, wisely perhaps, does not attempt an inventory of this third category. It is anyway plain what subclass he is interested in: assertions that do not yet have the certainty of the past but are nevertheless certain, propositions of the form ". . . must happen," for example, "Congress must declare independence." Such a proposition is true, he says, if and only if it can appear as the apodosis of a true proposition of the form "Since . . . , . . . must happen," where the protasis has one of the first two sorts of certainty.[26] An instance might be: "Since the stamp tax has been reaffirmed, Congress must declare independence." And "this," he says, "is the necessity which especially belongs to acts of the will." [27]

To these stipulations, Edwards appends yet a further set. The necessity pertaining to a yet-future event may be, he says, "moral" or "natural," depending on whether the established event from which its necessity derives is a "moral" or "natural cause." A "moral" cause is simply an event of the sort which in ordinary usage we will judge morally: a disposition, a choice or a motive.[28] So if the proposition is true, "Given the chance, John will take chocolate every time," then so soon as chocolate's availability moves into the certainty of the past tense, as in "John has just noticed the chocolate," the future event "John will choose the chocolate," has "philosophical necessity" of the "moral" sort—all else, as Edwards stipulated to begin, being equal.

The word "cause" has appeared. Edwards postpones his analysis of this concept to later in the book,[29] but we had best consider it here. He stipulates that he will "use it in a sense which is more extensive than that in which it is sometimes used." [30] He does not say whether he thinks his use is closer to everyday use or farther away. And I think the reason is discernible: precisely in his time, everyday use was itself uncertain, displaced by opposing philosophical proposals. Edwards, as has been often remarked,[31] goes analytically with David Hume: a "cause," according to Edwards, is any event that appears in the protasis of a true proposition of the form "If . . . happens, then . . . will happen." There need be no "positive productive influence" of the "cause" on its "effect."[32] Unlike Hume, however, he does not find such "invariable connection" a mere postulate, for he apprehends in the invariable connections of events the orderliness of God's thinking. Whether God ordains rain, and *so* ordains "the earnest prayers of his people," or ordains his people's prayers and *so* ordains rain, comes to exactly the same: he ordains the events' beautiful conjunction.[33]

With this sequence of analyses Edwards is up to something. He is adumbrating, as in accord with "the more natural notions of mankind," a conception of historical determination, but of a very particular kind. In that the past "necessarily" is what it is, the future will "necessarily" be what the past causes it to be. But this necessity is strictly of the philosophical sort; in speaking so, we are not speaking naturally and must always remind ourselves of that. If we do, we will not be betrayed into supposing that future events' necessity is of the sort that might be *imposed* by their causes, as if the past *made* the future be what it will be, perhaps in spite of us. For in Edwards' conception, to say that every event has its causes is simply to say that all events are in principle predictable by observation of antecedent events, that reliable correlations are there to be discovered. The "necessity" with which history proceeds is, so far as we have yet come, simply that such predictions may be of what "must" occur. And both the causality and the necessity may be and in the cases here relevant will be of the "moral" sort.

How then *will* we speak naturally about these same matters? With that question we arrive, finally, at Edwards analysis of "freedom" and "liberty," which he can now perform with dispatch. "The plain and obvious meaning of the words 'freedom' and 'liberty,' in common speech, is power, opportunity, or advantage, that anyone has, to do as he pleases. . . . And the contrary to liberty . . . is a person's being hindered . . . to conduct as he will."[34] Two points are immediately to be noted. First, it will then make nonsense to speak of the *will* being "free"; the *person* who wills is or is not free, to do what he/she wills.[35] Second, when we in ordinary language say, for example, that "John is free to go," nothing whatever is said about how John, supposing he chooses to go, comes to choose so. To the freedom of a person's willed act, it is entirely irrelevant whether his/her willing so "was determined by some internal antecedent volition, or whether it happened without a cause; whether it was necessarily connected with something foregoing, or not connected. Let the person come by his volition . . . how he will . . . if he is able [to execute] his will, the man is perfectly . . . free, according to the primary and common notion of freedom.'' [36]

And now at the very end of this part of his book, Edwards overtly introduces his target. ''Arminians, Pelagians and others, who oppose the Calvinists,'' create for ''liberty'' ''an entirely different signification.'' [37] On Edwards' principles, they are free to do this, if they do not simultaneously trade on ''the usual . . . acceptations of the word.'' But that is what the philosophical use proposed by Arminians in fact does, in Edwards' judgment—and in mine. Edwards' description of his opponents' use is intended to show their linguistic confusion without much need of comment. ''These several things belong to their notion of liberty: 1. That it consists in a self-determining power in the will, or a certain sovereignty the will has over itself, and its own acts, whereby it determines its own volitions; so as not to be dependent in its determinations, on any cause without itself, nor determined by anything prior to its own acts. 2. Indifference belongs to liberty in their notion of it, or that the mind, previous to the act of volition be in *equilibrio*. 3. Contingence is another thing that belongs . . . to it; not in the common acceptation of the word . . . but as opposed to all necessity, or any fixed and certain connection with some previous ground or reason of its existence.'' [38]

III

Edwards' language-analysis may be suspected of bias, toward the material position he has in mind—and so may the more elaborately ''empirical'' efforts of recent practitioners. Be that as it may, his analysis sets up both his refutation of ''free will'' and his own positive interpretation of freedom.

Each of the three determinants of Arminian ''liberty'' is separately dissected. Edwards first considers the notion that the will is free in that it is ''self-determined.'' [39] The confusion in this notion Edwards had already noted in the course of the linguistic analyses: it misplaces the adjective ''free'' from the person to the person's ''will.'' In common usage, freedom is freedom to do what one chooses; and no one has achieved a philosophical use quite bereft of this connection. But if the *will* is free, what then is *it* free to do? To choose, evidently. Thus we arrive at a choice to choose, without which the will would be unfree: more euphemistically, we posit a *self*-determining by the will, that is, by the person's determining.[40]

The notion is, Edwards thinks, "plainly absurd,"[41] for it must generate a regress of explanation that cannot be terminated except by contradiction. "[I]f the freedom of the will consists in this, that its own volitions are determined by itself, it will follow, that every free volition arises from another antecedent volition, directing and commanding that and if that directing volition be also free . . . , that directing volition is determined by another before that; and so, till we come to the first volition in the whole series: and if that first volition be free . . . , then that is determined by another volition preceding that, which is a contradiction."[42]

There is, we should note, one way of stopping the regress. The question on the table is: What causes the will to choose as it in any instance does? One could answer that *nothing* does, "that the soul's exertion of such a particular act of will, is a thing that comes to pass of itself, without any cause."[43] And that answer in turn could mean one of two things. One is that the soul is *a se,* that it is itself the opposite of nothing, that is, that it is divine; and indeed the tradition had often finally terminated the regress of freedom at a "participation" in God at the "depth" of the soul. But Scripture had closed that answer both for Edwards and for his immediate opponents, and Edwards never considers it. If the absurdities to which Edwards pointed were to be avoided, this left only the position that each free choice simply "start[s] out of nonexistence . . . without any cause or reason."[44] Edwards sees that this is the position to which Arminianism is in fact driven.[45]

But—and so we come to a second determinant of Arminian "liberty"—is it any less absurd to think of choice as "contingent" in this philosophic sense?[46] That many events are "contingent" in the everyday sense is obvious and nothing to the Arminian purpose. An event genuinely contingent in the philosophic sense would have no reason why it should have occurred rather than some other; also "moral" causes must be excluded, so that to a "contingent" choice motives would be simply irrelevant. In a world in which "contingent" events of this sort were to be expected, there could, Edwards points out, be no empirical knowledge at all, no "reasonings about the existence of things, past, present or future," beyond "what we have by the most direct and immediate intuition."[47] And if the Arminians are right, "millions of millions" of such events, that is, all human free choices, occur daily. Here Edwards' reversal of Arminian moral and political concern dawns: their position is morally nihilistic, there can be by their lights no argued discourse about what is to be done.[48]

One motif of Arminian "freedom" remains: that the pure model of freedom is an ability to choose also "in cases wherein no prevailing motive is presented . . . between . . . things, that are perfectly equal in the view of the mind."[49] When, asks Edwards, is the will supposed to be *in* this state of "indifference?" It cannot be at the moment of choice, for since choice is inclination, this would be to say that the mind inclines when it is not inclining.[50] Thus the actual Arminian position is that choice, to be free, *supercedes* on a state of indifference. But here is disaster, for if indifference defines freedom, if I am unfree to the extent that motives and predilections incline me, choice thus comes to be seen as *foreclosing* freedom: the exercise of freedom becomes the enemy of freedom's possession.[51] Edwards regards such a position as preposterous. And so no doubt it is, but it has nonetheless become the practiced conviction of American society, in which commitment is avoided because freedom must be preserved.

Edwards' own position is already before us. To another than the ordinary sense of "liberty," Edwards can assign no meaning. I am free when no "natural" cause frustrates my choice. That this choice may itself be determined by "moral" causes is irrelevant to my freedom. The position is both commonsensical and modern: I choose, and if I can do what I choose, know myself free; that I or you can also explain how I came so to choose does not alter this knowledge.

Thus space is left for the doctrine that *all* choices are in fact determined by moral causes. Edwards espouses the doctrine, as a Calvinist for whom the choice of choices is the gift of Another, for whom there is an encompassing moral order.

The "determinism" Edwards constructs is very different than we are likely to suppose it. In *Freedom of the Will*, he creates it by the axiom that every event, choices included, is as it is on account of its causes, and that the chain of causes always reaches to past events, which *must* be what they are.[52] But this is merely a polemic mode of constructing the metaphysical vision we have had before us from the first: of the harmony of all temporal events in the musical mind of God.[53] In God's mind each event has its "necessary" place, in that he knows with grounded certainty why it happens as it does.[54] It is from *this* vision that Edwards' Humean analysis of causation derives, according to which the causes and effects every event must have are simply those other events by relation to which it becomes intelligible. Nor is Edwards' universal determinism mechanistic or reductionist; there are truly the *two* orders of "natural" and "moral" causation and necessity.[55] In *Freedom of the Will*, Edwards says little about their relations, but we already know it: natural and moral causation are the modes elsewhere distinguished as God's "natural" and "moral" government, within the one fugal harmony of his natural and supernatural providence.

IV

The scenario is enacted in American courtrooms daily: "Your Honor, my client surely pulled the trigger. But he is innocent of murder, by reason of insanity." "What is the evidence of insanity?" "That he did this insane thing: to kill someone." Again: "Your Honor, my client took the money, but he should be treated with leniency, because of his deprivation." "What is the evidence of deprivation?" "That he took the money." Edwards foresaw the society in which such argument would be convincing. It would, he thought, be produced by the demand for Arminian "freedom," and it would be unfree.

Arminianism asserts that freedom "not only from coaction," but from necessity in the philosophic sense, is "essential . . . to an action's being culpable":[56] if I am "unable" to desist from an act, also in the moral-philosophical sense of "unable," I am thereby excused for the act. The generality of humanity supposes and Edwards fully agrees that if a natural cause, a cause "external" to the will, prevents me from desisting, this "wholly excuses" my act.[57] The problem is that, in the specifically American form of self-alienation, by which we become observers and manipulators of our own actions, we see also our own past choices and abiding inclinations, the moral determinants of our choice, as extrinsic to ourselves, as natural causes. We will say "My marriage has failed" in exactly the same mode as "I have been smitten by cancer," so that the act of divorce is praised as "honesty." It is apparent that within this self-understanding it will be only by inconsistency that any act at all can be blamed or praised. Inconsistency has been enforced by the circumstance that communities cannot exist without mutual praise and blame; but practiced inconsistency can be enforced only with ever diminishing effect. As we act more by our principles, our community dissolves.

Or as Edwards put it, "If the influence of moral . . . inability be the same, to excuse persons in not doing, or not avoiding anything, as that of *natural* inability . . . , then undoubtedly . . . *moral difficulty* has the same influence to excuse with *natural difficulty*. But all will allow, that natural impossibility wholly excuses, and also that natural difficulty excuses . . . in proportion to the difficulty.''[58] The consequence is that on Arminian principles I am excused for my act in proportion to my motivation to the act,[59] which means that I am always to be excused. The law in an Arminian society will be able consistently to demand only such obedience as I am moved in fact to produce; then the law cannot actually be broken, no matter what deeds are performed.[60]

Indeed, it is not just law, but all moral discourse which is emptied by Arminian freedom. For if the inducements and deterrents presented to the actual act of choice do not determine it, but rather the choice is determined by a prior act by which the will determines itself, this act will have its own and different inducements and deterrents, and so on to infinity. Which is to say that no inducements or deterrents ever acquire any purchase on choice.[61] So why argue or present them? Or if choice simply ''starts into existence'' for no reason, the presentation of reasons must be a priori irrelevant.[62]

Edwards must, to be sure, meet the converse Arminian charge: If each choice can in principle be so explained that we see why it *must* be as it is, does it make any sense to say to each other what we should choose? Does it make any sense to command someone to do what he/she is unable to do? According to Edwards, it does, in case the inability is moral-philosophic. For in *every* case when I disobey a command, I am just so morally unable to obey it; and this is not paradoxical or against the meaningfulness of moral discourse, as we will see if we do not confuse the various sorts of necessity.[63] The ''end of commands is to turn the will one way,''[64] that is, to be a cause determining choice. In the total motivating situation of which the command is a factor, the person chooses, and the choice will either be in accord with the command or not; that is, the command will either have succeeded or failed to determine the will. Let us suppose I choose against the command. The act of choice is an inclination of the will, and if the will inclines one way, it—philosophically!—cannot simultaneously incline ''the other way, and so can't choose to be made to go the other way,'' that is, to obey the command.[65] The will may indeed choose to obey a command to do something which the person turns out to be ''naturally'' prevented from doing; and the will may indeed ''oppose some future . . . act that it is exposed to.''[66] But I cannot will to obey a command I willingly do not obey— and so what?

Since ''the . . . very want of will to a thing commanded, implies a moral inability to that thing,'' and since it is precisely the inclination of the will that can be commanded, ''those things may properly be commanded, which men have a moral inability for.''[67] It is the opposite view which empties moral discourse: "If merely that inability will excuse disobedience, which is implied in . . . defect of inclination, remaining after the command is exhibited, then wickedness always carries that in it which excuses it.''[68]

There is a reason why despite the Arminian position's absurdity American society has adopted it, so as to act as if wickedness were its own excuse. To the total motivating situation belong the established tempers of the chooser's heart. That I can only choose what I choose when I choose it sounds less harmless when I remember that this "I" is an historical reality. My moral-philosophical "inability" to respond to any command otherwise than I in fact do is co-constituted by the fact of my past moral life and the abiding inclinations it has given me. Can someone meaningfully be commanded to do what we may with certainty know from knowledge of his/her history he/she will not do? Yet the absurdity of a negative answer remains also when we make this consideration explicit. The passage cited to conclude the previous paragraph continues: " 'Tis evermore so, that by how much the more wickedness there is in a man's heart, by so much is his inclination to evil the stronger, and . . . so much the more therefore has he of moral inability to the good required. His moral inability, consisting in the strength of his evil inclination, *is the very thing wherein his wickedness consists* [my emphasis]; and yet according to Arminian principles, it must be a thing inconsistent with wickedness.''[69]

That Arminian understanding of freedom must silence the community's moral discourse can be shown also by starting with the "indifference" which according to it "belongs to liberty of will.''[70] If, contrary to what Edwards takes to be the fact, we suppose "there may be an act of will in a state of indifference," this must be "the will's determining to put it self out of the state of indifference." Thus if indifference belongs to liberty, and liberty to praiseworthy or blameworthy actions, this pre-dispositional act "is that alone wherein virtue consists.''[71] All "that is done after the mind, by any means, is once out of its equilibrium and already possessed by an inclination, and arising from that inclination . . . is worthy of neither blame nor praise.''[72]

Thus "virtue and vice are wholly excluded out of the world.''[73] For on this understanding, precisely to the extent that my will is abidingly inclined, I am not responsible for what I do following that inclination.[74] "No propensity . . . can be virtuous or vicious . . . because they, so far as they take place, destroy the freedom of the will, the foundation of all moral agency, and exclude all capacity of either virtue or vice. And

. . . neither can the exercize of these dispositions be so: for the exercize of *bias* is not the exercize of *free self-determining will.*"⁷⁵ The dispositions, "which used to be called" virtues and vices, are farthest from being so. "The more violent men's lusts are, the more fixed their pride, envy, ingratitude and maliciousness . . . the further they are from being blameworthy."⁷⁶ Precisely those acts which by "the universal sense of mankind" are virtuous, because they "proceed from a heart *well disposed* and *inclined,*" are worthless.⁷⁷

Moral persuasion and inducement, exercised among the members of a community, must, if Arminians are right about liberty, be babble. For persuasions and inducements cannot be addressed to that pre-dispositional act of will which is alone supposed to be free and the bearer of moral value. From the other side, "This notion of liberty frustrates all endeavors to draw men to virtue by instruction, or persuasion, precept, or example: for though these things may induce men to what is *materially* virtuous, yet at the same time they [according to the Arminians] take away the form of virtue, because they destroy liberty; as they, by their own power, put the will out of its equilibrium." Acts of will "excited" by "motive and inducement" cannot "be virtuous; because so far as they are from them, they are not from the will's self determining power."⁷⁸

Or, as we now say, I must not "impose my values" on you, lest I infringe the freedom that is "yours." Edwards' delineation is precise: we may claim *liberum arbitrium,* the freedom each of us possesses as an individual self-determiner, or we may discourse morally with each other and find freedom when our mutual responses sometimes find a path to action; we cannot do both. We cannot be possessors of "free will" and live as a community. How far we have chosen [!] the former mode may be shown by a prophecy of Edwards along the way of his main argument.

Edwards remarked a possible alternative Arminian position: "the supposition that liberty consists" not in the power to resolve equilibrium but "in a power of suspending action for the present, in order to deliberation."⁷⁹ He thought it a sufficient debunking of this possibility to point out that "According to such a supposition, the most horrid crimes, adultery, murder, buggery, blasphemy, etc. do not at all consist in the horrid nature of the things themselves, but only in the neglect of thorough consideration before they were perpetrated."⁸⁰ He had not read the moral pronouncements of mainline denominations, according to most of which abortion, for example, is a terrible thing which may yet become the right thing to do if only it is preceded by sufficiently lengthy and agonized counseling and self-examination.

V

It is possible to read *Freedom of the Will* and feel that Edwards' victories over modernity's ethics are won too easily. The Arminian position is truly absurd, and Edwards' dialectics, even if they occasionally slip a cog, expose the absurdity. But absurdities do not triumph historically sheerly in that capacity. It is not any and every contrary position from which Arminianism can be so easily dialectically vanquished. Edwards' arguments have a material supposition that is not simply common sense.

Throughout, Edwards conflates the act of the will with the *state* of the will. His most telling points will not work without the identification of "inclination" as a movement with "inclination" as an attitude. That is, it is *virtues* that are commanded in moral discourse, by Edwards' supposition. The position from which the standard Enlightenment can be overcome is what is currently called "an ethic of virtue." And Edwards' discussion shows this more plainly as it advances. The fourth and last part of *Freedom of the Will,* devoted to the "chief grounds of the Reasonings of the Arminians," draws back to yet another fundamental statement of the issue: whether what is "praiseworthy" or "vicious" in our choices is the structure of their determinants or their "nature" as "dispositions or acts of the will."[81]

Edwards disposes of the Arminian position with his customary moves.[82] It is the position he now espouses that arrests us: what makes sin deserve punishment is whatever "makes sin hateful," and what makes virtue "fit to receive praise and reward" is whatever makes it "lovely." "Tis a certain beauty or deformity that are *inherent* in that good or evil will, which is the *soul* of virtue and vice . . . which is their worthiness of esteem or disesteem."[83] We have come to the matter of the next chapter.

What is "true virtue?" That is indeed the question. *That is:* Wherein lies the beauty of human life? *Freedom of the Will* prophecies America's moral nihilism. *True Virtue* adumbrates the alternative.

14

True Virtue

Edwards wrote the treatise on *The Nature of True Virtue* in 1755. It was not published in his lifetime; but appeared quickly thereafter and has been continuously read and admired since. In isolation from Edwards' metaphysics of musically beautiful communal consciousness, it has not perhaps been so continually understood. The question posed in this work is: What makes the difference between the mutual balancing of egocentric "interests" and the bonding of hearts in community? Between the theory by which Madison and his colleagues were about to create our polity, and the passion that moved them to create one?

II

Edwards believes he but reports the opinion of humankind,[1] as enshrined in common language,[2] by defining: virtue is "the beauty of an intelligent being."[3] This must be the beauty which is the mind's own, and not merely that of its products.[4] That is to say, for Edwards, that virtue "is the beauty of the qualities and exercizes of the heart." What is it that makes these beautiful, when they are?[5]

Only the heart's "general" and not merely its "particular" beauty can be truly *its* beauty. A "particular beauty," as Edwards here distinguishes, is any thing's harmony with a limited sphere; its "general beauty" is its harmony "with everything to which it stands related."[6] It is each thing's "general beauty" that is its beauty "as it is in itself";[7] this is dictated by Edwards' metaphysics but not here argued abstractly. Instead, he argues from a telling metaphor: whereas general beauty comprehends particular beauty, particular beauty "may be without and against" general beauty, as "a few notes in a tune, taken only by themselves and in their relation to one another, may be harmonious, which, when considered with respect to . . . the entire series of sounds they are connected with, may be very . . . disagreeable."[8]

If now we remember that it is consciousness whose beauty we want to specify, that we seek the heart's sort of harmony with all, we have our answer. "True virtue . . . consists in *benevolence to being in general.* Or perhaps, to speak more accurately, it is that consent, propensity and union of heart to being in general, which is immediately exercized" in general benevolence.[9]

That the beauty of minds is the heart's uniting sense, a "benevolence," Edwards carries over from previous work and hardly considers here. His concern in this work is the *generality* of true moral beauty's attachments. He notes and rejects as circular, proposals to locate virtue in consciousness' response to the intrinsic worth of objects. Then "there is room left for no other conclusion, than that the primary object of virtuous love is being, simply considered."[10] The beauty of consciousness is love to each thing that is, simply in that it is. And this, by Edwards' Platonizing warrants of thought, immediately implies that "being in general," the total system of existents, is the object of true benevolence. True virtue will "seek the good of each individual being unless it be conceived as not consistent" with the good of the whole.[11]

Within being in general, a "secondary" object of universal benevolence appears. Some of the beings that appear to me are themselves consciousnesses, and of these some, God at least, are themselves truly benevolent. By their benevolence, these consciousnesses are united to all being, and so present being to me localized. Thus my love of being in general, if I have it, coalesces with love of these other consciousnesses.[12]

Now, says Edwards, "let it be supposed that some beings, by natural instinct or by some other means, have a determination of mind to union and benevolence to a particular person, or private system, which is but a small part of being: and that this disposition . . . is independent [of] benevolence to being in general."[13] What ails such benevolence? Edwards' analyses are somewhat cumbersome at this point, but may be summarized so: "private affection" is not "true" virtue because it cannot be counted on to transcend the limits of its initial group when new groups must be reckoned with. It will sooner or later "set a person against general existence, and make him an enemy to it."[14] "[A]mong the Romans, love to their country was the highest virtue; though this affection . . . was employed. . . for the destruction of the rest of mankind."[15]

This tendency comes to its head over against *God.* If there is God, "a benevolent propensity of heart to being in general, and a temper . . . to love God supremely, are in effect the same thing."[16] This must be so on both counts analyzed, for God both includes being in general and is the supreme instance of benevolent consciousness.[17] Thus any stop to the expansion of our benevolence is rejection of God;[18] and when the demand is known "that the supreme, infinite, and all-comprehending Being requires a supreme regard to himself," persistence in partial affection "must unavoidably . . . fix us in a stated opposition to the supreme Being."[19] Vice versa and politically decisively, it is seeking God's glory as our "supreme, governing and ultimate end"[20] which alone breaks the partiality of affection, which opens our benevolence to intrusions from beyond its momentary boundaries.[21]

III

It is what political theory sometimes calls "the problem of the stranger" with which Edwards here labors. It is an ancient observation: social coherence makes each group opaque to the value of those beyond the group. If outsiders become interlopers they will be attacked, and if their challenge cannot be quelled, the group's very coherence will become the group's solvent. Democracies, also by ancient observation, are especially blind to the stranger and especially damaged by their blindness.

What can free our love to transcend the boundaries of our groups, while maintaining community? What can open us to the world as the world each time intrudes, other than alienation? As the Marxists put it: What can universalize solidarity, without making us merely "cosmopolitan?" It is not apparent, despite all praise of religious pluralism, that Edwards can be rebutted. The joint worship of God can do it; and no other plausible suggestion is yet on the table. If it is argued that God is regularly invoked by each people to valorize its enmity to others, those of Edwards' opinion will reply that only idols can be so invoked, not the true, that is, "all-comprehending God." Indeed, Edwards could surely agree with a central insight of Wolfhart Pannenberg's very modern thought: that the biblical God's claim to be the true God is verified precisely by his infinite capacity to transcend his own momentary worship and to free his own people from their momentary boundaries.

The matter is especially piquant with America and Jonathan Edwards. It is now a dogma of our accepted public philosophy: America's former consciousness of mission beyond its borders, of a "manifest destiny" given by God, made us a dangerous member of the community of nations, and we are well rid of this delusion. Those who know of Edwards' part in creating the dream of America's providential destiny, are likely to regard it as a blot on his record.

Edwards did not create the sense of American mission; it was what brought Puritans to this land in the first place. In "New" England they proposed to complete what had been begun in old England but frustrated at the last moment by king and bishop: the Reformation of Christianity. In his labor to discover in Scripture the agenda of that providence, Edwards differed from his countrymen only by scholarly energy. The question was bound to occur: if America was prepared and given to the children of Reformation to perfect their work, what could come next, when they had done it? It needed only the combination of Puritan self-understanding with the new post-millennialist exegesis to suggest that America was the place reserved by providence for the beginning of the millennium. The suggestion once made, the mystery would have been if the suggestion had not prevailed, as it did for over a century.

In 1742,[22] in the last of his pieces directly on the revivals, *Some Thoughts Concerning the Present Revival of Religion in New England,* Edwards, with painful caution, took the step. He noted that the discovery of America was "about the time of the Reformation . . . : which Reformation was the first thing that God did towards the glorious renovation of the world, after it had sunk . . . under the great . . . apostasy."[23] Perhaps out of dawning desperation, he could no longer refrain from apocalyptic praise of the awakenings: "The New Jerusalem . . . has begun to come down from heaven, and perhaps never were more of the publications of heaven's glory given upon earth."[24] So he proposed: " 'Tis not unlikely that this work of God's Spirit, that is so extraordinary . . . is the dawning, or at least a prelude, of that glorious work of God, so often foretold in Scripture, which . . . shall renew . . . mankind."[25] And: "This new world is probably now discovered, that the new and more glorious state of God's church on earth might commence here."[26]

Edwards' successors would not be so circumspect. A grandson, Timothy Dwight, president from 1795–1817 of a Yale geared for the training of evangelists, and only more or less an Edwardsean, fancied himself a poet and produced an apostrophe to America which included:

> Hail Land of light and joy! Thy power shall grow
> Far as the seas, which round thy regions flow.
> No more on earth shall Rage and Discord dwell,
> But sink with Envy to their native hell.
> Then, then a heavenly Kingdom shall descend,
> And light and glory through the world extend.

We have already noted how easily the millennial vision in its post-millennial construal is secularized, whereupon it can quickly become a naked proposal to save other peoples by our works and to our advantage. There is indeed a development that finally arrives at the self-righteous imperialism of the Spanish-American War.

It is not, however, so often asked what America would have been like *without* such vision. It is surely worth noting that the one great American enterprise so far undertaken by leaders thoroughly disabused of "moralism" in public policy, was the Indochinese intervention. America cannot deny power; the only question is by what warrants we will determine its use. One need not share politically recrudescent evangelicalism's mission to save the world from Communism, to think America must have *some* mission, if God's providence lives.

If, as chastened and demythologized post-millennialists, American Christians were still to insist that there can be a better future also in this world, and this by the standards and energy of the gospel; and if we were to think that God's providence can hardly have left our nation with no role in the coming of this future; what might that mission be? The suggestion that can come from Edwards is surely: advocacy and practice of a human solidarity whose very principle is its transcendence of all barriers of interest or historically momentary affiliation. There has never been a peace-loving nation. But why should there not be?

And if indeed, as seems likely, only common worship of the true God could enable such endlessly self-transcending mutuality, the question of civil religion is reopened. Is it really so, as mainline American denominations have recently agreed, that a civil religion can only be a despicable "lowest common denominator" of various real faiths? Might there not be an appropriation of the biblical eschatology, and even a civil worship appropriate thereto, which can be shared also with those not called to baptism or the prayer of the synagogue?

IV

It is time to return from such speculation to *True Virtue*. According to Edwards, the beauty of human life is such mutual benevolence as can be restricted by no barriers or particularities, because it is in fact identical with love of God. Yet Edwards saw as plainly as we do that human communities commonly unite and prosper by a mutuality which can hardly be so described, yet which enables human life and even has "something of the general nature of virtue." [27] The remainder of his inquiry is devoted to this gift of common grace.

Where does natural civil order come from? Edwards does not propose any one answer. In his account, several factors cooperate within God's one providence; and there is nothing in the account to prevent him from adding others, if the phenomena should suggest it.

The *possibility* of natural virtue is, according to Edwards, aesthetic. A well-ordered society, in its "just" proportions and reciprocities, is merely as such a beautiful object, and God ordains that we shall apprehend this beauty as we do any other. This we do even when we are not ourselves truly benevolent and so do not love the encompassing benevolence that is the final meaning and fulfillment of community.[28] Thus it becomes possible for well-ordered societies to be created and penultimately sustained also by partial benevolence.

This then actually happens in that self-love, following ordained natural regularities of our behavior, expands to embrace wider groups. Natural perception of the need for social contract makes self-interest into mutual interest. So Edwards both receives contract theory, so dominant in his time, and denies that it can explain communal reciprocity by itself, apart from more direct aesthetic response to social harmony.[29]

Next in Edwards' discussion is conscience. His derivation is remarkable. Love, he begins, is union with the other; thus self-love is union with oneself, and will be discomforted by any awareness of "inconsistency" with oneself. Given natural love of justice, I will be discomforted by such inconsistency whenever I become aware of behaving to another as I would be unwilling to be treated in his/her place; and this discomfort, with its converse pleasure, is conscience.[30]

It is, in Edwards' account, the phenomenon of conscience in which, among all natural moral principles, natural virtue is most dialectically related to true virtue. For on the one hand, conscience cannot fail to agree with the valuations of true virtue, and if fully illumined by nature and common grace would be entirely congruent with them.[31] Yet on the other hand conscience is not at all a love of the good itself, but only of my own comfort. It can therefore be defied; in the language of *Freedom of the Will*, it constitutes only a "moral difficulty" to adverse actions and not a "moral inability."[32]

Lastly, Edwards adduces "various . . . inclinations natural to men, which depend on particular laws of nature, determining their minds to certain affections . . . towards particular objects; which laws seem to be established chiefly for the preservation of mankind, and their comfortably subsisting in the world. These dispositions," he stipulates, "may be called instincts."[33] He discusses only two particular cases: pity[34] and attraction between the sexes.[35] Notably, he does not limit specifically sexual love to mutual sensual attraction, but makes the unity in difference of male and female foundational for comradeship and mutual assistance generally. I will diverge to report an early journal entry, for its own sake: "How greatly are we inclined to the opposite sex! nor doth an exalted . . . love to God hinder this, but only refines . . . it. God has created the human nature to love fellow creatures, which he wisely has principally turned to the other sex; and the more exalted the nature is, the greater love of that kind that is laudable, is it susceptive of." [36]

Nature and common grace thus provide abundantly, according to Edwards, for the reasonable if only penultimately enduring mutuality of human community and for the reasonable happiness of those within it. Many then and now will think this enough. Yet the whole scope of Edwards' analysis is to prevent mistaking this natural virtue for true virtue. His gravamen is variously developed, but may be fairly summarized: none of these natural dynamics break through the egocentric predicament. [37]

By Jesus' wisdom, and by the general wisdom of the race, we are not to let our left hand know that our right hand is doing good. As Confucianism had it, deeds preserve their virtue only when carried on the back, out of sight. But how do we get them there, without just so bringing them very much into sight? How do I determine to act selflessly, except by an itself very self-aware decision? There is, plainly, no possible answer to that question. *I* cannot determine to be selfless, to be universally and self-transcendently benevolent, if I am once less than selfless. Then, only an other than I can thus determine me. That, finally, is Edwards'—in itself, patent!—point.

That an other than I comprehensively determines me to benevolence is the same as that God determines me to benevolence—to argue in an Edwardsean way. Or, what is again the same, more than partial benevolence is a miracle. And that is both the truth of Edwards' thought, and the point where it fails us. It is surely and plainly the case that true virtue is a miracle, that transcending the egocentric predicament is inexplicable by any factor within it. But can the miracle be as *private* as it is by most of Edwards' accounts, and its assertion have any meaning in an analysis of communal love? Can this matter be worked out without mention of the word?

We have regularly come upon this impasse; in the present context it ceases to be tolerable. "Supernature," "special grace," "the heart's sense" for God, "union to Christ," "true virtue"—all have been descried as the brute unverifiable fact of the Spirit's new relation to the secret soul, which he does or does not take up, in either case telling no one. This doctrine is something of which other Christian confessions have always complained in Calvinism. But whatever may be the right of the complaint in other instances, Edwards was one Calvinist who could hardly defend the position.

In Edwards' system, community is a defining character of reality. He must therefore to be consistent, regard a putative event which is supposed to be entirely private as a non-being. He can of course say that the event of true virtue is real in the system because it is the community of God and soul. But can faith, interpreted as an event exclusively between God and each soul separately, be plausibly presented also as the base of humans' true community with each other? Precisely if we understand that community as Edwards does? Is the egocentric predicament broken between humans by an event which has no actuality between them?

In *True Virtue*, Edwards provides an empirical and in large part convincing account of the *discourse* in which "natural" community occurs. How can he do less for the real thing?

The End

I

One way to understand *True Virtue* might be as description of strictly new creation, of a new community not at all of this world. The problems pointed out at the end of the last chapter could be eliminated by saying that true virtue has no evidence in this world because it is the defining character of another one. The whole of *True Virtue* could then be read as a purely critical essay, as demonstration of the penultimacy of all historically actual virtue, by contrast with a limiting ideal endlessly approachable in history but never realized in it. Such a reading, however, would contradict Edwards' plainly stated intent with the book. Perhaps the most that can be said is that the temptation to read *True Virtue* in this way demonstrates the powerful eschatological pull that always animates Edwards' reflections on human authenticity.

We may begin discussion of Edwards' eschatology, more narrowly conceived, by reminding ourselves of Edwards' central and controlling vision of salvation: "Christ has brought it to pass that . . . he and his Father, and his people, should be . . . one society, one family; that the church should be as it were admitted into the society of the blessed Trinity," that we should be "in a sort partakers of (the Son's) relation to the Father."[1] Between Christ and the church, this means: "there shall be no more distance. . . . [The church] shall then be brought . . . to dwell eternally in his embraces. Then Christ shall give her his love; and she shall . . . swim in the ocean of his love."[2]

With this vision, Edwards recreated the eschatology of the Greek fathers, in its decisive difference from that usual in the West. For whereas Western theology has conceived human fulfillment as the perfecting of what each of us is in him/herself, the eastern fathers proclaimed our "deification," meaning thereby our inclusion in the divine life. For Edwards as for the ancient Greek church, our perfecting destiny is not primarily to be understood as our becoming more what we severally ought to be, or even as our becoming more "like" God, but as our coming to live in God, to be embraced by his life. A chief difference between this

vision of fulfillment and that usual in the West is that the Eastern vision
cannot be secularized; it is irremediably the vision of an End. Yet neither
is or can it be made unhistorical: we enter a new relation to God and one
another, and precisely that event is our fulfillment.

It is the church, an actuality of the history we now live, whose
inclusion in new relationships constitutes the End. We may say: the End,
according to Edwards, is but the final twist of the church's career under
God's rule. The personalist metaphor in "career" is appropriate. For
according to Edwards, the work of redemption is carried on from the fall
to the end doubly: "with respect to the effect wrought in the souls of the
redeemed; which is common to all ages" and "with respect to the grand
design in general . . . , by many successive works and dispensations."[3]
The successive events of providential history follow "very much after the
same manner as the carrying on of the same work . . . in a particular
soul, from . . . its conversion, till it is perfected . . . in glory."[4]

Indeed, the history of the world, as Edwards tells it, just *is* the
history of the church on its way from sin to deification. In the present
connection, it is in what the *History of the Work of Redemption* calls the
"finishing" epochs of the story that we are most interested. These begin
with the Crucifixion, and accomplish the dismantling of the church's
"carnal" state and the "establishing" of a "spiritual state"—terms which
we must remember to interpret "not of the heart" and "of the heart."
First "an end is brought" to the "carnal ordinances" and national exclu-
sion of old Israel. Then "an end is brought to the old Heathen empire"
by Constantine, "which is another . . . degree of the winding up . . .
of the world"[5] and one by which Edwards sets much store in all his
writings.[6] Then "is the finishing of Satan's visible kingdom in the world"
and "the calling of the Jews." And "last will come the destruction of
the outward frame of the world itself, at the conclusion of the day of
judgment."[7] The millennium does not appear here under a separate rubric, so much is the sequence one continuous narrative. At every step,
great and small, God's pragmatism is to triumph through adversity,[8] by
"remarkable pourings out of the Spirit."[9]

II

The last judgment itself begins with the return of Christ and the general
resurrection of the dead. "Christ will appear in the glory of his Father,"[10] "probably first . . . at a great distance as a star" then "as the
sun"; and "it shall be the beams of Christ's glory . . . shining on the

dead that shall raise them . . . and change the living."[11] Then "shall
the whole church of saints be caught up in the clouds to meet the Lord
in the air, and all wicked men and devils shall be arraigned before the
judgment seat," and "sentence shall be pronounced upon the righteous
and the wicked." Finally, "upon this, Christ and all his church of saints
. . . shall leave this lower world, and ascend . . . towards the highest
heaven."[12]

The point of this scenario is the public, and indeed political and
historical character of the judgment. Christ's appearance as a human judge
and the cosmological framework of the judgment make the judgment an
intersubjective event. "Although God now actually exercizes the most
sovereign dominion over earth . . . , ordering all things as seemeth to
himself good; and although he is actually judge in the earth . . . yet he
rules after a more hidden manner. . . . Many of the kings and great men
of the earth . . . look upon themselves as supreme, and therefore tyran-
nize over mankind."[13] This hiddenness must be lifted, that the final beauty
of God's works, which consists above all in "the moral beauty and regularity of his disposals of the intelligent world," may be revealed. The
"causes and controversies that must be decided by the supreme Judge"
are all public in that they are individuals' violations of our "union and
regulations in society." And many are "of a most public nature," "causes
between one nation and another"—as for example, between "the Span-
iards and Portuguese" and "all nations of South America"—or even
between one generation and another, so "that men that live now on the
earth may have an action against those that lived a thousand years ago."[14]

The cosmology of this scene doubtless now needs some explaining.
Edwards adhered to the classic pre-Copernican interpretation of "heaven,"
according to which it is a part of the created universe, spatially related to
the rest of the universe;[15] thus Christ's ascension to it was a *journey*, as
will be ours. By Edwards' account, this part of creation was made to be
God's own "residence" within his creation,[16] and the sphere of angels
and glorified humans.[17] Thus there are fundamentally two regions of the
universe: "this lower world," with its visible "heaven," corruptible[18]
and spoiled by sin;[19] and the now invisible[20] "heaven" or "highest
heaven," kept incorruptible by "the divine will and grace"[21] the abode
of holiness. Through the previous history of Christianity, this cosmological-
metaphysical division had been easily plotted on the "Ptolemaic" cosmic
map and was in no way an unsophisticated concept. Copernicus made the
plotting very much harder—ultimately impossible—but at Edwards' time
one could still, with a bit of strain, make it work by thinking of the
complete Copernican-Newtonian universe as *enclosed* in God's heaven.

Thus the corollary of final judgment is a great cosmological separation. "As there are two spiritual worlds, the elect and the reprobate, so there are two material worlds that are to be the everlasting . . . places of those spiritual worlds."[22] "This lower world" will become the place of the lost, transformed into flame by cosmic collapse.[23] The devil will have outfoxed himself again; his efforts to bring the lower world to ruin will by God's judgment succeed, and so prepare his own place of torment.[24] The new "heaven and earth" of Christ, his church and the good angels, will be that high heaven to which "Christ will come and take [us] away." This will then become also a new "earth" in that it will be the place of Christ's and his saints' resurrected bodily communion.[25] As the place where "Christ the great Redeemer shall be most perfectly glorified,"[26] it will itself "be exalted exceedingly in its nature."[27]

We should pause here to note how within Edwards' thought the political and cosmological realities of final judgment require each other. The judgment is the separation of two "spiritual worlds," two incompatible communities of consciousnesses, which are the outcome of history. A "material world," for Edwards, is the "between" of such a community, the condition for a unity of separateness and sharing which God thinks in thinking a plural mutuality of persons; therefore the great historical-political separation must be just as such a cosmological separation. With our longer experience of Copernicus, no amount of explanation and understanding will let us share Edwards' cosmological scenario as written, but its metaphysical parameters may nevertheless be exactly what we need. I will come back to these questions; first, we must contemplate his vision of the final glorification itself, for which we must turn mostly to journal entries.

III

"[A]t that day the moral world shall be settled in its final state."[28] The settlement will be a christological event: Christ will "deliver up to his Father . . . his representative kingdom," that is to say, his delegated exercise over the fallen creation of that absolute authority which within the triune life itself is proper to the Father. No longer will the saints need to have the "majesty" of the Father be "softened" for them by representation in the human nature of the Son. This does not mean that Christ's rule ends or that his human nature drops from the divine picture. For Christ's "mediatorial kingdom" will continue; that is, "he will cease to be 'viceroy' but remain 'spouse' ''; [29] he will eternally be the God-man whose reality enables the mutual love and happiness of God and creatures, as friends in all their awe-laden difference. [30] "Christ God-man" will be eternally the "head of [the saints'] enjoyment of God; as it were, the eye to receive the rays of divine glory and love," [31] "their organ" to "enjoy God as their portion." [32]

Just this abandonment of mere power will be Christ's own final glorification. Now, his glory is but that of "an honorable work, under the Father," then, precisely as God-man, he will live solely in the "mediatorial" role proper to the Son in the triune life: of pure contemplation and reflection of the Father's glory. His own glory will be purely the "glory of an high enjoyment of the Father"; [33] and this one human's contemplation of the Father and glorification by the Father will be the means of the saints' glorification, who enter the triune life *with* him.

It also follows from the continuing reality and mediatorial role of the Incarnation, that the saints' contemplation of God will be both "by an intellectual view" and "with their bodily eyes." [34] Edwards thought there is nothing to prevent minds immediately apprehending one another's beauty, if God so orders it; and so in fact it will be in the final community, "one of another and of the supreme Mind." [35] But also another "end is obtained by Christ's Incarnation, viz., that the saints may see God with their bodily eyes." [36] And this seeing also is among all mutually: "in all probability . . . there shall be external beauties . . . altogether of another kind from what we perceive here, and probably these beauties will appear chiefly as the bodies of the man Christ Jesus and of the saints." [37] The very medium of heaven "will be the light of the brightness of Christ's glorious body . . . , ravishingly sweet to . . . the external perception or sense" which the elect will indeed have. And in that light, their "pleasure from external perception will in a sense have God for its object." [38]

That the saints must have bodies, and so need and be capable of an "external view" of God's glory in Christ and each other, is so obvious within Edwards' interpretation of reality, that he hardly notes the matter. The glory will be communal glory; the sainted minds will be both intimate to and distinct from one another. Therefore they must be parts of a somehow material reality. Yet the gross entities we now lug about will hardly do for such communication as Edwards evokes; there will need to be a transformation of the saints' bodies, "by the beholding of Christ's glory," exactly coordinate to the transformation of their souls. [39]

Obviously, Edwards here must struggle for language and concepts.

What is to be posited is that, as the saints are bodies, "in heaven the glorified bodies of the saints will be . . . most flexible, moveable and agile, most easily susceptible of mutation, both from the acts of the in-dwelling soul and also from the influence of Christ";[40] and that, as they are consciousnesses apprehending these bodies, both "the medium" of sight and hearing "be infinitely fine and more adapted to a distinct and exact representation," and the "organ . . . be immensely more exquis-itely perceptive."[41] Edwards once speculated: the saints "will be able to see from one side of the universe to the other" because they will see not "by such slow rays of light that are several years travelling . . . from the fixed stars to this earth," but by the light "emitted from the glorified body of Christ."[42] Generally, the entities of the final reality must be thought of as having properties and obeying laws analogous to those we now know, but such properties and laws as render them "as it were, spiritual," by virtue of "infinite" liveliness.[43] The struggle shows in the threatened meaninglessness of those key modifiers, "most," "infinitely," and the like.

Finally, the two great themes of Edwards' general vision of reality decisively constitute his characterization of the saints' lively contempla-tion. It will suffice here simply to remind ourselves of them.

The final reality will be perfected *music*. Let me bring one more journal entry: "Singing is amiable, because of the proportion that is per-ceived in it. . . . There will doubtless, in the future world, be that which . . . will be a far more lively expression of this harmony, and shall itself be vastly more harmonious . . . than our air or ear . . . is capable of."[44] Edwards' speculations on glorification work with the traditional metaphors of light and seeing, but transform this seeing into a sort of perceptual dance.

The "final state" of the moral universe will be a *history*. "It seems to be quite a wrong notion of the happiness of heaven that it is in that manner unchangeable that it admits not of new joys upon new occa-sions."[45] The glory that God "is to receive" in the last heaven is "infi-nite," as it must be to suit its subject; thus "those that shall render him his tribute of glory will to eternity be increasing in their knowledge of his glory and so in the degree of their love and praise."[46] And just be-cause "the saints will be progressive in knowledge and happiness to all eternity,"[47] all will not be equal or equivalent in glory;[48] the truly com-munal character of their being will be that the "exaltation of some in glory above others will be so far from diminishing . . . the perfect . . . joy of the rest . . . that they will be the happier for it."[49]

IV

The gospel is the news that Jesus the Israelite is risen from the dead and must therefore finally be the Destiny of all creatures. Thus the gospel is essentially an "eschatological" proclamation, a promise of the final outcome of the human enterprise. A de-eschatologized Christianity is not merely incomplete or perverted; it has ceased.

Yet a process of de-eschatologizing has been continuous in American Christianity from Edwards' day to the present. In part this represents our participation in the general course of western Christianity, but America's foundation in the Enlightenment has given our history special features also in this respect.

In the period immediately after the Civil War, American preachers changed in remarkable lockstep from postmillennial to premillennial views; this expressed disillusion with efforts to transform America into the millennial paradise, and may be regarded as conversion to a soberer and more biblically realistic hope. Yet the millennial agenda of reform, reaching from completed abolition through women's suffrage and prohibition all the way to the post-World War I peace movement and the Black movement of the 1960s, continued to provide the actual moral life of the American nation. Thus the abandoning of postmillennialism must also be seen as a secularization; Christianity's affirmation of Christ's final victory lost its previous animating connection with America's moral-political life. Labor in this world on behalf of the moral vision enabled by the gospel came to be one thing, and the "heaven" to be brought by Christ's "return" to be simply another—whatever the latter might conceivably then be.

The faith's eschatological hope had of course, been denatured long before the Enlightenment, by the individualism of typical Western eschatology. Given who it is from whom Christianity awaits humanity's fulfillment, the End was biblically and patristically proclaimed as a fulfilled *community,* a "Kingdom" or "City." Western theology, however, conceived salvation as the perfecting of the defining virtues of the substance each of us is in him/herself; thus it conceived a salvation into which each of us might, so far as the concept is concerned, enter as the only initiate. So long as heaven remained one *place,* into which all the saved would be brought together, the disintegrative effects of this theology were somewhat checked. Copernicus removed the check.

How are we to conceive the fellowship of the resurrected, if there is

no place beyond the spheres for them to gather? There is to be, say
Scripture and creed, a *gathering* of transformed persons, and just therefore they will be somehow *embodied* for each other and their transformation to that end will be a "resurrection of the body." But what is a
body with no place for itself? How are bodies to meet outside space? In
fact, under the Copernican pressure, we have ceased to conceive a fellowship of the bodily resurrected, whatever formulas we recite, and conceive instead a survival of souls in some purely "spiritual" dimension.

That is, we conceive the survival of minds bereft of the means of
mutual presence and fellowship, of all that makes life righteous. Edwards
knew: "To be without a body is in itself an evil, because tis a want of
that which the soul of man naturally inclines to."[50] It is not surprising
that also those who "believe" in disembodied "life after death" display
no great eagerness to experience it; and that the rest abandon the conception not so much because it is intrinsically implausible—who knows?—
but because it is trivial and unworthy. One other move, to be sure, is still
widely made: *concepts* are abandoned altogether, and it is simply said,
but then not thought, that there is heaven some place. The difficulty is
that connections in life are made by thought, so that this sacrifice of
intellect is notoriously irrevelant to the moral content of life.

Perhaps the Christian hope has been refuted by astronomy. It has
been unless "body" and "place" may properly be used in theology and
philosophical reflection for aspects of reality now actualized as material
substances moving and colliding in a container-universe but actualizable
also otherwise. Intersubjectivity simply as such, the simultaneous distinction and mutual availability of consciousnesses over against each other,
is all that is necessary for science, *and* for the embodiment proclaimed
by the gospel. Edwards reduced body and space to just this root posit,
by demythologizing "matter" and identifying space as God's field of
awareness. Thus so long as God thinks his creatures' intersubjectivity by
some regularities, analogous to those explored by Newton, these need not
be the very same ones.

Edwards himself continued in the tradition according to which Newton's space and heavenly space are related in ways themselves describable according to Newton. But by his own lights, he would not have had
to plot the matter so. All that his system requires is that the same God
think the embodiment of this world and the different embodiment of the
Fulfillment.

For decades, much theology has been content, even when it has not
altogether lost the gospel's hope, to deal in "metaphors" and "symbols"
of the Kingdom. It will not do, at least not in America. Either the gospel

is empty, or there will be a final transformation of the parameters of being, creating a community in which time and space enable mutuality but no longer terminate it. Christians of the Enlightened nation must learn to *conceive* that transformation. In my judgment, Edwards has shown what must be done: we must understand the transformation of time and space not as a separate event from the last perfecting of love, but as one aspect of it. When the miracle happens that we love one another, we just thereby will "see from one side of the universe to another," and the we that so communicates will be the total human historical community. It is my good fortune and excuse that in this book I may praise Edwards for pointing out what to do, and need not myself do it.

16

Recovery of the Word

I

Other Christians have always objected to Calvinism's separation of the "means" of God's communication, "the Word," from the transforming act of the Spirit. On its face, the separation is biblically implausible; the Spirit may "blow where he wills," but it is the unpredictable dynamism of the church's proclamation and sacraments that is so described. When the pastor tells me, "Your sin is forgiven," does he/she thereby forgive me, or does he/she merely "prepare" me intellectually for a hidden spiritual event that may or may not ensue? When someone is baptized, is this verbally and symbolically speaking event itself the neophyte's initiation into new life, or does the event only signal that, to cite Edwards, "we may argue" that these persons "stand fair for being really God's people . . . in God's ordinary way of dealing"?[1] Does the Supper "contain the grace it signifies," as ecumenical doctrine has it, or does it not?

My purpose here, however, is not a general evaluation of the "extra Calvinisticum" as the old Lutherans called it; it might be found that within the complete systems of standard European Calvinist theologies the separation has been harmless. But Edwards was not a standard Calvinist and he worked in America. We have repeatedly encountered places where within the system of his reflection he needed to do what he did not do: give the *word* of the gospel the ontological weight of the transforming Spirit.

Our study of Edwards does not end in churchly esoterica. The relation of the word to the Spirit is not only a chief question of the church's own life, it is also the politically and socially decisive theological question. And Puritanism's answer to this question has been the curse to accompany the blessings it bestowed on America. There were not only two incompatible understandings of freedom at the base of American nation making, the constructive one of which was supported by Puritanism; there were also two incompatible understandings of communal spirit, Puritanism's relation to which was more ambiguous.

The line of democratic theory which stems from Jean-Jacques Rousseau does not require that the people *discourse* mutually for there to be a communal spirit; for this line, word and spirit are *not* thought of as inseparable. Rather, communal spirit is identified with shared impulse and interest which is there with or without joint effort to reach consensus; there is a "common will" antecedent to the verbally discoursive life of the group.

It is this line of democratic theory which has justified the totalitarian democracies that are modernity's characteristic polity. The "leader" is the one who just knows what "the people" want; he *divines* it without needing an exchange of words within actual assemblies. It is the same theory that justified Mr. Madison's machine-polity of checks and balances. As the engineers of our polity knew more clearly and stated more bluntly than we have since managed, it is only interests and impulses that can be mechanically balanced on the analogy of inertial forces. Thus what the political machinery can produce cannot be and was not supposed by its designers to be a consensus in the good but only a balance of the premorally wanted. This product can then be presented as what the community *should* do, as good for which to labor, only on Rousseau's hypothesis, that the group's grasp of its good subsists with or without moral argument and discussion and expresses itself most clearly in sheer simultaneous desire.

The other line of democratic theory does not suppose that communal spirit simply subsists; according to this interpretation, communal spirit must come to pass in actual moral discourse. *Words* must create the spirit's habitation among us; in that we argue what we as one community *should* do, the community we are has one spirit. It is polity shaped on this belief which Madison and others labelled "democracy" and which they excluded, together with religion, from the polity, to find its American place in the "private" sphere. As polity, our founders thought, discoursive democracy is altogether too spirited for the state's stability and is anyway impractical for properly massive political entities.

It was especially by the Puritan towns that the democracy of discourse was represented in America's founding period; it has been in the Puritan legacy of reform movements and organizations that it has maintained a somewhat shadowy reality in Madison's nation-state; and it has been in Puritan theology of mutual covenant that it has found limited theoretical expression. But Puritan theology could if hard pressed allow for the subsistence of community and the divining of common good also apart from the democratic discourse practiced in the Puritan towns. And it is that aspect of Puritanism that has been decisive. If we must talk with each other to be with each other, we cannot remain the moral atoms of political Newtonianism. But if, as Puritan theory insisted, the word and the spirit are essentially independent from one another, if communal discourse and communal spirit are different things, then we can at need withdraw from discourse into impermeable individuality and let polity-physics work out our communal interactions. Puritanism did not create, but could justify our mechanistic community.

I must begin by recording that Edwards too taught, for most of his career, a standard or even exaggerated version of the disastrous Puritan doctrine of the word. In the great sermon "On a Divine and Supernatural Light," which has formed so much of this book's analysis and provided the occasion for so many of its praises, Edwards said of the heart's true sense that teaching and exhortation "are not truly any second causes of it; but it is produced by God immediately. The word of God is no proper cause of this effect; it does not operate by any natural force in it. The word of God is only made use of to convey to the mind the subject matter of this saving instruction . . . it is the cause of the notion of [divine things] . . . but not of the sense of the divine excellency." [2]

In a journal entry, Edwards laid out the doctrine in greater generality and greater detail. Not just preaching but "means" generally "have no influence to produce grace." What they do is supply the soul "with matter for grace to act upon when God shall be pleased to infuse it." More particularly: "1. They supply the mind with notions . . . of the things of religion. 2. They may have an effect upon mere natural reason in a measure to gain the assent of the judgment. 3. They may have an effect upon the natural principles of the heart to give . . . a sense of the natural good or evil of those things that they have [given] a notion of." [3] It must be so in Edwards' scheme as he normally cast it; while "God produces all effects," it is the very definition of "natural events" that he "ties" them "to the operation of . . . means . . . according to fixed determinate rules. . . . And thus it is that natural means are the causes of the exercizes of natural principles. But means of grace are not means of the exercize of grace, in such a manner, for the actings of the Spirit of God in the heart are more arbitrary and are not tied . . . by such laws." [4] That Edwards by such ruthless clarity goes beyond the saving ambiguities of ordinary Puritanism, may be attributed to his occupation with Locke.

When he is on this theoretical line, Edwards, like some other Puritans, can be led away from the Reformation itself. A relatively late draft [5] is an elaborate analysis of the freedom of God's grace; in it he argues that it is not contrary to free grace for works to be required as prerequisite for justification, so long as these are not supposed to "do something for God's . . . benefit, that shall in some measure answer for . . . the ben-

efit we receive from God," or possess some "amiableness . . . that
recommends as to the benefit" of justification, or involve some "trouble"
that is to "balance the benefit we receive." Now this is all well and
good, and was the teaching of the best medieval scholastics, but the hearer
of such doctrine actually preached must from his/her standpoint instantly
inquire, as Edwards formulates it: "Why are we said to be saved by grace
without works since our works . . . are prerequisite to our going to heaven,
as much as if heaven were given for the amiableness of our works?"
Having posited this telling objection, Edwards has no answer but repeti-
tion of the position which provokes it. He cannot answer, for the place
of the actual hearer or speaker is unoccupied by his theory. Precisely that
place, however, was the standpoint of the Reformers.

What, after all, is—to instance the "means" central to Edwards'
own career—preaching to *do?*[6] As actual personal address, its function
is not plausibly described as only the providing of matter for a living
contact that is to occur otherwise. It was the great question about the revival: Why do we need such direct and exhortatory, and not merely informative, preaching? Edwards once answered in contradiction of theory:
"The main benefit that is obtained by preaching is by impression made
upon the mind in the time of it; and not by an affect that arises afterwards
by a remembrance of what was delivered."[7] Nor is this "impression"
invariably described as strictly "notional"; in the *Treatise on Religious
Affections,* Edwards' final reflection on the revivals, the "great and main
end for which God has ordained that his Word . . . should be . . .
applied and set home upon men, in preaching," and not merely be read
and studied, is "the impressing divine things on the heart and affections."[8] Yet when he preached farewell to Northampton, theory ruled
and he defined the whole purpose of preaching as a purely notional business, as discovering in Scripture and describing "the distinguishing marks
of true piety," so that "professors of religion" may have the standards
by which to "best discover their state, and more surely . . . judge of
themselves."[9]

Edwards' words to his people are in fact usually addressed on the
one hand to the unconverted, threatening and encouraging them to *be*
converted—with, as we have seen, the hidden understanding that their
efforts will succeed only when they fail—and on the other hand to the
converted, praising their blessings. The conversion falls between; there is
no word to which it would be the response. In a letter of spiritual coun-
sel, of 1741, a new young convert is advised on the one hand not to
"leave off seeking, striving and praying: for the very same things that
we exhort unconverted persons to pray for," namely, spiritual illumination[10]

and humiliation over sin.[11] On the other hand, she is to concentrate on the vision of Christ, of his love[12] and his glory.[13]

Thus Edwards' preaching does become immediate and performatively vital, but only in evoking the reality and end of sin—which is, of course, what has given him his hell-fire reputation. "Be entreated to consider attentively how great and awful a thing eternity is." When "you shall have worn out a thousand . . . such ages, yet you . . . shall know that you are not one whit nearer to the end of your torments."[14] Since faith is apprehending the beauty of Christ, one would think that the chief purpose of the preacher would be to make Christ audible in this beauty. But just at this point, Edwards instead becomes abstract. And why should even the preaching of unconverted "strivings" be "affectionate"? Edwards' struggle with the old Puritan problem of "preparation," of the *use* of the "humiliations" that precede grace, was incessant and unsatisfying.[15]

II

Edwards could write in mid-career: "Thus it is evident, that the special end for which God has made man, is something wherein he has nextly to do with his Creator, as an intelligent voluntary agent." This is: "communication between God and man."[16] But *how* do these communicate? Without "means"? That is, without a common reality *in* which to come together?

In the 1338th of his entries in the *Miscellanies,* written in the final years at Stockbridge, Edwards redrafted his conceptual system.[17] He begins the entry by introducing a new ruling category: "Definition. By *conversation* I mean intelligent beings expressing their minds one to another, in signs intentionally directed to us for our notice, whose immediate and main design is to be significations . . . wherein these . . . are evidences distinguished from works done by them, from which we may argue their minds." Here the words of conversations are still "signs"; in this Edwards is still at one with Locke. But *these* "signs" are now distinguished from "evidences" of the speakers mind; I do not *conclude* from what you utter to what you intend. Rather, according to Edwards now, in "conversation" intelligent beings so open to one another that such outwardness is transcended.

The distinction cuts especially deep in the case of God. Until this entry, Edwards apprehended the *word* of God, for all the praise he bestowed on it, as a device by which God gives us information about him-

self—information that he may or may *not* turn into communion with us.
But now we read: "Thus I distinguish God's communicating his mind to
us by word or conversation, from [his] giving an opportunity to learn it
by . . . arguing the nature and will of God by God's works." Before,
whether my knowledge that, for example, God is merciful came from
"nature" or "revelation" was thought to make no difference in my relation to God; either way, the relation must wait for its authenticity upon
a miracle which the revealing word had "no influence to produce." Now,
revelation as *word* is precisely not mere evidence; and this character *is*
its authenticity.

The concept of conversation established, Edwards immediately uses
it to reconstrue his ruling insight into the reality of community. What had
before been abstract assertion can now become concrete. A new analysis
is established of "moral agents as united in society, in a commonwealth
or kingdom." Of these, the foundational point is now: "So far as we can
see, all moral agents are conversible agents." "Especially do we find
conversation . . . requisite between intelligent creatures concerning moral
affairs." "Moral agents are social agents."

Edwards treats first the role of conversation in any society at all. He
moves in three steps; of the first two we have heard before. First: "Tis
needful in order to a proper moral government, that the head or heads
. . . of the society should enforce the rules of the society, by threatening
the just punishments and promising the most suitable rewards; but without words . . . there is no threatening or promising." Second: "[T]is
needful not only that the general . . . good should be known" as just
noted, "but also the particular design" of governing policy; this knowledge is even more exclusively shareable only in conversation.

So far so legalistically, familiarly, and "naturally" good. But now
Edwards discerns a third level at which conversation functions communally, transcending and enabling the two first noted: "The special medium of union and communication of the members of the society" which
is to say, the "being of society as such, is conversation." This is new
thought; the being of community had before depended on words but had
by no means consisted in them. And Edwards plunges on: "And the well-
being and happiness of the society is friendship. Tis the highest happiness
of all moral agents; but friendship, above all other that belongs to society,
requires conversation . . . the felicity of friendship is *tasted* and enjoyed
by that." [my emphasis] These two sentences contain an entire political
theory. Here community in words is itself at the level of the heart's "taste";
it is no longer the prerequisite of moral agents' "highest happiness," it
is itself that happiness. And this happiness is "friendship," the unity

which in Edwards' more strictly theological thinking is between God and the soul the fruit of Incarnation. The gulf between words and the miracle of the heart's sense has been overcome, by the discovery that words in actual use are not just a repertoire of signs to stand for other things, but *conversation,* themselves the reality of our mutuality.

Since conversation is now the actuality of that friendship which God in Christ takes up with us, Edwards can reconstrue also the divine society of God with us by the new category. He hastens to do so; and it seems apparent that the new general doctrine of society was set up to enable this. Conversation plays the three roles just noted also in "God's moral government of a . . . society of intelligent and willing creatures, to which society he is united as its Head, ruling for its good." About the two "natural" roles, he repeats what he had said before: God communicates by his words both his promises and commands, and the course and plot of his historical providence.

It is again at the third, supernatural level that new insight appears. Also of "God's moral kingdom" it is now seen that its "happiness" is directly "in the members' enjoyment of each other's friendship" and "in the enjoyment of the friendship of their head." And also of *this* happiness it holds: "Therefore here . . . above all is conversation requisite." It is first the life of the church in this world which Edwards is thereby enabled newly to interpret: "God's word on his part, and prayer on ours" are no longer mere means of our fellowship with God, they *are* the communion between us. But even more remarkable and metaphysically telling is what Edwards can now say about the *final* community.

"If God's moral kingdom, or the society of his friends and willing subjects, shall be . . . in another world, in the most perfect social state, united in the most complete friendship . . . with God their Head . . . , is it reasonable to suppose any other than that they will fully enjoy the sweets of their friendship . . . ; in the most perfect conversation, either by words or some more perfect medium"? Before, Edwards supposed that it was only the saints' outward apprehensions of one another that would require a medium, perfected or not. The saints' "intellectual" view of one another's minds was to be unmediated. Now that split is overcome; precisely their "highest" fellowship is conversation, mediated in and through an intersubjective space. Now it is clear not only that but *why* the saints must be eternally embodied for one another. Now it is clear how they at the last will attain to a perfect "intellectual" view of one another's consciousnesses without after all becoming but one consciousness; also our "intellectual" fellowship does not bypass a world between us, for it is *conversation*. The ancient dualism of soul and body

is overcome at what is for Christian thought the metaphysically paradigmatic level, the vision of the End.

Edwards takes the last step: "And shall [the saints] have . . . no
conversation . . . with their glorious Head, the fountain [of] all the felicity of their society, in friendship with whom their happiness chiefly
consists?" Edwards at the start of his reflection reconstrued the "beatific
vision," apprehending it not on the paradigm of seen beauty but on that
of heard beauty. Now he reconstrues it once more: God and we will
indeed *sing* to one another, beatitude will be the perfected eternal chant-
ing of "God's word and prayer."

I will not do as I have been tempted, and recapitulate each chapter
of this book, showing how it could be rethought by Edwards' new central
category. That would be tedious; and where Edwards' work on a particular matter cried out for him to recognize the word's metaphysical weight,
this was noted, Moreover, it would be idle. I do not know how such a
rethinking of, say, Trinity or the religions would have worked out in
Edwards' fecund mind. Indeed I obviously do not even know *whether,*
given the opportunity, he would have attempted such a comprehensive
reconstrual of his system. I do not know whether the summa would have
been a theology of the End *and* its Word. I therefore conclude with the
report of *Miscellany* 1338, and with the following.

III

At this end of my commendations of Edwards, the questions must again
surface: How are citizens of the Enlightenment's nation to be the church?
And how is that nation itself ever again to be a polity, and not merely an
economy in arms? The answer is perhaps the same to both questions.

We cannot and should not retreat from the Enlightenment's vision
of cosmic harmony, of order that both is pervasive and basic in reality
and is open to our intersubjectively testable discovery. But it has been
the disaster of the American church that we have been able to conceive
the church's God only as the ancient author of this order, and perhaps as
the present sometime meddler in it. The same debility has been the disaster of our wider community, since God and political freedom go together; it is again only as origin once upon a time and perhaps as occasional and feared eruption that our "system" can condone free political
life. What we must have, lest we ossify, is the apprehension—not the
mere concept—of another harmony that transcends and includes and val-

idates the harmony of the spheres, and that moreover *so* includes and
validates Newton's world as to enable within it the discourse that is freedom.

Perhaps there is no such harmony. Then the American enterprise is
lost; deciding to behave *as if* there were such harmony would be self-
defeating. Nor will the transformation of physics into Taoism or Bud-
dhism liberate us, except from the very roots of our national history. But
perhaps there is God—the God, that is, of the trinitarian creeds. Edwards
apprehended and proclaimed the triune God himself as a music that transcends, includes and validates all the atemporal harmonies of the cosmos.

What for most of his life Edwards was seemingly not able to do,
was so to construe this encompassing musical harmony as thereby to
understand and enable the actual life of human community, even though
the ultimacy of community was always his other great metaphysical conviction. As community, he said, we *sing* to and with one another, but
one might, for so long as Edwards' remained bound to the traditional
Calvinist doctrine about words, have supposed that we were merely to
hum or whistle. Thus the actual, conversational and communal life of the
church remained astonishingly uninterpreted in his reflection; and the great
books which in fact are about the American polity never quite admit that
they are, or fully connect to the vision that is explicit in all his other
thinking.

It is indeed musical order, as the mind's encompassing object, that
can both encompass the orders known to the Enlightenment, and set freedom loose around them. But the music that can do this—and, if Edwards
is at the last right, does—is a *choral* music: the Trinity is a fugued hymn.
It is Edwards' discovery of the category of conversation which frees Puritanism from its own bonds and finally makes of his reflection a complete yet liberating interpretation of reality.

This book has contained so much polemic against the Enlightenment
that some readers may suppose I want simply to repeal it. The contrary
is my intention, as it must be the intention of every Christian who is a
citizen of this nation and of every citizen who loves this land's community. America has no foundation but the Enlightenment and the Puritanism of which Enlightenment was the secularization.

The Enlightenment unleashed the critical function of the mind over
against all appearances of truth. Who would now wish to restrain it? Or
even to challenge its autonomy? None, anyway, faithful to the gospel's
insatiable critique of all religion and of all human pretensions to truth.
The Enlightenment dreamed of universal order, and set out to adumbrate

it. And it dreamed of constructing humane polities in the course of the same quest. Surely Edwards was right to recognize that the dreams are fitting, because the universe's Creator is *triune*.

Jonathan Edwards undertook *critique* in the service of the *gospel* and the adumbration of universal *harmony* as encompassed in *triune* harmony. He is America's theologian because he so astonishingly accomplished both undertakings. And at the last he penetrated to the ancient dualism, perpetuated in both Puritanism and Enlightenment, which has made critique destructive and harmony silent and impersonal, and transcended it.

Notes

Preface

1. Lamentably, this remains the case even though the critical edition from Yale, *The Works of Jonathan Edwards* (New Haven: Yale University Press, 1957–), has now reached six volumes. The long-delayed volume(s) of the *Miscellanies* is the most serious lack; Edward H. Davidson, *Jonathan Edwards: The Narrative of a Puritan Mind* (Boston: Houghton Mifflin, 1966) may serve as an example of sympathetic study undone by not using this material. I doubt that publication of the unpublished sermons will fundamentally change the situation. But I must not be too certain, since I have deliberately restricted my use of sermonic material to the many published items; a plunge into that vast body of untranscripted material would have postponed completion of this book to another life.

2. Perry Miller, *Jonathan Edwards* (New York: W. Sloane, 1949).

3. I will name some of the main studies in the notes as I go, at those places in my text where it first seems appropriate.

4. Miller, 50–51.

5. Particular points on which Miller has been corrected are also, though secondarily, important. He misunderstood Calvin and original Calvinism, thus creating an illusory foil for Edwards. Nor was Edwards even slightly "naturalistic"—whatever that might be—though he was a sort of demythologizer. The charge that Miller misrepresented Edwards by portraying him as genuinely involved in the Enlightenment and so as "modern," whereas Edwards was really "medieval," is, on the other hand, just silly. The gravamen turns out to be that Edwards believed in the Christian God and regarded the Bible as authoritative. Certainly, if to be Christian is by definition to be medieval, Edwards was medieval—and so what?

Chapter 1

1. Among recent studies, James Carse, *Jonathan Edwards and the Visibility of God* (New York: Scribner's, 1967) is written most from a similar point of view. I suppose that is why it seems to me at once so full of remarkable insight and so wrongheaded.

2. If there are any grounds to think that the melancholy story of decline told by Joseph Haroutunian, *Piety versus Moralism* (New York: Henry Holt, 1932)

need not have happened, or might even yet be countered, it must lie in recovery of Edwards' full vision, or something like it. Haroutunian's book is a remarkable exception to the chronology of Edwards-scholarship; appearing in 1932, it might have been written yesterday, and should be read by any with interest in Edwards.

3. *The Federalist,* ed. of 1832, 39.

4. Karl Barth, *Die protestantische Theologie in 19. Jahrhundert* (Zurich: Evangelischer Verlag, 1952), 19.

5. Thomas Jefferson, letter to Benjamin Rush, 1800.

6. John Adams, *Dissertation on the Canon and Feudal Law.*

7. E.g., The *Federalist,* 39, 43–45, 283, 241.

8. For an expanded version of the following, with bibliography, Robert W. Jenson, "The Kingdom of America's God," *Dialog,* 15 (1976), 12–20.

9. It should not be but has become necessary to insist explicitly that Newton and Locke, and not simply the whole company of seventeenth- and eighteenth-century thinkers, were indeed the decisive interlocutors of Edwards' thinking, as a reading of the manuscripts on "Natural Philosophy" and "Mind" instantly makes clear. What was once a salutary reminder that Edwards did not grow up in an intellectual desert, and that nearly the whole battery of eighteenth-century intellectual life must be supposed to have had its various effects on him—see, e.g., William Sparks Morris, "The Young Jonathan Edwards: A Reconstruction" (University of Chicago dissertation, 1955)—is in danger of turning into the kind of scholarship that treats thoughts as if they were viral strains and equates all influences as if they differed only in weight. Norman Fiering's very learned and informative study, *Jonathan Edwards' Moral Thought and Its British Context* (Chapel Hill: University of North Carolina, 1981), suffers from such method. It suffers also from a refusal to take it seriously that Edwards wanted to talk about God, not about "moral philosophy."

10. "Memoirs of President Edwards," *Works* (New York: Leavitt, 1849), I: 51.

Chapter 2

1. Edwards' works will be cited by page from the Yale edition (e.g., YE4: 103), where this exists. Works not yet in the Yale edition will be cited by their own internal systems of division, to enable utilization of various editions; only where this is not possible will older editions be cited by page. Finally, the *Miscellanies* will be cited by number.

2. "Memoirs of President Edwards," *Works* (New York: Leavitt, 1849), I: 16.

3. Ibid., 18.

4. Edwards' concept of beauty is exhaustively analyzed by Roland André Delattre, *Beauty and Sensibility in the Thought of Jonathan Edwards* (New Haven: Yale University Press, 1968), 15–114.

5. *Miscellanies,* a.

6. "Memoirs," 16.
7. YE6: 305.
8. By what written or oral paths this part of the tradition reached Edwards is disputed. To the whole subject of Edwards' education, see now pp. 7–87 of Wallace E. Anderson's excellent introduction to YE6.
9. *Miscellanies,* 901–931.
10. YE6: 305.
11. *Miscellanies,* 901–931.
12. YE6: 305.
13. *Miscellanies,* 42.
14. Ibid., 182
15. Ibid., 232.
16. E.g., ibid., 864.
17. Ibid.
18. Ibid., 1007.
19. "Memoirs," 21.
20. Sydney E. Ahlstrom, *A Religious History of the American People* (New Haven: Yale University, 1972), 131.
21. William Ames, *Medulla Theologica,* I, IV, 31: VI–X.
22. There is a survey of this history by Bruce M. Stephens, "A Theological Patois: The Eternal Sonship of Christ in the New England Theology," *American Religion: 1974 Proceedings* (Tallahassee: American Academy of Religion, 1974), 44–55.
23. *Miscellanies,* 259.
24. Ibid., 182.
25. Ibid., 108.
26. YE6: 151. See also 490–493.
27. "Memoirs," 17.
28. *Miscellanies,* 188.
29. Ibid., 182.
30. YE6: 202.
31. Ibid., 203.
32. Ibid., 202–203. To the sources of Edwards' doctrine of space, see Anderson, 98.
33. Ibid., 203–204. It is worth noting that Edwards never abandoned this ontological sort of proof for God. See *Miscellanies,* 650, 880. We may formalize his latter argument as follows. Only assertions of existence that can appear as one side of a true disjunction can be false; God's simplicity gives no handle for constructing a "q" in "p v q" when "p" is "God is" and "q" then "not p."
34. Ibid., 1340.
35. Ibid., 1297.
36. Ibid., 1304.
37. Ibid., 1298.

38. Ibid., 383.
39. So Patricia J. Tracy, *Jonathan Edwards, Pastor* (New York: Hill and Wang, 1980), 51–69.

Chapter 3

1. Wallace E. Anderson, intro. to YE6, YE6: 188–192.
2. YE6: 230.
3. Ibid., 231.
4. Ibid., 230.
5. Ibid., 289.
6. Ibid., 332–338.
7. Ibid., 344.
8. Ibid., 332.
9. Ibid., 336.
10. Ibid., 337.
11. Ibid., 336.
12. Ibid., 336–337.
13. Ibid., 336.
14. Sections of these drafts were in fact published in *True Virtue*.
15. YE6: 216.
16. Ibid., 215.
17. Ibid.
18. Ibid., 353.
19. Ibid., 208.
20. Ibid., 198.
21. Ibid., 211–212.
22. Ibid., 211.
23. Anderson, 66.
24. YE6: 214.
25. Ibid., 215.
26. Ibid.
27. Ibid., 216.
28. Ibid., 377–380. This passage is from "Mind," and is an interpretive key for the whole essay on atoms.
29. Ibid., 234–235.
30. Ibid., 234.
31. Anderson, 325–329.
32. YE6: 342–343.
33. *Miscellanies*, 267.
34. YE6: 343–344.
35. Ibid., 343–344, 350–351.
36. Ibid., 350.
37. Ibid., 344. The resemblance of Edwards' view to that of Bishop Berkeley

has often been noted. To what extent this can depend on influence is unclear;
Anderson, 36, 76n, 100–103, 123, 176.
38. YE6: 354.
39. E.g., ibid., 339.
40. Ibid., 344.
41. Ibid., 345.
42. Ibid., 351–352.
43. *Miscellanies*, 1.
44. YE6: 206.
45. Ibid., 388.
46. Ibid., 374.
47. Ibid.
48. Ibid., 345.
49. Ibid., 389.
50. *Miscellanies*, 238.
51. YE6: 238.
52. *Miscellanies*, 150.
53. YE6: 385–386.
54. See below, pp. 150–152.
55. YE6: 398.
56. Ibid., 381.
57. Ibid., 364.

Chapter 4

1. I owe full clarity on this point to a paper by a then student at Gettysburg
   Seminary, David Yaego.
2. *Miscellanies*, 867.
3. Ibid., 896.
4. Ibid., 867.
5. Ibid., 547.
6. Ibid., 867.
7. Ibid., 1. See also, e.g., ibid., gg.
8. E.g., ibid., 547.
9. Ibid., 1296.
10. E.g., ibid., 931.
11. Ibid., 900.
12. Ibid., 901.
13. E.g., ibid., 952, 954.
14. Ibid., 804.
15. Ibid., 744, Or see ibid., 845.
16. E.g., ibid., 681, 710.
17. Ibid., 651.

18. *Dissertation Concerning the End for which God Created the World*, I, I, 3–5.

19. Ibid.

20. *Miscellanies*, 247.

21. *End*, I, II, 1.

22. Ibid., I, II, 1–4; I, III.

23. *Miscellanies*, 1127.

24. Ibid.

25. *End*, I, III.

26. Ibid.

27. Ibid. See also, e.g., I, IV, Obj., 4.

28. There is an entry in the *Miscellanies* which is the draft of those parts of the *End* drawn on for this paragraph, and which contains the following: "all God's love may be resolved into his love to himself and delight in himself, as asserted in my Discourse on the Trinity." *Miscellanies*, 679.

29. *End.*, II, VII.

30. *Miscellanies*, 1066.

31. *End*, I, IV, Obj., 1.

32. Ibid., II, VII. Or see the paroxysm of emanationist language in *Miscellanies*, 1082.

33. *End*, II, II.

34. E.g., ibid., II, III–V.

35. *A History of the Work of Redemption*, Doc., II, 1.

36. *End*, II, VII.

37. *Miscellanies*, 448.

38. Ibid., 1004.

39. Ibid., 710, App.

40. Ibid., 103.

41. Ibid., 86.

42. *History*, Imp., I, 3.

43. Ibid., Per. I, Pt. IV, IV.

44. *Miscellanies*, ff.

45. Ibid., 741.

46. Letter of Oct. 19, 1757.

47. Karl Dieterich Pfisterer, *The Prism of Scripture: Studies on History and Historicity in the Work of Jonathan Edwards* (Bern: Herbert Lang, 1975), argues this very point, successfully, I think.

48. *History*, Per. I, Intro.

49. Ibid., Per. I, Pt. I, XVI.

50. E.g., *Miscellanies*, 803, 804.

51. *History*, Per. I, Pt. III, I.

52. Ibid., Per. I, Pt. VI, XVIII.

53. Edwards notes this; *Miscellanies*, 1295.

54. Sermon, "The Final Judgment," Doc., I, 1.

55. *Miscellanies,* 864.
56. Sermon, "God Glorified in the Suffering of the Damned," Use, 1.
57. *Miscellanies,* 508.
58. Ibid., 172.
59. Ibid., 156(146).
60. Sermon, "The Justice of God in the Damnation of Sinners," Doc., II, 1.
61. *Miscellanies,* 156(146), 172.
62. Ibid., 320, 344.
63. Ibid., 710, App.
64. Ibid., 931.
65. Ibid., 1340.
66. Ibid., 907.
67. *History,* Per. I, Pt. IV, II; Pt. VI, XIX.
68. Ibid., Per. III, Pt. II, I–II.
69. Ibid.
70. To Edwards' historiography, see Pfisterer, *Prism,* 165–224.
71. *History,* Per. I, Pt. I, I.
72. *Miscellanies,* 833.
73. *History,* Per. I, Pt. I, V.
74. *Miscellanies,* 64.
75. Ibid.
76. Ibid., 1364.
77. Ibid.
78. E.g., in Edwards himself, ibid., 531.
79. Ibid., 362.
80. Ibid.

Chapter 5

1. YE4: 148–149.
2. See now C. C. Goen's introduction to YE4, YE4: 1–65.
3. "Farewell Sermon," 1844 ed., 79.
4. Sermon, "The Justice of God in the Damnation of Sinners," App., IV. Obj.
5. *Discourses on Various Important Subjects,* Intro.
6. Sermon, "Justification by Faith," Intro., 1.
7. Ibid., e.g., Doc., II, Third.
8. Ibid., e.g., Intro., 3.
9. Sermon, "The Manner in which the Salvation of the Soul is to be Sought," Doc., I, Inq., 1.
10. Sermon, "The True Christian's Life," App., I, 3.
11. *Inquiry concerning Qualifications for Communion, Works* (New York: Leavitt, 1849), I: 117.
12. For a complete and I think definitive presentation of Edwards' understanding of "preparation" and the most closely related subjects, I may refer to two

studies: John H. Gerstner, *Steps to Salvation: the Evangelistic Message of Jonathan Edwards* (Philadelphia: Westminster, 1960); and John H. Gerstner and Jonathan Neil Gerstner, "Edwardsean Preparation for Salvation," *The Westminster Theological Journal,* 42 (Fall, 1979): 5–71.

13. Gerstner, *Steps,* 96–102.
14. "Manner," Doc., I, Inq., 2.
15. YE4: 30ff.
16. "Justification," Doc., X, First, 2.
17. Ibid., Doc., II, First, 1.
18. Ibid., Doc., I, First.
19. Ibid., Doc., II, Third, 2.
20. Ibid.
21. Ibid.
22. Ibid., Doc., I, Sec., 1.
23. Ibid., Doc., I, Sec., 2, 3.
24. Earlier, in the *Miscellanies,* 2, Edwards entered a different and vastly better explanation of why "faith" as a "condition" of the covenant of grace is not a work.
25. "Justification," Doc., Sec., 1.
26. YE4: 39.
27. Ibid., 28.
28. Ibid., 160ff.
29. Ibid., 29ff.
30. Ibid., 32.
31. Ibid., 164.
32. Ibid., 165ff.
33. Ibid., 32.
34. Ibid., 33.
35. Ibid., 34.
36. Ibid., 35.
37. Ibid., 36–48.
38. Ibid., 36.
39. Ibid., 60.
40. Ibid., 64ff.

Chapter 6

1. On this point, see Conrad Cherry, *The Theology of Jonathan Edwards* (Garden City: Doubleday, 1966), 12–15, and the bibliography there. Cherry unrolls the whole of Edwards' theology from Edwards' understanding of faith as the heart's sense of a new "idea" of God—as will be articulated also in this chapter. The appropriateness of this starting point is proven by the comprehensive interpretation that results.

2. See the introduction to Edwards' philosophical writings by Wallace E. Anderson; YE6:128ff.
3. Sermon, "A Divine and Supernatural Light," Doc., III, Sec., 5.
4. Ibid., Doc., I, Sec., 1; III, Sec., 5.
5. Ibid., Doc., I, First, 1.
6. Ibid., Doc., I, Sec., 1.
7. Ibid.
8. *Miscellanies*, 782.
9. Sermon, "That Great Care Is Necessary, Lest We Fall into Some Way of Sin," App., I, 2nd.
10. "Light," Doc., I, Sec., 1.
11. E.g., sermon, "The Importance and Advantage of a Thorough Knowledge of Divine Truth," Doc., III, 1.
12. *Miscellanies*, 782.
13. YE1: 142.
14. Ibid., 144–147.
15. YE2: 96.
16. Ibid., 272.
17. "Light," Doc., I, First, 3.
18. *Miscellanies*, 284.
19. "Light," Doc., I, Sec., 1.
20. *An Humble Inquiry*, Pt. 2, II, 2.
21. "Light," Intro.
22. Above, pp. 48–49.
23. "Light," Intro.
24. *Miscellanies*, 537.
25. "Light," Doc., I, First, 3–4.
26. YE2: 208.
27. Ibid., 214ff., 228.
28. "Light," Doc., I, First, 1.
29. Ibid.
30. *Miscellanies*, 732.
31. Sermon, "True Grace Distinguished from the Experience of Devils," Imp., Sec., Inq.
32. *Miscellanies*, 628.
33. "Light," Doc., II, 2.
34. Ibid., 3.
35. Ibid.
36. *Miscellanies*, 539.
37. Ibid., 826.
38. YE4: 386–387.
39. *Miscellanies*, 396.
40. Ibid., 397.
41. "Light," Imp., Thirdly, 4.

42. Ibid., 2.
43. E.g., *Miscellanies,* 628.
44. "Light," Doc., I, sec., 2.
45. *Miscellanies,* 628.
46. "Light," Doc., I, Sec., 2.
47. YE4: 185.
48. Ibid., 160–161.
49. *Miscellanies,* 393. In the Narrative, YE4: 170.
50. Ibid., 170–175; see also 563–564.
51. Ibid., 332.
52. Ibid., 332, 335, 340.
53. Ibid., 334, 337.
54. Ibid., 341.
55. Ibid., 105.
56. Ibid., 231.
57. YE2: 131–133.
58. Charles Chauncy, *The Late Religious Commotion in New England Considered* (Boston: T. Fleet, 1743), 13ff.
59. Ibid., 9ff.; Charles Chauncy, *Twelve Sermons* (Boston: T. Leveratt, 1765), 217.
60. YE2: 95.
61. Ibid., 100.
62. Ibid., 101.
63. Ibid., 106.
64. Ibid., 121.
65. Chauncy, *Commotion,* 9ff.
66. YE4: 297.
67. YE2: 253.
68. YE4: 183.

Chapter 7

1. Charles Chauncy, *Twelve Sermons* (Boston: T. Leveratt, 1765), 201–219.
2. Ibid., 217.
3. Compare Charles Chauncy, *The Late Religious Commotion in New England Considered* (Boston: T. Fleet, 1743) and Edwards, YE2: 228–260.
4. Chauncy, *Commotion,* 22.
5. Ibid., 16ff.
6. Chauncy, *Sermons,* 182ff., 204ff., 252ff.
7. Chauncy, *Commotion,* 20.
8. YE4: 467.
9. Ibid., 244.
10. Ibid., 453ff.
11. Ibid., 241.

12. Ibid., 101.
13. *Miscellanies,* 1010.
14. Sermon, "An Inquiry into the Qualifications for Church Membership," 117.
15. Sermon, "Man Naturally God's Enemies," Doc., III.
16. Sermon, "God Glorified in the Suffering of the Damned," Use, 3.
17. See the entire sermon, "True Grace Distinguished from the Experience of Devils."
18. YE4: 570.
19. *Miscellanies,* 530.
20. Ibid., 301.
21. "True Grace," Doc., II.
22. There are two documents especially: the *Treastise on Religious Affections* and *True Virtue.*
23. *Miscellanies,* 472.
24. Ibid., 1183.
25. "True Grace," Imp., Sec., Inq.
26. Ibid., Imp., Sec.
27. YE2: 245.
28. Ibid., 246.
29. "True Grace," Imp., Sec.
30. *Miscellanies,* 369.
31. YE2: 149.
32. Ibid., 264–265.
33. Ibid., 319.
34. Ibid., 336.
35. *Miscellanies,* 534.
36. YE2: 315.
37. Ibid., 127–181.
38. Ibid., 197–208.
39. Ibid., 205.
40. Ibid., 240–248.
41. Ibid., 266–310.
42. Ibid., 311–324.
43. Ibid., 340–442.
44. Ibid., 365.
45. Ibid., 383–453.
46. Ibid., 254–261.
47. Ibid., 262–265.
48. Ibid.
49. Ibid., 344–348.
50. Ibid., 357–364.
51. Ibid., 376–379.
52. YE4: 285.
53. See, e.g., the sermon, "Hypocrites Deficient in the Duty of Prayer."

54. *Miscellanies,* 771.
55. "True Grace," Imp., Sec., Inq.
56. YE2: 251.
57. "True Grace," Imp., Sec., Inq.
58. *Miscellanies,* 141.
59. Ibid., 79.
60. Ibid., 739.
61. Ibid., 567.

Chapter 8

1. *Miscellanies,* 182.
2. This is perhaps the place to acknowledge the contribution of Douglas C. Elwood, *The Philosophical Theology of Jonathan Edwards* (New York: Columbia University, 1960), while also recording doubt that Edwards' theology is usefully located as a "third way" between "theism" and "pantheism."
3. YE2: 298.
4. *Miscellanies,* 117.
5. "Memoirs of President Edwards," *Works* (New York: Leavitt, 1849), I:16.
6. To the following, see Robert W. Jenson, *The Triune Identity* (Philadelphia: Fortress, 1982), 57–159.
7. YE5: 118.
8. Sermon, "God Glorified in Man's Dependence," Doc., I.
9. Ibid., Doc., II, Use, 1.
10. Ibid., Doc., II, 1.
11. *Miscellanies,* 402.
12. Ibid.
13. Ibid., 1151.
14. Ibid., 958.
15. Sermon, "Divine Wisdom Displayed in the Work of Redemption," II, II.
16. Ibid., I, 1.
17. *Miscellanies,* 614.
18. Ibid., 293.
19. Ibid., 94.
20. Ibid., 179.
21. Ibid., 238.
22. Ibid., 117.
23. Ibid., 94.
24. YE6: 364.
25. *Miscellanies,* 116 (136).
26. For a few special questions he did pursue, see ibid., 94 at the end, and ibid., 308.
27. *A History of the Work of Redemption,* Doc., First, 1.

Chapter 9

1. YE2: 513.
2. YE3: 343–349.
3. Sermon, "God's Sovereignty," Doc., IV, 2.
4. Sermon, "Sinners in the Hands of an Angry God," Doc.
5. *Miscellanies,* 702.
6. *History of the Work of Redemption,* Imp., I, 3.
7. *Miscellanies,* 702.
8. Ibid., 704.
9. Ibid., 1218.
10. Ibid., 1266.
11. Ibid., 704.
12. Ibid., 1064.
13. Ibid., 710.
14. Ibid. For a published version of the same point, *History,* Doc., II, 1.
15. *Miscellanies,* 781.
16. Sermon, "The Wisdom of God, Displayed in the Way of Salvation," I, 1.
17. *Miscellanies,* 1091.
18. Ibid., 1245.
19. Sermon, "The Final Judgment," Doc., III, 1.
20. *Miscellanies,* 769.
21. Ibid.
22. Ibid., 1245.
23. Ibid., 1340.
24. YE3: 387–388.
25. *Miscellanies,* 581.
26. See also ibid., 156 (146), 330, 344.
27. YE2: 485.
28. *Miscellanies,* 809.
29. Ibid., 1177.
30. Ibid., 894.
31. Ibid., 407.
32. Ibid., 398.
33. Ibid., 741.
34. For a brief statement of the principle, ibid., 62.
35. Sermon, "God Glorified in the Damnation of Sinners," Doc., I, 1.
36. Sermon, "The Eternity of Hell Torments," Doc., I, 2.

Chapter 10

1. *Miscellanies,* 952–958, 1358.
2. Ibid., 958.

3. Ibid., 1358.
4. Ibid., 791. See also ibid., 512, 518.
5. Ibid., 1044.
6. Ibid., 180.
7. Ibid., 516.
8. Ibid., 949.
9. Ibid., 721.
10. Ibid., 1122.
11. Ibid., 460.
12. Ibid., 721.
13. Sermon, "On the Excellency of Christ," Doc., Intro.
14. Ibid., Doc., I.
15. Ibid., Doc., I, 1.
16. Ibid., Doc., II.
17. Ibid., Doc., III.
18. Ibid., Doc., Sec., II.
19. Ibid., Doc., Sec., III, 1.
20. Ibid., Doc., Sec., IV–V.
21. *Miscellanies*, 2.
22. Ibid., 510.
23. Ibid., 398.
24. See, e.g., the exhortation that closes "Excellency," App., I–II.
25. *Miscellanies*, 190.
26. Ibid., 487. We may note that Edwards held to these relatively early formulations; ibid., 709, 738.
27. Ibid., 764b, 766.
28. Ibid., 487.
29. See also ibid., 205.
30. Ibid., 513.

Chapter 11

1. Ignatius of Antioch, *To the Magnesians*, VII, 1–2.
2. This is perhaps the central question of Clyde A. Holbrook's *The Ethics of Jonathan Edwards* (Ann Arbor: University of Michigan, 1973). It may be thought that his polarity of "objective"/"subjective" is not the clearest way to stipulate Edwards' position.
3. *Miscellanies*, 392.
4. E.g., ibid., 791.
5. Ibid., 398.
6. Ibid., 483.
7. Ibid., 764a.
8. Ibid., 1352, 1360.
9. Ibid., 244, 245, 299. The following returns to 1352, 1360.

10. Ibid., 1304.
11. Ibid., 986.
12. Ibid., 864.
13. Ibid., 1338.
14. Ibid., 986.
15. *History of the Work of Redemption,* Per. I, Pt. IV, II.
16. YE2: 322.
17. *Miscellanies,* 979.
18. E.g., ibid., 853–876, 1181.
19. E.g., ibid., 992.
20. *Inquiry into the Reasons for Which God Created the World,* Third, Obj. XI, Ans.
21. *Miscellanies,* 1162.
22. Ibid.
23. E.g., ibid., 979.
24. Ibid., 1157; see also 1335.
25. *History,* Per. III, Pt. II, Sec. I, III, 4th.
26. Ibid.
27. YE5: 136–137. The following returns to *History,* op. cit.
28. *History,* Per. III, Pt. II, Sec. I, III, 3rd, 2, (4).
29. E.g., ibid., Per. III, Pt. II, Sec. I, III, 2nd, 1, (1); sermon, "Man's Natural Blindness in the Things of Religion," II, 3.
30. *History,* Per. I, Pt. VI, 1.
31. Ibid., Per. III, Pt. II, Sec. I, I, 3, (2).
32. Most of the manuscript material is now available; YE5: 97–205.
33. For the history, see the now standard work by E. L. Tuveson, *The Redeemer Nation* (Chicago: University of Chicago Press, 1968).
34. There is a seminal article which must be recognized: C. C. Goen, "A New Departure in Eschatology," *Church History,* XXVIII: 25–40.
35. *History,* Per. III, Pt. II, Sec. I, III, 4th.
36. Ibid., Per. III, Pt. II, Sec. II, Doc.
37. E.g., *Miscellanies,* 835.
38. YE5: 317.
39. The document is in YE5: 309–436.
40. *Miscellanies,* 835.
41. Ibid., 1339.
42. E.g., ibid., 1064. Carl W. Bogue, *Jonathan Edwards and the Covenant of Grace* (Cherry Hill: Mack, 1975), provides a complete analysis of Edwards as a "covenantal" or "federal" theologian.
43. E.g., *Miscellanies,* 1215.
44. Above, pp. 108–109.
45. *Miscellanies,* 1091.
46. E.g., ibid., 1118.
47. Ibid., 1353. This is consistent; see ibid., 1358, 1287, 1283.

48. Ibid., 1353.
49. *History,* Per. I, Pt. IV, IV.
50. Ibid., Per. I, Pt. IV, V.
51. Ibid., Per. I, Pt. IV, I.
52. Ibid., Per. I, Pt. V, XII.
53. Ibid., Per. I, Pt. I, III.
54. *Miscellanies,* 1335.

Chapter 12

1. *Miscellanies,* 97.
2. Ibid., 96.
3. Ibid., 824.
4. Ibid., 936–937. See also 710, 744.
5. Ibid., 1281. This is an obsession in the journals; see, in one stretch, ibid., 822, 824, 827, 848, 866, 871.
6. That this book is a *political* work, an "indictment of utilitarian liberalism," is Perry Miller's abiding insight; *Jonathan Edwards* (New York: W. Sloane, 1969), 276.
7. Sermon, "The Sin of Theft and of Injustice," Doc., Sec., 2.
8. Ibid., Doc., Sec., 3 (2).
9. Sermon, "The Peace which Christ Gives His True Followers," Doc., III.
10. YE4: 514.
11. *Miscellanies,* 369.
12. Ibid., 1163.
13. YE4: 556ff.
14. YE3: 107.
15. To the history, see now Clyde A. Holbrook's introduction to YE3.
16. YE3: 108.
17. Ibid., 113.
18. Ibid., 109.
19. Ibid., 221–349.
20. Ibid., 351–370.
21. Ibid., 120–129. Holbrook, in his note 1 at 121, appears to miss this distinction.
22. Ibid., 129.
23. Ibid., 128.
24. Ibid., 130.
25. Ibid., 133.
26. Ibid., 125
27. Ibid., 126.
28. Ibid., 125.
29. Ibid., 196.

30. Ibid., 134ff.
31. Ibid., 139ff.
32. Ibid., 147ff.
33. Ibid., 158ff.
34. Ibid., 169ff.
35. Ibid., 167.
36. Ibid., 375.
37. Ibid., 380.
38. Ibid., 389.
39. Ibid., 383ff.
40. Ibid., 380–381.
41. Ibid., 381–383.
42. Ibid., 382.
43. Ibid., 386ff.
44. Ibid., 387.
45. Ibid., 389.
46. Ibid.
47. The following depends on ibid., 390–394.
48. Ibid., 189ff.
49. Ibid., 391.
50. Ibid., 390.
51. Ibid., 391ff., n. 1.
52. Ibid.
53. Ibid., 394.
54. Ibid.
55. Ibid., 397.
56. Ibid., 394.
57. Ibid., 397.
58. YE6: 398.
59. *Miscellanies*, 18.
60. Ibid.
61. Ibid.
62. Ibid., 184.
63. YE3: 397–405.
64. Ibid., 401ff.
65. Ibid., 401.
66. Ibid., 400–403.
67. Ibid., 403.
68. Ibid., 402–404.
69. Ibid., 404–405.
70. Ibid., 405.
71. Ibid., 406.
72. Ibid., 407.

Chapter 13

1. See now Paul Ramsey's introduction to YE3, 68ff.
2. Ibid., 2.
3. YE3: 169.
4. Ibid., 137–167.
5. Ibid., 137.
6. Ibid., 138–139.
7. Ibid., 139–140.
8. Ibid., 141.
9. Ibid.
10. Ibid.
11. Ibid., 143.
12. Ibid., 144.
13. Ibid.
14. Ibid., 145–147.
15. Ibid., 149.
16. Ibid., 150–151.
17. Ibid., 149.
18. Ibid., 155.
19. Ibid., 151.
20. Ibid.
21. Ibid., 150–151.
22. Ibid., 151–152.
23. Ibid., 152.
24. Ibid., 153.
25. Ibid.
26. Ibid., 153–154.
27. Ibid., 154.
28. Ibid., 156–157.
29. Ibid., 180–182.
30. Ibid., 180.
31. Ibid., Ramsay, 34ff.
32. Ibid., 180–181.
33. *Miscellanies,* 29.
34. YE3: 163.
35. Ibid.
36. Ibid., 164.
37. Ibid.
38. Ibid., 164–165.
39. Ibid., 171–179.
40. Ibid., 171.
41. Ibid.

42. Ibid., 173.
43. Ibid., 178.
44. Ibid., 183–184.
45. Ibid., 179.
46. Ibid., 180–189.
47. Ibid., 181.
48. Ibid., 195–212.
49. Ibid., 195.
50. Ibid., 198.
51. Ibid., 206–212.
52. Ibid., 180–185, 213–269.
53. For Edwards explicit statement of the connections, see the Conclusion of *Freedom of the Will,* YE3: 430–439.
54. YE3: 257–269.
55. Ibid., 157–161.
56. Ibid., 295.
57. Ibid., 309.
58. Ibid., 297.
59. Ibid., 297–300.
60. Ibid., 300–301.
61. Ibid., 302–304.
62. Ibid., 304.
63. Ibid., 304–308.
64. Ibid., 304.
65. Ibid., 304–305.
66. Ibid., 305.
67. Ibid., 308.
68. Ibid., 309.
69. Ibid.
70. Ibid., 320–333.
71. Ibid., 320.
72. Ibid., 321.
73. Ibid., 326.
74. Ibid., 324–325.
75. Ibid., 326.
76. Ibid.
77. Ibid., 321.
78. Ibid., 331.
79. Ibid., 329.
80. Ibid.
81. Ibid., 337.
82. Ibid., 337–342.
83. Ibid., 340.

Chapter 14

1. *The Nature of True Virtue* (Ann Arbor: University of Michigan Press, 1960), 1.
2. Ibid., 104–107.
3. Ibid., 6.
4. Ibid., 1.
5. Ibid., 2.
6. Ibid., 2–3.
7. Ibid., 3.
8. Ibid.
9. Ibid.
10. Ibid., 8.
11. Ibid.
12. Ibid., 9–13.
13. Ibid., 18.
14. Ibid., 19.
15. Ibid., 88.
16. Ibid., 24.
17. Ibid., 14–15.
18. Ibid., 20–23.
19. Ibid., 21.
20. Ibid., 25.
21. Ibid., 23–26.
22. For a careful account of Edwards' whole series of utterances before and after this, see Stephen J. Stein's introduction to YE5: 19–29.
23. YE4: 355ff.
24. Ibid., 346.
25. Ibid., 354.
26. Ibid.
27. *True Virtue*, 86.
28. Ibid., 27–41.
29. Ibid., 42–60.
30. Ibid., 61–66.
31. Ibid., 67–70.
32. Ibid., 71–74.
33. Ibid., 75.
34. Ibid., 80–84.
35. Ibid., 79–80.
36. *Miscellanies*, 190.
37. *True Virtue*, 85–97.

Chapter 15

1. Sermon, "The Excellency of Christ," App., III, 2.
2. Sermon, "The Church's Marriage with Her Lord," Doc., II, 1.
3. *A History of the Work of Redemption*, Doc., II, 3.
4. Ibid., Per. I, Pt. I, VII.
5. Ibid., Per. III, Intro., III.
6. *Miscellanies*, 1327.
7. *History*, Per. III, Intro., II.
8. E.g., ibid., Per. I, Pt. VI, XIX.
9. Ibid., Per. I, Pt. I, V.
10. Ibid., Per. III, Pt. II, Sect. II, Doc.
11. *Miscellanies*, 949.
12. *History*, Per. III, Pt. II, Sect. II, Doc.
13. Sermon, "The Final Judgment," Doc., II, 1.
14. *Miscellanies*, 1007.
15. E.g., ibid., 743.
16. Ibid., 833.
17. Ibid., 743, 952, 889.
18. Ibid., 952.
19. Ibid., 806.
20. Ibid., 809.
21. Ibid., 952.
22. Ibid.
23. Ibid., 863, 900, 901, 929, 931.
24. Ibid., 931.
25. Ibid., 809.
26. *History*, Per. III, Pt. II, Sect. II, Doc.
27. *Miscellanies*, 952.
28. Ibid., 1356.
29. Ibid., 742; see also 957.
30. Ibid., 571.
31. Ibid., 742.
32. Ibid., 1072.
33. Ibid., 742.
34. Ibid., 460.
35. Ibid., 182.
36. Ibid., 460.
37. Ibid., 182.
38. Ibid., 721.
39. Ibid., 1079.
40. Ibid., 1296.
41. Ibid., 263.
42. Ibid., 926.

43. Ibid.
44. Ibid., 153 (143).
45. Ibid., 372.
46. Ibid., 1099; for a nearly identical entry at the opposite chronological extreme, 105.
47. Ibid., 435.
48. Ibid., 430.
49. Ibid., 431.
50. Ibid., 644.

Chapter 16

1. *Miscellanies,* 849.
2. Sermon, "On a Divine and Supernatural Light," Doc., II, 3.
3. *Miscellanies,* 539.
4. Ibid., 629.
5. Ibid., 1020.
6. On Edwards' preaching generally, see Wilson H. Kimnach, "The Brazen Trumpet: Jonathan Edwards's Conception of the Sermon," *Jonathan Edwards: His Life and Influence,* ed. Charles Angoff (Rutherford: Fairleigh Dickinson, 1975), 29–44.
7. YE4: 397.
8. YE2: 115.
9. Farewell Sermon, 1844 ed., 74ff.
10. *Advice to Young Converts* (New York: Religious Tract Society, 1819), 2.
11. Ibid., 5.
12. Ibid., 18.
13. Ibid., 10.
14. Sermon, "Eternity of Hell Torments," App., 2.
15. For yet another set of passages, *Miscellanies,* 325, 337, 354, 369, 488, 674, 776, 862. Or see the sermon, "Pressing into the Kingdom of God," App.
16. *Miscellanies,* 864.
17. Ibid., 1338.

Index

Where a chapter title provides sufficient guidance, pages within the chapter are not indexed.